Approaches to *Paradise Lost*

THE YORK TERCENTENARY LECTURES

To
the Students of
the University of York

Approaches to *Paradise Lost*

The York Tercentenary Lectures

by

John Arthos J. B. Broadbent Philip Brockbank Bernard Harris
Merrit Y. Hughes Frank L. Huntley Brian Morris F. T. Prince
Mary Ann Radzinowicz Irene Samuel T. J. B. Spencer
Joseph H. Summers J. B. Trapp

edited by
C. A. Patrides

Edward Arnold, London

© *University of York*, 1968

First published 1968,
by Edward Arnold (Publishers) Ltd.
41 Maddox Street, London, W.1

SBN: 7131 5418 7

Printed in Great Britain
by W & J Mackay & Co Ltd, Chatham

Contents

The Contributors	ix
Preface	xi
Frank L. Huntley: Before and After the Fall: Some Miltonic Patterns of Systasis	1
Irene Samuel: *Paradise Lost* as Mimesis	15
Mary Ann Radzinowicz: 'Man as a Probationer of Immortality': *Paradise Lost* XI–XII	31
F. T. Prince: Milton and the Theatrical Sublime	53
Joseph H. Summers: The Embarrassments of *Paradise Lost*	65
T. J. B. Spencer: *Paradise Lost:* The Anti-Epic	81
J. B. Broadbent: Milton's 'Mortal Voice' and his 'Omnific Word'	99
Bernard Harris: 'That soft seducer, love': Dryden's *The State of Innocence and Fall of Man*	119
Brian Morris: 'Not without Song': Milton and the Composers	137
John Arthos: Milton, Andreini, and Galileo: Some Considerations on the Manner and Form of *Paradise Lost*	163

Merritt Y. Hughes:
    Beyond Disobedience   181

Philip Brockbank:
    'Within the Visible Diurnal Spheare': The Moving World
    of *Paradise Lost*   199

SPECIAL CONTRIBUTION

J. B. Trapp:
    The Iconography of the Fall of Man   223

List of Illustrations

The plates are illustrations to the essay by J. B. Trapp, 'The Iconography of the Fall of Man', and appear between pages 228 and 229.

1. Mantegna, *Madonna della Vittoria*. Paris, Louvre
2. *Fall of Man*. Dura Europos, Christian Chapel, wall painting
3. *Adam and Eve*. Cameo. Paris, Bibliothèque nationale, Cabinet des médailles
4. *Fall of Man*. Detail from the sarcophagus of Junius Bassus. Vatican, Grotte Vaticane
5. *Temptation of Eve, Fall of Man, Rebuke, Expulsion* and *Toil of Adam and Eve*, from the Grandval Bible. London, British Museum, MS. Add. 10546, fol. 5v
6. *Temptation* and *Fall of Man*. Detail from the mosaics of the narthex, Venice, S. Marco
7. *Temptation* and *Fall of Man*. Octateuch. Istanbul, Seraglio Library, cod. viii, fol. 43v
8. *Temptation* and *Fall of Man*, from the 'Caedmon' MS. Oxford, Bodleian Library, MS. Junius xi, p. 31
9. *Fall of Man*, from the St Albans Psalter, Hildesheim, St Godehard, p. 17
10. *Temptation of Eve, Fall of Man, Rebuke* and *Expulsion*, from the *Très riches heures du duc de Berry*. Chantilly, Musée Condé, MS. 1284 [65], fol. 25v
11. Fall of Man and moralisations, from the *Bible moralisée (Gen. 3)*. Oxford, Bodleian Library, MS. Bodl. 270b, fol. 7v
12. Temptation of Eve, from *Speculum humanae salvationis*. Paris, Bibliothèque nationale, MS. lat. 9584
13. The First Temptation of Christ and its types, from the *Concordantia caritatis*. Lilienfeld, Stiftsbibliothek, MS. 151, fol. 33

LIST OF ILLUSTRATIONS

14. *Fall of Man* and *God's Rebuke of Adam and Eve*. Hildesheim Cathedral, bronze door, detail
15. Ghiberti, *Creation of Adam and Eve, Fall* and *Expulsion*. Panel from the 'Porta del Paradiso' of the Baptistery, Florence
16. Dürer, *Fall of Man*. Woodcut from the *Small Passion*
17. Batholomaeus Spranger, *Adam and Eve*. Drawing. Stuttgart, Kupferstichkabinett
18. Michelangelo, *Fall and Expulsion*. Vatican, Sistine Chapel, Ceiling fresco
19. Raphael, *Fall of Man*. Vatican, Stanza della Segnatura, Ceiling
20. Titian, *Fall of Man*. Madrid, Prado Museum
21. Rubens (with Jan Breughel), *Paradise*. The Hague, Mauritshuis
22. Tintoretto, *Fall of Man, with Expulsion*. Venice, Accademia
23. Hans Holbein the Younger, *Fall of Man* and *Toil of Adam and Eve*. Woodcuts from the Dance of Death—Old Testament suite
24. Rembrandt, *Fall of Man*. Etching
25. Berthold Furtmeyer, *Tree of Life and Death*. Munich, Staatsbibliothek, clm 15710, fol. 60v
26. Jean Cousin, *Eva prima Pandora*. Paris, Louvre
27. *Adam and Eve*, attributed to Bronzino. Balcarres, Collection of the Earl of Crawford and Balcarres
28. Lucas Cranach the Elder, *Fall of Man*. University of London, Courtauld Institute Galleries, Lee Collection

The Contributors

JOHN ARTHOS, Professor of English, University of Michigan.

J. B. BROADBENT, Professor of English, University of East Anglia.

PHILIP BROCKBANK, Professor of English, University of York.

BERNARD HARRIS, Professor of English, University of York.

MERRITT Y. HUGHES, Professor of English, Emeritus, University of Wisconsin.

FRANK L. HUNTLEY, Professor of English, University of Michigan.

BRIAN MORRIS, Senior Lecturer in English, University of York.

F. T. PRINCE, Professor of English, University of Southampton.

MARY ANN RADZINOWICZ, Fellow of Girton College, Cambridge.

IRENE SAMUEL, Professor of English, Hunter College, The City University of New York.

T. J. B. SPENCER, Professor of English and Director of The Shakespeare Institute, University of Birmingham.

JOSEPH H. SUMMERS, Professor of English, Michigan State University.

J. B. TRAPP, Librarian, The Warburg Institute, University of London.

Preface

The lectures published here were delivered at the University of York in 1966 and 1967 to mark the occasion of the 300th anniversary of the publication of *Paradise Lost* (1667).

With one exception—the special contribution by Mr Trapp—all the lectures are published in the order they were delivered. This order was not premeditated, and neither was the nature of the series. Our lecturers were simply invited to speak on *Paradise Lost*; the particular approach was subject only to their interests.

The response was certainly gratifying. Every lecturer accepted our invitation with impressive enthusiasm. The few who declined were obliged to do so because of previous commitments (as in the case of Professors M. C. Bradbrook, D. J. Gordon and F. R. Leavis) or because of an inability to cross the Atlantic at the time their presence was required at York (as in the case of Professors Douglas Bush, Northrop Frye and Louis L. Martz). Even so our initial aim has been achieved. The present tribute to Milton remains a joint Anglo-American enterprise, in keeping with our ever-increasing awareness that our study of *Paradise Lost* (as of all great literature) is advanced most when we expose ourselves to one another's insights.

Our gratitude is extended in the first instance to the lecturers who agreed to join us, and in the second, to the University of York which supported this series from the outset.

The lectures in their transit from oral delivery to print underwent minor changes only, gaining in particular a minimum of documentation. The only exception is Mr Trapp's lecture, the very nature of which demanded a broader frame of reference than was possible within the time at his disposal.

Quotations from Milton's prose are from *The Works of John Milton*, gen. ed. F. A. Patterson (New York, 1931–40), 20 vols., hereafter cited as *Works*. Milton's poetry is quoted from *The Poetical Works of John Milton*, ed. Helen Darbishire (Oxford, 1952–5), 2 vols.—a text whose use in the present volume is particularly meaningful to those of us at York since our Library's collection of Miltoniana is based on a generous bequest of books from the late Miss Darbishire.

The sources of the illustrations reproduced here are as follows. Plates 1, 4, 6, 15, 18, 19, 20, and 22: Mansell Collection, London; 3: Bibliothèque nationale, Paris; 5: The British Museum; 9 and 24: The Warburg Institute, London; 10: Giraudon, Paris; 8 and 11: The Bodleian Library, Oxford; 14: Bildarchiv Foto Marburg; 17: Württembergische Landesgalerie, Stuttgart; 21: Stichting Johan Maurits van Nassau, The Hague; 25: Bayerische Staatsbibliothek, Munich; 26: Archives photographiques, Paris; 27: The Scottish National Portrait Gallery, Edinburgh; and 28: The Courtauld Institute, London.

The only lecture delivered in the series but not collected here is my own on 'The Comedy of *Paradise Lost*' which, as editor, I decided not to include.

C.A.P.

Langwith College
University of York
20 August 1967

Before and After the Fall: Some Miltonic Patterns of Systasis

Frank L. Huntley

Few will deny that the justification of God's ways to man involves a paradox. Thirty years ago Professor Lovejoy's gloss on the *felix culpa* or fortunate fall satisfied for a time. But voices have been raised against that explanation, on intellectual, theological, or dramatic grounds. My purpose here is to suggest yet another solution, one which seems almost too simple to be true, but which is grounded in the intellectual history of the Renaissance, in Milton's own thinking, and in the structure of *Paradise Lost*. It is the pattern of systasis or the union of two complementary opposites.

Some examples of the pattern will remind us how familiar we are with it. Matthew Arnold, for one, opposes the 'spontaneity of consciousness' of the Hellenic race to the 'strictness of conscience' of the Hebraic. But throughout his discourse, Arnold appeals to his fellow Englishmen to be more perfect than their too Hebraic selves and their too Hellenic neighbours the French: they must become Hellenic-Hebrews or Hebraic-Hellenes, truly combining the two opposites, 'sweetness and light'. Another example is Dryden's definition of a play as 'a just and lively image of human nature'. Though Crites of the *Essay* may boast of the 'justness' of the Ancients and Lisideius of the 'liveliness' of the French, Neander wins the argument by pointing to Ben Jonson as the playwright who best combines 'justness' and 'liveliness' to give England the victory adumbrated from the beginning in the sound of naval guns off shore. The Horatian ends of poetry, again, are that it not only teach but also delight, opposite functions really, but 'right' poetry, as Sir Philip Sidney makes quite clear, teaches by delighting, a doctrine which for Milton makes Spenser a better teacher than Aquinas. Complementary opposites create that love-poetry of the

Renaissance which seeks a balance between a marriage of true minds and a marriage of male and female. This would not be Marvell's *A Definition of Love,* on the one hand, nor *To His Coy Mistress,* on the other, but Michael Angelo's *Gli occhi miei vaghi delle cose belle* or Donne's *A Valediction Forbidding Mourning.* Coleridge, finally, wrote that the poetic faculty 'reveals itself in the balance or reconciliation of opposite or discordant qualities; of sameness, with difference; of the general, with the concrete; the idea with the image; the individual with the representative; the sense of novelty and freshness, with old and familiar objects. . . .'[1]

In short, the pattern we describe is everywhere in Western thought. Let us define it: there is a division into two universal terms; these terms are opposites; at the outset one of them is usually given a higher value than the other; and they must be of such a kind as to allow their combination to produce an ideal, a *tertium quid* which is greater than the mere sum of the two parts. Certain pairs are more susceptible than others to such treatment. *Black versus white* or *being versus non-being* might well be left in their initial state of contrariety. But *scholar-and-gentleman, soul-and-body, theory-and-practice, pride-and-prejudice* obviously lend themselves to combinations. Sometimes the best of each opposite is taken to form the third; at other times the lower term is the means to the end of the higher; at still other times what initially appears to be all bad, like *culpa,* is gradually shown to be the cause of a good effect, which makes of it a *felix culpa.*

This dialectic especially characterises the writings of Plotinus, the Cabbala, Hermes Trismegistus, St Augustine, Marsilio Ficino, and a host of others, but primally the conversations of Socrates and the letters of St Paul and hence the Christian humanism of the Renaissance. Plato takes us from the visible shadows to the invisible Ideas, and the genius of Christian thought is the linking of two energies in its central dogma, the Incarnation. In Plato the pattern involves the twice-bisected line of the sixth book of the *Republic,* the doctrine of forms and bodies, the participation of a lower in a higher value, and the actual passage, as in the *Phaedo,* of one opposite, like sleeping, into the other, waking, or of death into life. The ultimate source for Milton's description of the creation of the world by the Demiurgic Son and for the double consciousness of God, Adam, and Satan, may well be the following passage in the *Timaeus* which describes the union between the indivisible or divine, on the one hand, and the divisible or corporal, on the other:

[1] *Biographia Literaria,* Ch. XIV.

Out of the indivisible and unchangeable, and also out of that which is divisible and has to do with material bodies, he compounded a third and intermediate kind of essence, partaking of the nature of the same and of the other. . . . He took the three elements of the same, the other, and the essence, and mingled them into one form, compressing by force the reluctant and unsociable nature of the other into the same. . . . This entire compound he divided lengthways into two parts, which he joined to one another at the centre like the letter 'X' [*chi*], and bent them into a circular form, connecting them with themselves and each other at the point opposite to their original meeting.[2]

In 1658 Dr Thomas Browne used this passage at the end of the fourth chapter of *The Garden of Cyrus* to create an emblem of the Greek *theta* in solid geometry: two circles placed on a globe like the equator and the meridian, the outer circle representing immortality; the horizontal line that meets the eye, mortality; 'and the third [the intersections at 0 and 180 degrees], which was the *Systasis* or harmony of those two, in the mystical decussation', the Greek 'X' [*chi*] symbolising the Incarnation. By means of this emblem he was able to combine death, accident, and the vanity of human wishes (*Urn Burial*) and their opposites—life, design, and 'the mystical mathematics of the city of Heaven' (*The Garden of Cyrus*), to form a single piece. Hegel, as all know, did not invent the thesis, antithesis, and synthesis; Plato did. And having quoted Coleridge once, it is instructive to quote him again:

He for whom Ideas are constitutive will in effect be a Platonist—and in those for whom they are regulative only, Platonism is but a hollow affectation. . . . How little the commentators of Milton have availed themselves of the writings of Plato, Milton's darling.[3]

So much for Plato; Christian examples will come later.

That the pattern exists no one will dispute. We must now show that it functions centrally in *Paradise Lost* through a comparison of the pre- and post-lapsarian states of its two human characters. Milton, a Renaissance Christian humanist, weaves into his doctrine and his art at least four separate modes of systasis between pairs of reconcilable opposites. In an order of increasing depth and significance these modes are (1) the marriage between *male* and *female*; (2) the conflict and reconciliation in plot of the *union-with* and the *separation-from* good; (3) the terms *good* and *evil* within the propositions of his 'great argument'; and (4) the relationship between *Creator* and *creature* in theology.

[2] *Timaeus*, 35–37; tr. B. Jowett.
[3] *Coleridge on the Seventeenth Century*, ed. R. F. Brinkley (1955), p. 553.

I

In the first place, *Paradise Lost* describes the mating before and after the Fall of the wisest and most handsome man and the most beautiful woman, in figure and spirit, that can be imagined. They are opposites, in sex, in dominion, in divided responsibilities, and yet theirs is a union in prosperity and adversity. It is only part of Marvell's wit outside the three central stanzas of *The Garden* that can argue that 'Two paradises 'twere in one/To live in Paradise alone'. Adam calls his wife 'Best Image of my self and dearer half' (V, 95), and Eve's beautiful paean to Adam in the form of a cancrizone that lists the beauties of nature up the scale and then down depends, perhaps too much, upon her husband (IV, 641–56). Nature is created in a kind of *yang* and *yin*, with other suns and their attendant moons 'Communicating Male and Femal Light,/Which two great Sexes animate the World' (VIII, 150–1). Conscious of this law of nature even before Eve is born, Adam tells God that he needs a fellow human being for 'harmonie or true delight' 'Which must be mutual, in proportion due/Giv'n and receiv'd' (VIII, 384–6). And part of the divine plan for this union is that Adam be the superior term, Eve the inferior, a pattern which Adam recognises but which he, like the rest of us, cannot always believe (VIII, 540–60).

How nicely Milton prepares for their tragic separation on that fatal day by assigning to these two of a single pair their opposite yet conjoined tasks in Eden! The Creator's extravagance must be met by man's prudence, and all the economy of this couple consists of binding up and lopping away, as if the only tools in that first potting shed were a ball of twine and some pruning shears. Their 'sweet Gardning labour' (IV, 328) and 'delightful task' (IV, 437) is this pair of opposite duties; 'To prune these growing Plants, and tend these Flours. . . .' (IV, 438–9).

Adam's job seems mostly to bind up and cut away the excess branches of the fruit-trees for their growth, while Eve's is to prop up the flowers and to pluck the fruit. In her dream (IV, 450–81) she sees herself amid the flowers and her husband under a plantain tree. As she leaves him in an ill-fated attempt at *division* of labour, she busies herself binding up roses, while her husband, we hope, was staking up the tomato plants. Satan not only hears them talk of the Forbidden Tree, but he learns from this first school of agriculture that 'Nature multiplies/Her fertil growth, and by disburd'ning grows/More fruitful' (V, 319-20). In that rash hour, therefore, Eve comes to her more responsible self, and plucks the apple; she has been trained to gather the fruit for Adam's table that more fruit may grow. While she temporarily leaves her flowers for the fruit, however, Adam, who has finished his morning labour in the orchard, is spending his noon hour weaving for his wife a garland of flowers (IX, 840).

Though Milton avoids a systematic division of labour, the simple male and female tasks of Adam and Eve become a metaphor for the whole poem. Paradoxically, Satan lops away their innocence that God's grace may burgeon. And the punishment for disobedience is that mothers create fruit within their wombs and fathers support the children with the sweat of their brows while it is Death who holds the pruning shears. Yet, after the Fall, the Father and Son enter into a kind of husbandry that did not exist before:

> See Father, what first fruits on Earth are sprung
> From thy implanted Grace in Man . . .
> Fruits of more pleasing savour from thy seed
> Sown with contrition in his heart, then those
> Which his own hand manuring all the Trees
> Of Paradise could have produc't, ere fall'n
> From innocence.   (XI, 22-30)

The traditional term for this restoration was 'engrafting', or as Milton's God says to the Son, man shall 'live in thee transplanted' (III, 293).

In the psychology of marriage between male and female, two opposites, capable of a tragic split, are joined to create a harmony. Eve, female alone, consistently seeks earth and self; Adam, male alone, tends toward airy abstractions and metaphysical conceits of reality. The two together in their bower of bliss and supporting love keep the central concern both earthly and heavenly, a union of bodies and minds. When Eve confesses her fault and raises her husband from despair, we see how male and female join to create a whole that is greater than the mere summation of the two parts. Finally, the very love Adam has for Eve is the cause not only of his fall but also of his salvation. If Adam typologically is Christ then his willingness to die with and for Eve foreshadows the Son's promise to die out of God's love for man. Thus Milton's drawing of these two characters is a systatic pattern of a life that can spring out of a death.

II

Adam and Eve, of course, are the hero of *Paradise Lost*, and the story takes them from their creation to the loss of Eden. Our second point is that the plot Milton 'invents' is, like most great plots, a necessary reconciliation of the two opposing forces which initially create the conflict. Adam and Eve become the centre between a cause and a result, as in the setting of this mighty plot the earth, on which the action takes place, swings pendulously below the ramparts of Heaven and yet far above Hell. Book IX, the temptation and the fall, is the climax of the story with two great waves of causation before it and two great waves of result after it. Satan's desire for revenge is the immediate cause, and the ultimate cause is his own revolt from awe and expulsion from good. After the Fall, the lust instead of love and the recriminations instead of harmony are the immediate result, while the ultimate result is their redemption and that of mankind.

More specifically, the plot of *Paradise Lost* follows that age-old pattern of a relationship with good in three stages: first, the hero has a relationship with good that is mostly stable: in the second stage, there is an almost complete separation from that good; and finally, there is a re-establishment of that union with the good in a form more challenging and yet more stable than it was before.

A few examples will illustrate this kind of plot. In the *Iliad*, Achilles first has an apparently stable union with the Greek host, which is precarious because of his capacity for wrath; in the second stage, of separation, Achilles sulks in his tent until the Trojan forces almost win the war; and finally, after the death of Patroclus, the re-establishment of the union with the Greeks brings about the victory that was impossible before. Again, Oedipus at first is the proud and passionate king of Thebes in a union with his people that hangs on ignorance and an ability to solve childish riddles; next, there is the complete separation from his wife, his daughters, his people; until finally, at Colonus, he is reunited with good in a more stable union, embraced, as it were, by the gods themselves. The hero of Milton's *Samson*, which begins in the fifth act, also cries as a sign of discovery and reversal, 'My riddling days are past' (*S.A.*, 1064). One more example of the familiar plot will suffice, Fielding's *Tom Jones*. The first six books show Tom in a rather precarious union with his natural benefactor, Allworthy, in what might be called a state of semi-innocence. Then a series of events separate Tom from Allworthy, and he travels for six books on the road to London becoming more experienced along the way. Finally, in London, he learns the truth that re-establishes him with Allworthy in a real union, so that with his garden-innocence of good nature enhanced by his knowledge of the world he can truly become Allworthy's heir, marry his beloved Sophia, prudently double the acreage of his estate, and live happily as a real squire to its people.

In the first stage of the plot of *Paradise Lost,* the union with God is good and stable because it is beneficent and easy and natural for Adam and Eve constantly to affirm it. But for them to remain in that stage would rob them of a more difficult perfection. There must be, therefore, signs that lead us to expect the separation from that good, and Adam and Eve are given a capacity to disobey even before Satan steals into their fold. Thus, almost from the beginning their morning and evening prayers and repasts of both food and love are threatened. Immediately after the famous paean 'Haile wedded Love' (IV, 750 ff.), Milton tells us the Cherubim 'from their Ivorie Port. . . . Forth issuing at th' accustomd hour stood armd/To their night watches in warlike Parade' (IV, 777–80). They find Satan, the inventor of gunpowder, squatting like a toad at Eve's ear, and:

> As when a spark
> Lights on a heap of nitrous Powder, laid
> Fit for the Tun som Magazin to store
> Against a rumord Warr, the Smuttie graine
> With sudden blaze diffus'd, inflames the Aire:
> So started up in his own shape the Fiend.   (IV, 814–19)

During the initial union with God, appearance continually clashes with reality, dreams and fancies with truth. Telling Adam her dream, Eve describes the voice she heard—'I thought it thine' (V, 37); it wasn't. As for the interdicted tree, she says, 'Fair it seemd,/Much fairer to my Fancie than by day' (V, 52–53). The unforgettable presence of the moon in the night-scenes of Eden anticipates change. The moon rising in 'clouded Majesty' is 'apparent queen' in two senses, manifest and in appearance only. And all night long the nightingale, that 'solemn bird', sings a song that to Milton and to us, though not to Adam and Eve, is a song of passion, pain, separation, change, and eventual triumph. Such urgings of the plot bring to mind Wallace Stevens' line, 'Let *be* be the finale of *seem*'.

Similarly after the Fall, in the middle stage of plot, things must seem worse than they actually are, as this kind of irony, which always consists of a disproportion of knowledge between us and the actors in the drama, knits part to part. Before the true equilibrium can be attained, Adam and Eve have to become almost all flesh with very little of the divine. Hence Adam's uxoriousness, apart from Biblical and patristic precedent, becomes necessary to Milton's plot. 'I feel/The Link of Nature draw me: Flesh of Flesh,/Bone of my Bond thou art' (IX, 913–15), cries the distracted husband truly beside himself, that is, close to the extreme of the lower half of his nature. So great is their despair that they contemplate suicide. Then, 'Submitting to what *seemd* remediless' (IX, 917–19), Adam comforts his wife by the belief that despite their sin God cannot destroy them utterly. Where Satan was once 'stupidly good' (which means good for the wrong reasons), Adam here is stupidly wise: since he does not yet know of the plan for redemption, Milton makes him instinctively guess at the next and final stage of his own plot. After the Fall, the bond with God is more difficult, involving as it does free choice and a struggle against all environmental pressures. And yet the final reconciliation makes for a stronger bond because of the covenant between God and man.

In plot, then, the union-with and the separation-from good is laid out in the three inevitable stages of thesis, anti-thesis, and synthesis from the very beginning: first, the union—'Say first . . . what cause/Mov'd our Grand Parents in that happy State,/Favour'd of Heav'n so highly'; secondly, the tragic separation from that good—'to fall off/From thir Creator'; and finally, '. . . till one greater Man/Restore us'. In this way the plot of *Paradise Lost* is a pattern of systasis between two opposites, a good that is not quite complete and an evil that does not deserve total damnation.

III

The plot, however, is only the formal proof of a great argument, which demands not only a series of propositions that are acceptable but also a certain manner of arguing. In the art of argumentation Milton knew well the difference between violently opposed points of view and those which, by being complementary rather than contradictory, can allow a reconciliation. Satan the adversary, we all recognise, is unequivocal evil in his steadfast pursuit of everything which is opposite to the good: 'the more I see/Pleasures about me, so much more I feel/Torment within me', he complains, 'as from the hateful siege/Of contraries' (IX, 120–22). These Milton had defined in his *Art of Logic*[4] as mutually exclusive, like *seeing versus blindness* or *motion versus rest*. The total separation between good and its avowed adversary is like the eternally separated bounds of hell that consist of intense heat and gelid cold:

> Thither by harpy-footed Furies haild,
> At certain revolutions all the damnd
> Are brought; and feel by turns the bitter change
> Of fierce extreams, extreams by change more fierce,
> From Beds of raging Fire to starve in Ice
>   . . . thence hurried back to fire.   (II, 596–603)

Again, wilfully separated evil and good become the siege of contraries:

>   the evil soon
> Driv'n back redounded as a flood on those
> From whom it sprung, impossible to mix
> With Blessedness.   (VII, 56–59)

When arguing only one side of a prolusion, such as whether night is better than day or whether the world is decaying or getting better, Milton or any schoolboy would not give an inch. Rhetoric demanded, in Professor Rajan's nice phrase, 'the kind of over-statement inevitable in a prolusion'. Some of us think that this is the way Milton argued with Salmasius or any other poor devil that came within the reach of his prose. On the tenure of kings and magistrates Milton is right, and the other is wrong; there are no two ways about it.

But in poetry Milton deals with *mixable* opposites. *L'Allegro* and *Il Penseroso* must dismiss the extreme contraries of each in order that they come together. 'Hence loathed Melancholy/Of Cerberus, and blackest midnight born', an exaggerated extreme at the beginning of the first poem, allows the real melancholy of studious concern to follow. Similarly, 'Hence vain deluding joyes,/The brood of folly without father bred', dismisses the extreme of what more temperately is that kind of joy which 'would have won the ear/Of Pluto, to have quite set free/His half-regain'd Eurydice'. This is because all of us can be both the joyful free man and the responsible contemplative; the latter is the

---

[4] I, xiv; in *Works*, XI, 117.

more valued term but the systasis of the two in our minds becomes that third, the true ideal of 'sweetness and light'. The same pattern had also been practised by Milton in the two brothers of Comus and the Attendant Spirit, whose final solution has some of the fear of real consequences that the younger brother divulges and some of the rational optimism of the elder brother, each brother being partial and individual but also contingent and fulfilling.

Milton was a disputant for a great part of his life, and *Paradise Lost* is his greatest argument, as it must be to justify the ways of God to man. But *Paradise Lost* as rhetoric displays the irenic disposition of Acontius' *Stratagemata Satanae*. Published in Oxford in 1565, this is not so much a work on theology as it is an *ars disputandi* for learned men on how to conduct a Christian enquiry into truth. 'Don't get the idea that you know everything', Acontius warns; for,

Unhinged by this conviction you will not be able to suffer any man to utter a complete sentence; scarcely has he opened his mouth, when you will think you have fathomed what the other is going to say, and even what he might say. And with a single word—a word, do I say? nay rather, with a single laugh or grim look or gesture of some sort you think you have more than sufficiently explained away any objection that may have been raised; and if any one dare so much as to hint disagreement with anything you have affirmed or denied, you regard him as guilty of high treason or sacrilege.[5]

In *Paradise Lost* arguments like those between the Father and Son, or between Adam and Raphael, or between Adam and Eve are, expectedly, Socratic dialogues bringing to fruition two opposites in the form of a newer truth. But Milton's core argument must prove that good can come out of evil. He has given the devil his due so generously that Dryden and others were misled into thinking the devil is the hero, an illusion that may be one of Satan's stratagems. Yet contrary though he is, Satan remains a son of God and an agent in the overall plan for His family of creatures, since the totality of the Creator is fulfilled in the myriad kinds of behaviour of His creatures. The final dramatic fulfilment will be the Son's assuming the heavenly throne and all creatures becoming God in Him. Apart from theology, therefore, this kind of rhetorical systasis differs from Satan's (and the logician's) 'siege of contraries' in the same way that St Augustine differentiated the two modes in his *Enchiridion* on faith, hope, and charity:

From this we deduce the curious fact that, since every being so far as it is a being is good, when we say that a faulty being is an evil being, we seem to say

[5] *Satan's Stratagems*, tr. W. T. Curtis (San Francisco, 1940), p. 50.

only that evil is good, and that nothing but good can be evil, seeing that every being is good and that no evil is possible if the very thing which is evil is not a real being. There can therefore be no evil thing unless it be something good. And although this seems to be a contradiction in terms, the logic of this reasoning seems inevitably to force us to make this conclusion. . . . Wherefore, in these contraries known as good and evil the rule of the logicians that two contraries cannot be found simultaneously in the same thing, does not hold.[6]

This rhetorical necessity to allow the closing of gaps between opposites rather than their widening into contraries supports the generally accepted thesis that *De doctrina* comes close in the time of its composition to *Paradise Lost*. Its mitigation of extreme Calvinistic positions on election, reprobation, and predestination, as well as the Arminian tendencies of both the Latin prose and the English epic as compared with the views that Milton had held in the early 1640s, illustrate once more a trend towards systasis in disputation as he prepared to write his great poem.

To argue the anti-synergistic propositions of a narrower Calvinism would get him into 'the siege of contraries'. Synergism means the joining together of two energies, opposite in that one is God's and the other man's, but complementary to each other.

IV

Which brings us at last to theology. The reconcilable opposites in the characters, in the plot, and in the argument have at their base the pairs, paradoxes, oppositions, and reconciliations of Christian theology. All the essential Christian doctrines are Platonic systases, as man and God, the Fall and the Redemption, visible and invisible, the summary of the ten commandments into two—to love God and to love one's fellow man. Thus many a tripartite division will sooner or later dichotomise itself, like the three theological virtues of faith-and-hope on one side (for God) and charity on the other (for man), which partially accounts for Milton's dividing his *De Doctrina* into two books. It is this conjunction of Creator and creature that Milton hopes for in his great pleas for inspiration, a voice from heaven 'above th' Olympian Hill' and 'the flight of Pegasean wing' (VII, 1-4). Only by God and man together will

[6] *Enchiridion*, IV, 13-14 (Migne, vol. XL; tr. L. A. Arand, *Ancient Christian Writers*, III [1955], 20-21).

> Earth be chang'd to Heav'n, and Heav'n to Earth,
> One Kingdom, Joy and Union without end.   (VII, 160–1)

As Michael prepares to give Adam his future history, he counsels man to moderate opposites:

> thereby to learn
> True patience, and to temper joy with fear
> And pious sorrow, equally inur'd
> By moderation either state to bear,
> Prosperous or adverse.   (XI, 360–4)

This reflects the pattern in heaven of the Father's tempering His justice with the Son's mercy:

> To them by Faith imputed, they may finde
> Justification towards God, and peace
> Of Conscience, which the Law of Ceremonies
> Cannot appease, nor Man the moral part
> Perform, and not performing cannot live.
> So Law appears imperfet, and but giv'n
> With purpose to resign them in full time
> Up to a better Cov'nant, disciplind
> From shadowie Types to Truth, from Flesh to Spirit,
> From imposition of strict Laws, to free
> Acceptance of large Grace, from servil fear
> To filial, works of Law to works of Faith   (XII, 295–306)

since Christ said, 'I come not to destroy [the law] but to fulfill [it]' (*Matt.* 5: 17). In *Paradise Lost*, as elsewhere, the theological pattern works in pairs of opposites, the lower terms drawn up to the higher, the two together forming systases of wholes greater than the summation of the two parts.

Experience of evil, as the child realises who learns that the stove is hot by burning his hand, costs us something. Not being gods but only men, we will go on paying that price—'Knowledge of Good bought dear by knowing ill' (IV, 222)—pausing wishfully with Adam on that too sudden reconciliation of opposites within his soul:

> O goodness infinite, goodness immense!
> That all this good of evil shall produce,
> And evil turn to good; more wonderful
> Then that which by creation first brought forth
> Light out of darkness!   (XII, 469–73)

Adam forgets that Michael, a few minutes before, had tried to warn him against sounding like the elder brother in *Comus*:

> nor can this be,
> But by fulfilling that which thou didst want,
> Obedience to the Law of God . . . and . . . love.   (XII, 395–404)

Just as, right after the Fall, Adam was too far over on the side of self-conviction—'his evil Conscience represented/All things with double terror' (X, 849–50)—so here he is too far over on the side of optimism. The final lesson of the poem is not that the Fall is fortunate but this:

> Henceforth I learne, that to obey is best,
> And love with feare the onely God . . .   (XII, 561–2)

'This having learnt', Michael tells Adam at the end of the poem, 'thou hast attaind the summe/Of wisdom' (XII, 575–6).

Adam and Eve after the Fall must become true warriors; to survive the battle they helped create the need to be well armed. Hence the vignettes that Michael shows them of future history imitate the epic arming of the hero to go forth to his greatest challenge. The vignettes mix events in future time and actions that are timeless and typical of the human scene: first Cain and Abel, and then a lazar-house; the descendants of Jubal and Seth, and then a general carnage. The two kinds of pictures combine the shields of Achilles and of Aeneas: the Greek (*Iliad*, XVIII) depicts general human scenes of no specific time, whereas the shield made for Aeneas (*Aeneid*, VIII) shows in relief actual events in the future founding of Rome.[7]

If the first shield is wrought by Hephaistos and the second by Vulcan, the 'shield' of the final book of *Paradise Lost* is 'the whole spiritual armour' of St Paul. It is a shield of systatic unions of apparent opposites, the shield of the St Paul of *Romans, Corinthians, Galatians,* and *Ephesians.* Michael assures Adam and Eve that 'the Law of Faith/Working through love' shall 'arme [them] With spiritual Armour, able to resist/Satans assaults, and quench his fierie darts' (XII, 488–92; cf. *Ephes.* 6: 11). This Pauline pattern finally is well illustrated in the sixth chapter of second *Corinthians,* which could describe Adam and Eve *after* 'They hand in hand with wandring steps and slow,/Through Eden took their solitary way'. The passage begins with a series of merely correlative

---

[7] L. A. Sasek, 'The Drama of *Paradise Lost*, Books XI and XII', in *Studies in English Renaissance Literature,* ed. W. F. McNeir (Baton Rouge, 1962), pp. 181–96.

pairs; in the middle it divides into 'right hand' and 'left', and then launches into pairs of antitheses which end in shocking oxymoron:

> . . . in much patience, in afflictions [wrote St Paul]; in necessities, in distresses; in stripes, in imprisonments; in tumults, in labours; in watchings, in fastings; by pureness, by knowledge; by long suffering, by kindness; by the Holy Ghost, by love unfeigned; by the word of truth, by the power of God; by the armour of righteousness on the right hand, and on the left by honour and dishonour; by evil report and by good report; as deceivers, and yet true; as unknown, and yet well known; as dying, and, behold we live; as chastened, and not killed; as sorrowful, yet always rejoicing; as poor, yet making many rich; as having nothing, and yet possessing all things.

Thus, from the confluence of those two mighty rivers of thought and feeling, the Graeco-Roman and the Judaeo-Christian, Milton has drawn a pattern of complementary opposites which is the pattern of systasis, by means of which he sustains the persons, the story, the argument, and the doctrine of *Paradise Lost*.

Paradise Lost as Mimesis

Irene Samuel

To spend our reading of *Paradise Lost* quarrelling with Milton's God is as futile as it would be to read *Hamlet* quarrelling with the theory of monarchy or the existence of ghosts. Perhaps there never ought to have been kings in Denmark, perhaps there never were ghosts; but the tragedy of Prince Hamlet is not a tract on either subject, and *Paradise Lost* is not a tract on theocracy. Like tragedy, comedy, and other modes of the literary art, epic poetry represents a human action; and like every such representation, assuming a reality to imitate, it implies a whole complex of desirabilities and undesirabilities in human life. Renaissance commentators on Aristotle's *Poetics* were for ever saying that there is little else for poetry to imitate but men in action. And Milton thought the matter so obvious that in his preface to *Samson Agonistes* he merely quoted and translated Aristotle's phrase, 'Tragedy is an imitation of a serious action, etc.,' saving his comment for more debatable matters.

In the eighteenth century Dr Johnson was the critic who most enjoyed complaining of Milton. Every era seems to have had at least one. And Johnson's every word on Milton can contribute to our understanding—if only we invert it. He criticised the 'want of human interest' in *Paradise Lost*, asserting

> The plan . . . has this inconvenience, that it comprises neither human actions nor human manners. The man and woman who act and suffer are in a state which no other man or woman can ever know. The reader finds no transaction in which he can be engaged; beholds no condition in which he can by any effort of imagination place himself; he has, therefore, little natural curiosity or sympathy.

Clearly Johnson expected 'truths too important to be new', truths 'taught to our infancy'—and found what he expected, a mere versifying of familiar Sunday school stories.[1] An odd choice that would have been for one of the most independent minds of the seventeenth century in his greatest poetical effort—an odd repudiation of every principle by which he lived and worked. The one time Milton undertook merely to set down someone else's views, in his translation of the *Judgement of Martin Bucer*, he affixed a postscript proclaiming that he

> could never delight in long citations, much less in whole traductions; whether it be natural disposition or education in me, or that my mother bore me a speaker of what God made mine own.

The unprejudiced reader will grant that Milton's mother did indeed bear him a speaker of what is his own.

As a Christian he of course held central Christian beliefs; but innumerable poems might be written out of the same beliefs, some of them as tedious as Dr Johnson thought *Paradise Lost*. Milton had thought hard about poetics, 'that sublime art which . . . teaches what the laws are of a true epic poem, what of a dramatic, what of a lyric', and enunciated at least one major law of an epic poem. In his *Second Defense* he declares:

> the poet who is called epic . . . does not undertake the whole life of the hero whom he proposes to sing, but just one action of his life, that of Achilles, for example, at Troy, or the return of Ulysses, or the coming of Aeneas to Italy . . .; the rest he leaves alone.

The one action he chose as subject of his epic poem is unmistakably the losing of Paradise, not universal human history, not a justification of God, not a versified *Doctrina Christiana*. The titles he gave his various earlier plans for tragedies on the theme make the point: *Paradise Lost, Paradise Lost, Paradise Lost, Adam Unparadiz'd*. The summary he prefixed to the several books of his completed poem in its second edition makes the same point:

> The first Book proposes, . . . in brief, the whole Subject, *Mans disobedience and the loss thereupon of Paradise*.

Like other Renaissance critics Milton divided poetics into invention and

---

[1] Yet presumably Johnson knew how distorted his own reading of Milton was, since he transcribes into his 'Life of J[ohn] Philips' from a Bodleian MS by Edmund Smith the revealing comment: 'False criticks have been the plague of all ages; Milton himself, in a very polite court, has been compared to the rumbling of a wheel-barrow; he had been on the wrong side, and therefore could not be a good poet' (*The Lives of the Most Eminent English Poets* [London, 1794], I, 431).

disposition.² Wherever the poet finds his subject he must still invent his fable and so arrange its parts that they represent a single unified action.

In *Paradise Lost* Milton professes to be undertaking 'Things unattempted yet in Prose or Rime', not old familiar matter in a new mode of unrhymed verse, but a poem never before written. And surely *Paradise Lost* never was written until he wrote it. If Dr Johnson could have let Milton write his poem, not guessing what this 'modern Greek' 'would or could or should have sung . . . in tolerable verse,' he might have found 'human interest' aplenty—and raised more relevant issues.

The first relevant questions about the poem of Milton's invention are: What Paradise? what loss? And then, as we read 'Of Mans First Disobedience': What disobedience? indeed what man? The answers can only be given by the entire unfolding action. Of course Milton assumes and plays upon our initial response. As soon as we hear the title and opening phrase, we will think *Genesis* 1–3, or even

> In Adam's fall
> We sinned all.

But he has written:

> Of Mans First Disobedience, and the Fruit
> Of that Forbidd'n Tree, whose mortal tast
> Brought Death into the World, and all our woe,
> With loss of *Eden* . . .

Whether or not we formulate it, the effect of that opening is to catch us up into the poem, less as the heirs of original sin than as members of the human species who desire joy, Eden, and have death and woe. The opening statement of the subject immediately infuses into the Biblical story universal human meanings—unless we prefer to say reads out of that story the universal meanings Milton recognised in the tale of Adam, Hebrew for man, losing Eden, Hebrew for bliss.

The invocation similarly fuses the Hebraic and Hellenic traditions. Here too Milton plays upon our initial assumption, that the poem is

---

² Not that Milton, or many Renaissance critics, felt bound by the division; but on the importance of invention to the Renaissance critics named by Milton in *Of Education*, see, for example: Castelvetro, *Poetica d'Aristotele vulgarizzata*, II, 2: 'la quale inventione è la più difficile cosa che habbia il poeta da fare, & dalla quale parte pare che egli prenda il nome, ciò è ποιητής' (Vienna, 1570, p. 43; Basel, 1576, p. 78); Mazzoni, *Difesa della Comedia di Dante* (Cesena, 1587), III, 5, p. 408; Tasso, *Discorsi del Poema Heroico* (Naples, 1594), II, p. 20, and III, p. 56.

going to present the Biblical story in the classical epic genre, to make us feel, whether or not we formulate it, that our whole western tradition is involved, less as Christian content in Greek form than as total civilised heritage. The Heavenly Muse accomplishes that just by being invoked—as Muse she is Greek, as Heavenly something more than Urania; the reference a few lines later to the familiar temple in Jerusalem as the unexpectedly Hellenic 'Oracle of God' helps; the explicit statement that the invoked Spirit prefers 'Before all Temples th' upright heart and pure' urges the point home. Human truths are not peculiarly Hebraic or Hellenic, but human; poetic values are not uniquely classical or Biblical, but poetic. The poem will 'soar/Above th' *Aonian Mount*'—not straight off to Mount Sion, also named in the invocation, but into a realm from which both mounts are beheld in a single landscape, the human scene.

The point can be made endlessly out of all Milton's habits as thinker, as writer; perhaps one high moment in *Paradise Lost* makes it best. At the grand climax of the creation of this universe, in Book VII, developed from Genesis, Plato's *Timaeus*, Ovid's *Metamorphoses*, and whatever else Milton found to his poetic purpose, Raphael tells Adam of the creation of man:

> There wanted yet the Maister work, the end
> Of all yet don; a Creature . . . endu'd
> With Sanctitie of Reason, . . .
> . . . self-knowing, and from thence
> Magnanimous to correspond with Heav'n,
> But grateful to acknowledge whence his good
> Descends. (VII, 505–13)

Perfect man is to be 'self-knowing', the great Socratic ideal, and 'from thence magnanimous' with the Aristotelian culmination of all the virtues, *megalopsychia*, in order to 'correspond with'—be like and thus able to communicate with—the Christian Heaven. Such a fusion of classical and Christian is implicit from the start in Milton's poem as it promises its human story.

And at once the action commences by plunging us into Hell—all too recognisably human, with every posture of Satan, every impulse of Moloch, Belial, Mammon, Beelzebub, the very architecture of Pandemonium, the diplomatic manoeuvrings at Hell's gate and in Chaos only too familiar. It takes no uncommon thinker to be against evil; it took a most uncommon poet to invent a Satan not damnable because he is damned, but damned because he is thoroughly damnable. Not the tags, the names, devil, Hell, Sin, but the death-producing deeds that merit the names carry the action forward. The propelling impulse of this entirely recognisable Hell is: Let the universe be smashed so I retain my eminence as Most Important Person. Typically self-important, Satan needs worlds, made by others, to destroy.

When the scene shifts to Heaven, again the names, the tags, God, Messiah, angel, do not carry the meaning; rather the deeds and words invented by the poet give their meanings to the names. Here wisdom rules, justice triumphs by acclaiming generosity, and if the heavenly life lived in admiration and love is more desirable than familiar, it is the humanly desirable Milton represents. Here the propelling impulse is: Let life be saved at whatever sacrifice. Humanly that is the one impulse we can all admire, and Milton's Heaven asks only that we admire it. It takes far less shift from our normal values to participate in the mimesis of this Heaven than in the Homeric or Virgilian Olympus, the best features of which Milton has quietly adopted.

The detail of Books I–III is designed to establish the values on which the losing of Paradise will turn. At the same time the purposes and plans of all the agents thus far involved make it of momentous importance that Paradise not be lost—as it is going to be—even if to be salvaged, as it is also going to be.

With tremendous poetic daring Milton delays Eden until Book IV, intensifying the reader's expectation as the whole universe concentrates its interest on that small stage. Like a wave gathering momentum as it moves from Hell through Chaos to the empyrean and thence through interstellar space to the sun, the action sweeps into Eden, to break there in a rippling calm, from which it soon starts to gain momentum for another great wave that will not break until the fall in Book IX, after which we 'only hear its melancholy, long, withdrawing roar' and are left stranded on 'the vast edges drear and naked shingles' of this world. Of the two great waves in which the action of *Paradise Lost* moves, the first does not break until it reaches Paradise in Book IV, the second until it crashes in the losing of Paradise. And it was poetically daring to gather so much momentum in Books I–III. For if this Eden proves scarcely worth the fuss Heaven and Hell are making about it, no propriety of theological conviction can save Milton's poem. If this Eden is a bore, by all means get Satan—or whoever—to the rescue. No sensible person wants to be bored.

If the innocence of Milton's Eden were a negative, or even partial state, the representation had better not pause as a great arrival. Obviously the brief tale in Genesis could now complete itself. Yet Milton delays the losing of Paradise through four more books, inventing even more lavishly than in the first three the developing action. Books I–III have been prelude, as Books X–XII will be aftermath. Books IV–IX enact the completeness of Eden and then the completeness of its shattering.

The opening words of Book IV show with what force the poet is thrusting off to Book IX the great crisis of the poem:

> O for that warning voice . . .
> . . . that now,
> While time was, our first Parents had bin warnd
> The coming of thir secret foe, and scap't,
> Haply so scap't his mortal snare.

A warning voice will in fact come in Book V and converse with Adam through Book VIII, making the event of Book IX all but impossible, while never letting us forget that it is coming. That is how the tensions of dramatic and narrative mimesis work: through our knowing what is to happen and straining against its happening. Where the issue is unknown curiosity leads us on; where it is foreknown, as in the greatest tragedies, dramatic and epic, it always is, not curiosity but involvement pulls us, unwilling-willing what is to come.

In the initial speech by an agent in Book IV, Satan soliloquising develops the motives he brings to the Garden: hatred for the universe that is, determination to dominate as much of it as he can, disdain as the pose behind which to hide self-contempt, self-pity for self-inflicted woes—the whole psychosis of the divided mind turning upon and rending itself because it cannot be the totality of things.

And only then at last we are allowed Eden. We behold it, not through the distorting lenses of Satan's eyes—that would be to mar the place fatally in advance—but over his shoulder. We see what is there to behold as he cannot; he sees 'undelighted all delight' (IV, 286); we can allow ourselves delight alloyed only by our sense of what lies ahead because of his presence. Among the poetic achievements of this Eden is that it almost makes us forget the danger. But perhaps the most remarkable achievement is that a poet in advanced middle age could so thoroughly give his mind to imagining two perfectly happy young people delighting so entirely in their lives.

Remarkably too, he includes varieties of response to this Eden. The same power that enables him to organise tremendous reaches of time and space without ever letting the single ongoing action lose itself in a map of the universe or a chronicle of universal history, much the same organising power enables him to represent something like the spectrum of possible human mood, motive, response to all manner of things—including Eden—without ever pausing to catalogue them. Each reveals its value as it plays its part in events. The first reaction to Eden that we witness is envious contempt, and that reaction Milton assigns to Satan. The comment of inhumanity on the pleasant garden is a curse:

> O Hell! what doe mine eyes with grief behold,
> Into our room of bliss thus high advanc't
> Creatures of other mould, earth-born perhaps . . . (IV, 358–60)

Why should other, inferior people know joy? That grudging of other people's pleasures Milton shows as allied to the determination to cause pain; so too he allies the contempt, rooted in envy, that calls other people inferior to the determination to use them for one's own purpose:

> League with you I seek,
> And mutual amitie so streight, so close,
> That I with you must dwell, or you with mee
> Henceforth . . . .
>   Hell shall unfould,
> To entertain you two, her widest Gates,
>   . . . there will be room,
> Not like these narrow limits. . . .   (IV, 375–84)

The villain is all but curling his mustachios as he gloats in advance over the suffering he is going to inflict. For Satan is doing his damnedest to turn the world into melodrama.

Did such malice and such sneers ever strike any reader as the voice of independent energy? Blake, who knew that energy is eternal delight? Shelley, who knew that moral energy is the ability to enter into the pleasures and pains of our species? It would be interesting to know how admirers of Milton's Satan read such lines.

And it would be interesting to know how Dr Johnson read the loving dialogue between Adam and Eve that follows. An Adam who argues from the fullness of his joys to the bounty of the universe, an Eve who thinks herself fortunate to have someone 'preeminent by so much odds' as Adam to live with, in their exuberant sense that all the world, save for 'one easie prohibition', is theirs to enjoy—perhaps they are unlike young Sam Johnson and his bride—and yet perhaps not unlike what young Sam Johnson and his bride, if they were happy, dreamed themselves to be.

In the following book, Raphael, far more at home in a far wider world than Satan, is also at home visiting Eden, and sharing Adam and Eve's pleasures can prepare them to share his. The action hardly stops to make such points; it makes them because the imagination that invented it had experienced, observed, pondered an extraordinary range of human affairs and manners, and poured his full human understanding into his poem.

Here, at the end of Book IV, the self-applauding, self-lamenting, envious-contemptuous threatener of Eden, so certain that he will immediately demolish the place, is soon put to ignominious flight. His confrontation by Ithuriel and Zephon, and again by Gabriel, in which he has to hear some home truths, simply ends with his removal. And with that thrusting out of Satan, and the thrusting off of the fall until Book IX, Eden can become increasingly Edenic, not merely the place that is going to be lost, but positively the state of joyous growth, for which innocence, not-hurt-fulness, is only the negative name.

In Book V, after coping with Eve's nightmare—and yes, this Eden can include a nightmare—Adam and Eve begin to range imaginatively through an expanding world as they entertain the sociable spirit Raphael. They hear and comment on his exposition of the great chain of being, his narrative of the war in Heaven, his account of the designing of the universe as their home. Then Adam has further opportunity to learn and grow as he further discusses with Raphael his own partially mistaken views on astronomy and life in Eden—for yes, this Eden can include even mistakes. Through Books V–VIII it becomes increasingly clear that this happy pair are not forbidden to think, to raise questions, to have impulses and notions, to correct false impressions, to deal with their world out of their own developing natures and knowledge. This Eden can contain whatever stuff of life may enable man to become more 'self-knowing, and from thence/Magnanimous to correspond with Heav'n'.

Of course Books V–VIII at the same time expand the poem to include events from the remote and near past in places beyond the scene of the action proper. Of course the war in Heaven serves also as an exemplum demonstrating a maxim, a parallel to the events of the future that will be foretold in Books XI–XII, a contrast to the details of the fall in Book IX. Of course the creation-story in Book VII also contrasts with the destruction-story in Book VI and with the destruction-reconstruction story in XI–XII. And we can work out a great many other relations. In a living organism it can be shown that the big toe of the left foot is interconnected with the right earlobe. But when we flatten out the organism to diagram its various networks, we may murder to dissect.

Mimetically, Raphael's visit is that part of the developing action 'where God or Angel Guest/With Man, as with his Friend, familiar us'd/To sit indulgent' in an expansive interchange through which the garden proves itself Eden. Books V–VIII are not attached as removable episode, but designed to make Book IX impossible—until it comes. By the time we have participated in the full mimesis of the first eight books, we feel—whether or not we formulate it—that the one possible impossibility is to throw Eden away. Everything else is permitted, encouraged, easily remedied. And that, I take it, is the point of the place: it can afford everything, include everything—a nightmare, a graphic account of war, even mistaken notions and impulses—everything but its own cancellation. And in Book IX Eve and Adam decide to cancel Eden out.

The opening phrase of the poem, 'Of Mans First Disobedience', stops a number of readers from ever reading further. They know what Milton's poem is going to say: it is going to recommend blind obedience as the desideratum, servile fear and trembling, being content in the station to which providence has assigned us. But these recommendations are hardly Milton's. His poem contravenes them as his whole life repudiated them. The phrase should of course raise the question Obedience/disobedience to what? to whom? *Paradise Lost* itself demonstrates through the Abdiel episode that Milton, far from requiring compliance to every so-called superior, thought such compliance might prove complicity in evil. But any reader of Milton's prose can supply evidence to disabuse us of false assumptions about his views:

'The general end of every ordinance . . . is the good of man.' (*Tetrachordon*)

'The greatest burden of the world is superstition . . . of imaginary and scarecrow sins.' (*The Doctrine and Discipline of Divorce*)

'God delights not to make a drudge of virtue.'
(*The Doctrine and Discipline of Divorce*)

'The property of truth is, when she is publicly taught, to unyoke and set free the minds and spirits of a nation.' (*The Reason of Church-Government*)

'[Under] tyrannical duncery . . . no free and splendid wit can flourish.'
(*The Reason of Church-Government*)

'This is a solid rule that every command given with a reason binds our obedience no otherwise than that reason holds.'
(*The Doctrine and Discipline of Divorce*)[3]

William Blake himself was hardly less willing to confuse Nobodaddy with God, more concerned to free men from customary errors. Evidently Milton equated the thing that costs man joy with a blind taking on of a yoke, not a splendid release to clear-sighted freedom.

By the end of Book VIII the action has made all such points and thereby made the losing of Paradise all but impossible. Yet by the end of Book IX Paradise has been utterly lost; without change of scene, with nothing done to Adam and Eve, the pair have somehow managed to do the damage to themselves.

Book IX, in which *Paradise Lost* concentrates its tensions, marks an absolute shift from a whole world to a world torn apart. It takes two moments to rend it: 'she pluckd, she eat:/Earth felt the wound'; 'he scrupl'd not to eat/. . . Earth trembl'd from her entrails' (IX, 781 ff., 997 ff.); and the rending is complete. A symbolic act—and the eating of the apple is clearly symbolic—can have many unlike meanings, depending on what the motives involved in it make it mean. In Book IX, the eating signifies 'Away with Eden'.

But not until late in Book IX, for again Milton thrusts off the crisis. The action recommences, as the whole mimesis commenced, with that prime exemplar of self-rending destructiveness, Satan. Dramatically, he whips himself yet again into the spitefulness he needs to carry out his plot; thematically, he represents the guilty anguish, loss of reason, physical diminution, and other modes of death opposed, in every sense, to the joys of Eden. He has reduced himself to the point where he cannot face the simplest fact, pursue the easiest line of reasoning. From a speech that abounds in self-delusion and self-contradiction, take just his atrocious mathematics in referring to his followers as 'well-nigh half' the angels, when the exact number is just one third; or take his great principle of artistic criticism:

> O Earth, how like to Heav'n, if not preferrd
> More justly, Seat worthier of Gods, as built
> With second thoughts, reforming what was old!
> For what God after better worse would build? (IX, 99–102)

[3] *Works,* seriatim: IV, 117; III, 373, 495, 272, 240, and 457.

It makes for some interesting judgements. Obviously the *Epitaph for Damon* must be a better poem than *Lycidas*, since what poet after better worse would write? Or shall we say that Albee must have a greater understanding of human nature than Shakespeare, since what literature after a better writer a worse would produce? The motive of Satan's critical pronouncement is simple: he is here on earth, can't get back to Heaven, wherefore earth must be the more artistic achievement—especially since he intends to take it over. He contradicts the pronouncement in a moment, as he increasingly contradicts himself with every other word. His one apparent certainty is that he is going to reduce all this joyous beauty to woe. But again, as in Heaven, Hell, and points in between, his certainties, though asserted in a very big voice—for Satan is nothing if not magniloquent—need not convince us. He was just as certain back in Book IV—and then had to slink muttering off. He was just as certain on the battlefield of Heaven—and then had to leap into the abyss. He will be equally certain that he has been entirely victorious when he reports his achievement in Hell—and will find his boasted victory dust and ashes in his mouth.

Paradise, in short, is not yet lost merely because Satan says it's going to be. It is still not lost in the following scene between Adam and Eve, which Satan knows nothing about, where the honeymooning couple have their first domestic spat. The scene is prelude, not cause of what follows, as Satan's prologue was prelude, not cause, ominous only in the event. With great poetic economy Milton uses their quarrel to draw the firmest of lines between the transient, trivial, momentary errors that Eden can contain and cure, and the kind of aberration that proves fatal. It is not because Eve insists on going off by herself that in the next scene she decides to wreck Eden and think she has on the whole improved the scenery; it is not because Adam finally lets her go that he later decides he too must destroy Eden and call the devastation gain. An entirely different Scene 2 and 3 could have followed Scene 1, with no irreparable damage.

The little impulse of self-assertion Eve shows in this first scene, the little laxness Adam shows when, after answering her every argument point by point, he throws in his hand out of an obvious reluctance to win the dispute and thereby win her displeasure—these impulses in the pair hardly destroy them. At the same time they make what follows likely—when it comes. For in what follows the temporary negligible impulse of each suddenly mushrooms into dominant motive, subduing or excluding every other, until it decrees 'This I must have though it cost me and everyone everything else.' The whole person now stakes the world for one purpose in an irrevocable deed.

The story Milton took from Genesis gave him the symbolic act; his own reading of the world, its men and women, and the many books written by and about them, gave the symbolic act its meanings. It is one thing for Eve to have indulged in a moment of petulant self-assertiveness, another completely different for her to say 'I *must* queen it over the universe, and if Eden by its very nature precludes my queening it, away with Eden.' It is one thing for Adam to have given in to her self-assertion lest he lose her good will, another entirely different for him to decide 'I *must* hold on to her, and if it costs Eden, away with Eden.' For as each concludes and enacts 'Away with Eden', Eden ends.

It took a poet of great human discernment to make the little pointless healable rift of the morning quarrel both antithesis and prelude to this destruction. The magniloquent prologue of Satan supplies only *his* motive, and that we have known for a long time. His one thesis: I, only I, I alone matter—no universe can be its home. He creates what he finally requires, that 'world of death' which is Milton's definition of Hell. But *his* motive for wrecking the human pair at this point hardly matters. Our concern is with them. In his attempt on Eve, he has rather noticeably to suppress every thought he thinks, every wish he wants. With the dulcet tones of a kind of cosmic Don Giovanni—and what a wrenching of his nature that must involve!—he turns confidence-man urging the seventy-five different reasons for buying his fraudulent stock. To break the bond that holds Eden together, he must get the woman to believe that the bond is bondage, that Eden is inferior to her deserts, that she is in shackles which she must tear off. We have seen no shackles, no subjection, no 'Down on your knees, slave', from Adam to Eve, or Raphael to Eve, or anyone else to Eve—we have seen no knowledge forbidden her—for that matter we have seen no universe in which she could be 'ador'd and serv'd by Angels numberless, [her] daily Train' (IX, 546-8). Nobody in the Miltonic Heaven goes around with any such entourage. But evidently the serpent's speech is highly persuasive: it conjures up for many readers the same illusory universe it conjures up for Eve. Told that she is shackled, she at once feels the shackles; told that she has been kept in ignorance, she at once feels painfully ignorant ('What fear I then, rather what know to feare/Under this ignorance of Good and Evil,/Of God or Death, of Law or Penaltie?' (IX, 773-5)). Told that she can have something better than Eden, and deserves it, and simply doesn't know what's what if she supposes Eden worth having, she immediately decides to improve her condition: 'Here grows the Cure of all . . ./ . . . what hinders then?' Told that the apple contains magic, and that magic is better than her realities, she hurls realities away.

But is it credible, the reader asks, that she would unless there is some truth in what the serpent says? Milton's poem allows no truth in what the serpent says, but makes the scene wholly credible. If we stop to ask, But why on earth should she believe such lies at this point? the answer is: She shouldn't, but she does. Milton asked the question in just that incredulous tone at the outset:

> say first what cause
> Mov'd our Grand Parents in that happy State,
> Favour'd of Heav'n so highly, to fall off
> From thir Creator and transgress his Will
> For one restraint, Lords of the World besides? (I, 28–32)

The losing of Paradise should be all but incredible—until the action of Book IX makes us credit it. And the impulse in Eve that Satan fans into overwhelming motive is so natural, human, familiar that we are only too likely to think it inevitable. Nothing in human affairs is inevitable; but poetry, dealing with our probabilities, need only make us accept what it represents.

Theologically, the fall involved all possible crimes; and Milton was theologian enough to touch every possibility into his representation. Poetically, the ongoing action uses Eve's outgrown narcissism and earlier moment of self-assertion, uses what she had already ordered within herself or could easily still set in order, and shows her choosing one motive in herself to the exclusion of the rest.

The fully gathered wave is at its crest and starting to break. It should also be impossible that Adam complete the destruction of Eden, yet credible that he does. And now with the daring of a poet who knows that he can carry off all his intended effects, Milton puts the specious arguments of the serpent in their place: though Eve parrots to Adam what the serpent said to her, Adam does not break the bond of Eden out of any like gullibility. Non-readers of Milton's poem go on talking as if Adam sought 'forbidden knowledge by forbidden means'; no scrutiny of Book IX bears them out.[4] His sole concern is to keep

[4] Adam's words in XII, 270–9, as in XII, 469–78 and 557 ff., if read *as Adam's* in a given mimetic context, do not contradict the representation in Book IX. If misread as Milton's own comment, they would involve serious inconsistencies.

Eve: she is his, not to be taken from him, his possession; and he can supply out of his own inventive brain, without help from her or the serpent, the ninety-nine reasons why he too must throw Eden away. He thus commits the greater folly, supplying momentum entirely from himself. Again, his 'How can I live without thee?' (IX, 908) is so compelling, so persuasive, that many readers ask 'How indeed could we expect him to live without her?' as though that were involved at this point. Evidently the arguments by which Adam persuades himself that he must do as Eve has done carry more than enough conviction to make his deed credible. His fear of loss, of solitude, his sense that what he cares for belongs to him—it is so natural, familiar, human that it seems virtually inevitable. And yet was 'How can I live without thee?' a helpful question to ask? Might he not instead have asked, What can I do *for* her?

As Adam quickly works out what God had better take into account 'lest the Adversary/Triumph and say; Fickle their State whom God/Most Favors; who can please him long?' (IX, 947-9), he persuades himself that he must leap into the trap to join Eve. His grand phrases, 'if Death/Consort with thee, Death is to mee as Life', and 'what thou art is mine/ . . . to lose thee were to lose myself' (953 f., 957 ff.), unhappily reveal the unwitting egotism of the romantic lover replacing his earlier 'domestic care' for Eve.

What the fall of each separately, of both together, comes to in Milton's version is 'all for self-love and Eden ill lost' enacted by a pair who can briefly dignify self-love with a variety of fine names—desire for knowledge, courage, devotion. They can also dignify their use of each other afterwards as an act of love. It proves an act of hate; and the wrangling couple on whom the curtain falls at the end of Book IX are almost ready to perform *Who's Afraid of Virginia*, etc. They don't, but they have shown the way.

Not that Milton is a vulgar poet. But evidently he had a large grasp of possible human vulgarities, as of other human possibilities. Translate the serpent's 'one man except,/Who sees thee? (and what is one?) who shouldst be seen/A Goddess among Gods' (IX, 545-7)—translate that into any age's equivalent of 'You should be on television', and the vulgarity is apparent. Or take Adam's 'if such pleasure be/In things to us forbidd'n, it might be wisht,/For this one Tree had bin forbidd'n ten' (IX, 1024-6) and translate it into the terms used by our advertisers—no one should be able to miss the vulgarity. Nor is 'I told you so' less vulgar when phrased 'Would thou hadst heark'nd to my words' nor 'Is this the thanks I get?' when phrased 'Is this the Love, is this the recompense?' (IX, 1134, 1163).

The 'mortal taste' of the forbidden fruit in Milton's poem involves some appallingly bad taste. And the action by representing Adam and Eve reduced to such dialogue tells how irrevocably Eden has gone. The expansive joy of the garden has contracted to a couple who sit glaring and snarling their hatred at each other.

From that low point there can only be some rise. But with the aftermath in Books X–XII I cannot here attempt to deal. The repercussions swing to Heaven, to Earth, to Hell, to outer space, to Hell, to Earth, to Heaven, to the solar world, to Earth again, to Heaven, to Earth—to the long future stretching ahead as the split rends the world. A healing begins in Book X, in fact began back in Book III before ever Eden was rent, and a final healing is promised in Book XII. Chiefly the aftermath involves one long *pathos*, a widening stain of suffering from an ever reopening wound, constantly healed, constantly to be healed, potentially closed by the atonement, actually closed only at far-off Doomsday. Against readers who want to rename the poem 'All for Salvation, or Eden Well Lost' we can only argue that cancer is not a great good because it enables surgeons to show their skill. But Books X–XII are crowded, and how we read them depends on many things.

In any event, at the end Adam and Eve go into exile to find a new home, 'though sorrowing, yet in peace'. Humbled and diminished they wander off into the distance: 'The World was all before them'. And suddenly that distance is foreground: the world before them is our world. They have left Eden to become more like us, when what the poem made us want was to become more like them. The reader who has experienced the full mimesis may well exclaim Infelix culpa! unfortunate fall! The happy pair have cut themselves down to our stature, have cut *us* down to our stature. Whatever may be said for the world they enter, it is not the Paradise they have lost.

'Man as a Probationer of Immortality': *Paradise Lost XI-XII*

Mary Ann Radzinowicz

The kind of literary critic who interests himself particularly in writing about the up-to-date relative popularity of great poets—who makes revaluations or chronicles dethronements—was greatly engaged with John Milton from 1920 to 1950. His work cloaked the work of another sort of practical critic, one who disliked the end of *Paradise Lost*, often irrelevantly because he disliked Christianity, and who explained his distaste by discovering imperfections in Milton's work. The first sort made a virtue of his modernity by excluding from the great tradition, and so from living interest, now this and now that writer whom other times had been unwilling to let die. Of his work I have nothing to say, except that not only the results are now called in doubt but even the method of inquiry. Of the second sort, however, I report in the tercentenary year of the publication of *Paradise Lost* that their dissatisfactions are largely answered. The poem ends, we say more and more confidently, with the perfect locking into place of Milton's epic plan, not with a suppositious 'ebbing and retreating' of his genius. In the forties and fifties it was fashionable to say that the last books versify dryly a useless or terrible dogma. That alleged versification of dogma really emphasises not dogma but the theme of man's education in liberty. The last books of *Paradise Lost* are Adam's and everyman's books, not theology's. It used to be said that the last books were divided and misshapen; they are not misshapen but are constructed to show that although the world to which Adam descends is all before him, the paradise he attains is all within. It used to be said that they were harsh and pessimistic; they are neither.[1] They oppose to one view of what is

---

[1] For the view that *Paradise Lost* XI–XII dogmatise a dreadful doctrine, see William Empson, *Milton's God* (London, 1961), pp. 242 ff.; J. B. Broadbent, *Some*

noble and heroic in man and hopeful in his fate quite another view of nobility and heroism.[2] In short the last books contain what Coleridge found in them, 'a love of man as a probationer of immortality.'[3]

To carry forward a step the new interpretations of the close of *Paradise Lost*, two things seem to me to demand special emphasis. First, the last books conspicuously show Adam being taught within time what God foreknows in eternity and being admitted without impairment of his free will to such share in foreknowledge as will send him forth though sorrowing yet in peace. They combine man's exercise of free will in time and God's foreknowledge in eternity. Adam is taught in them what has happened and what will happen not just so that he will be comforted, knowing that his end is peace, but so that action will be clearer to him as the essential condition for that peace. Not just to have attained the sum of wisdom but to have seen the deeds of fortitude which lead to higher victory is what brings Adam to a paradise within. How action gives meaning to time has not, I think, been sufficiently emphasised. Milton has shaped the last two books to show Adam that patience and heroic martyrdom are more than an inner condition; they are a species of ethical behaviour. The action proposed to Adam is

---

Graver Subject (London, 1960), pp. 267–95; John Peter, *A Critique of 'Paradise Lost'* (New York, 1960) pp. 138–66—to take only the most recent of its proponents. For the view that it is misshapen, see John Peter, *op. cit.*; E. M. W. Tillyard, *Milton* (London, 1961), pp. 256 ff.; C. S. Lewis, *A Preface to 'Paradise Lost'* (London, 1942), pp. 125 ff.; and variously, H. J. C. Grierson, *Milton and Wordsworth* (London, 1950), p. 120; Kenneth Muir, *John Milton* (London, 1955), p. 160; Grant McColley, 'Paradise Lost', *Harvard Theological Review*, XXXII (1939), 228. For the view that the poem ends in harsh pessimism, see Louis L. Martz, 'Introduction' to *Milton: A Collection of Critical Essays* (New Jersey, 1962), and *The Paradise Within* (New Haven, 1964), p. 150; B. Rajan, *Milton and the Seventeenth Century Reader* (London, 1947), pp. 82–85, 105–7.

[2] The recent criticism denying all these defects and substituting analysis for deprecation includes: F. T. Prince, 'On the Last Two Books of *Paradise Lost*', *Essays and Studies*, n.s., XI (1958); Berta Moritz-Siebeck, *Untersuchungen zu Milton's 'Paradise Lost'* (Berlin, 1963); George Williamson, *Milton and Others* (London, 1965); Joseph H. Summers, *The Muse's Method* (Cambridge, Mass., 1962); Northrop Frye, *Five Essays on Milton's Epics* (London, 1966); Helen Gardner, *A Reading of 'Paradise Lost'* (Oxford, 1965); Michael Fixler, *Milton and the Kingdoms of God* (London, 1964); as well as numerous essays by A. E. Barker, E. E. Stoll, Barbara K. Lewalski, Rosalie L. Colie, H. R. MacCallum, C. A. Patrides, J. E. Parish, Mother Mary Christopher Pecheux, W. G. Madsen, and J. M. Steadman.

[3] 'Milton', from Lecture X delivered in 1818, printed in *Literary Remains* 1836).

an inner and a public struggle between good and evil. Action supplies the sense in which man can be seen to be a probationer rather than merely a penitent or a prisoner of time. Secondly, Milton does not imagine that God's plan works out successively only or eventually, but rather that it works in the two dimensions of successive time and the immediate present. It is not only when history halts that good shall triumph over evil or that 'evil on itself shall back recoyl' but rather it is in the very moment of each act of virtue and love. In the last two books eternity and history intersect. To tell the story which shall be doctrinal to a nation is to tell a true story; it is to say nothing of what shall come to pass which lies beyond man's knowledge and is wrapped in God's inscrutable foreknowledge except what is sanctioned by what has come to pass before. *Paradise Lost* ends in scriptural history because (as William Haller has shown)[4] 'the uniqueness of scriptural authority lay in the fact that in scripture as nowhere else history was authenticated by prophecy and prophecy was confirmed by history'. God, Milton shows, has not changed his mind and abandoned history. Man's history with its repetitions of failure and its necessary chain of cause and effect takes on value and meaning when it is translated into spiritual biography. Man's probation, while national and historical, ends in immortality; that is, has an inner meaning in itself which will never diminish.

The intellectual beauty of the final books is, then, the beauty of a poetry concerned to shape ideas by controlling the smaller units of imaginative creation—catalogue, metaphor, pageant, vision, drama—through a great constructive principle which, by virtue of its exactitude, surprise and realism, never tires the reader but which moves him actively to the contemplation of moral values, more interesting and real than anything else creation might afford. Where some have claimed that Milton's imagination slept while with 'panoramic omnicompetence' he performed an assignment he had no taste for, it can rather be said that his mind was alive and called forth the most engaged and lively reading on the part of his audience. The reading was a participation in ethical imagining; the resultant poetry, the poetry of intellect. The final books which seem purely didactic to some are not didactic in any way that the whole poem isn't: they give the reader the opportunity to put into final order the epic context and the inner ethical system, and to perceive, when all is in place, how the inner ethical system boldly attracts

[4] 'The Tragedy of God's Englishman', *Reason and the Imagination*, ed. J. A. Mazzeo (New York, 1962), p. 203.

the mind, surrounded as it is by ring upon ring of lyric, dramatic, historical; fabular, scientific, mythic; sensory, cognitive and spiritual perspectives and contexts. The whole poem shows how vastly human behaviour makes a difference: the last two books give to the mind of the responsive reader the last sweep down the vistas of time not into an unknown futurity when all shall somehow be well but straight into the heart of significant human action.

I

'Refin'd by faith and faithful works'

It may seem idle to ask what Milton imagined that God had planned for unfallen man to do with his life in a poem whose opening words foretell first disobedience. But the question 'what might have been' is answered by the poem and makes sense of what happens. 'Grateful vicissitude'[5] was to have been the heavenly perfection in Eden, harmonious change not static perfection. Time began the moment creation was initiated, and the passage of time was joyous and circular. So one may ask, what did Raphael mean when before the fall he told Adam

> perhaps
> Your bodies may at last turn all to Spirit
> Improv'd by tract of time. (V, 496–8)

What was to fill the tract of man's unfallen time and how would it have been improving? And since in *Of Education* Milton wrote 'the end ... of learning is to repair the ruins of our first parents', can any clear distinction be drawn between improvement and amendment?

What was to fill the tract is clear: it was worship and work, within 'fellowship ... fit to participate all rational delight' (VIII, 389–91). Adam's lesson to Eve in Book IV as their first day in Eden drew to a close taught that.

> Fair Consort, th' hour
> Of night, and all things now retir'd to rest
> Mind us of like repose, since God hath set
> Labour and rest, as day and night to men
> Successive ...

[5] Cf. J. H. Summers, *The Muse's Method* (Cambridge, Mass., 1962), pp. 71–85.

> Man hath his daily work of body or mind
> Appointed, which declares his Dignitie,
> And the regard of Heav'n on all his waies. (IV, 610–20)

Men and creatures differ in that man is to work, work being the expression of his love and voluntary obedience to God. Work itself cannot be saving, but the unfallen man and woman work and share pleasant tasks, not made 'to irksom toile, but to delight . . . and delight to Reason joind' (IX, 242–3). They were to work together 'till younger hands ere long/Assist' (IX, 246–7), the work was to consist in the regulation of Eden, it was to be punctuated with

> Refreshment, whether food or talk between,
> Food of the mind, in this sweet intercourse
> Of looks and smiles, . . . of Love the food,
> Love not the lowest end of human life. (IX, 237–41)

—and it was to be accompanied by spontaneous worship of and communion with God.

How the tract of time spent thus was to improve is also clear. Simply by the actions involved in voluntary obedience, Adam and Eve would perfect themselves, as though the steps to heaven were not fixed but moving, so that to stand would be to ascend. They were to better themselves in love so they would ascend the scale of heavenly love, were to improve themselves in diet so that their very bodies would take on more spiritual qualities, were to better themselves so in the arts of fellowship that at will they could participate with angels and dwell either in Eden or Heaven. Milton explained this when he told how God had promised to repeople heaven after the fall of Lucifer and his band:

> [I] in a moment will create
> Another World, out of one man a Race
> Of men innumerable, there to dwell,
> Not here, till by degrees of merit rais'd
> They op'n to themselves at length the way
> Up hither, under long obedience tri'd. (VII, 154–9)

Like the angels, unfallen men might have dispersed themselves throughout the whole scope of creation, when they wished repairing to Eden as to a shrine to hear from Adam how God had visited him there. Then Eden had been

> Perhaps thy Capital Seate, from whence had spred
> All generations, and had hither come
> From all the ends of th' Earth, to celebrate
> And reverence thee thir great Progenitor.   (XI, 343-6)

Adam's fall incapacitates all creation for 'improvement by tract of time'. What is required after it is amendment. The opposition between improvement and amendment becomes clear enough in the last books of *Paradise Lost*, it seems to me, to make it unlikely that Milton attached to the paradox of the fortunate fall the meaning some have found. The most he says is that the fall cannot thwart God's power and glory. He does not hint that Adam and Eve receive a better reward for the struggle to repair what they needlessly defaced. They ultimately receive the final Kingdom of God which God planned all along. The inner garden or the paradise of the quiet conscience is their fulfilment in moral strength: it is not better than the Regnum Christi, it is better than an unquiet and disconsolate expulsion. Milton suggests that Adam and Eve shall cover their one bad deed with many good not to excuse them from the fall, but rather to throw stress on action, to make it plain that in the postlapsarian world man again has his responsibilities and freedoms even more taxing than they were before. For improvement by tract of time, the fall substitutes a new set of alternatives and it is the examination of these to which the last two books is directed. The alternatives are set forth in the vision Michael shows Adam and in the prophecy he delivers to him. They are staged in Books XI and XII as though they were demonstrations in a laboratory of historical time. Adam views, Adam reacts with emotion and hypothesis, his reactions are criticised, his hypotheses are corrected, and a subsequent demonstration takes the matter to a new stage.

The lessons of time have a double burden. On the one hand they are ethical demonstrations from which moral truths are drawn to guide Adam and hence every man. On the other they are political and historical demonstrations from which political and historical laws are deduced. The great epic design is meant to reveal how the free will of the individual interacts with historical necessity. Man, as he chooses this or that course in his freedom, becomes the second cause of what ensues. *Paradise Lost* prophesies at the end not a grand scene of anarchy in which upon an ever darkening stage a few regenerate men flash out to each other their points of light. Rather, many stages of history are passed in review to show what conditions the historical process affords for the exercise of choice. The panorama of time, which includes all historical time and all historical place, gives the setting in which the individual must perpetually repair injustice, his great moral and political responsibility. On the one hand is the universal process of God's ways; on the other the process of individual experience which is regenerative in so far as it corresponds with God's plan at each successive dispensation in history. The conclusion of *Paradise Lost* teaches not merely private righteousness but public righteousness as well, as both are dependent upon man's inner liberty.

So it is that Books XI and XII are framed in two solitary personal scenes, Adam and Eve alone with their future, and contain a circling through history which is their epic dimension. How the individual may act upon the flow of history is the subject of the epic, which gives to the poem its intellectual force. The ocean of time moves in its fluxion and refluxion by natural laws which Milton depicts in typifying scenes, and the man and woman alone together direct themselves in liberty to respond, in liberty to affect and alter, but in conformity to the laws of their being and the laws of historical change. The burden of a single episode will be multiple, therefore: the burden of the Nimrod episode, for example, will be, as Nimrod was evil and was overcome in his own day, usurp no authority over the freedom of other men, aspire to no unholy power; it will be also, oppose to Nimrod all your human force for Nimrod represents a variety of human malfeasance which shall arise to be opposed; detect in Nimrod the perpetual figure of the tyrant or anti-Christ who will emerge in some form in each historical dispensation and combat him, cast him down as King Charles when he appears.

The first lessons of the last books for Adam and Eve are of predominantly ethical bearing but in them the peculiar complexity of the historical stage is most carefully set. When Book XI opens, Adam and Eve are no longer prostrate and 'thir port/Not of mean suiters'

> nor important less
> Seem'd thir Petition, then when th' ancient Pair
> In Fables old, less ancient yet then these,
> *Deucalion* and chaste *Pyrrha* to restore
> The Race of Mankind drownd, before the Shrine
> Of *Themis* stood devout.   (XI, 8–14)

They are already free again not only before the crucifixion but before the flood, not only before the flood but before that other later metaphorical flood which Ovid treated, when the stones Deucalion and Pyrrha cast behind them were transformed into men. They stand praying and free while three stages of time in separate circles wait upon their next acts. In like manner after the prayers of Adam and Eve have been presented to the Father by the Son who has rejoiced that man's doom 'to better life shall yeeld him' (XI, 42), Milton again reminds his audience of the shifting location of the epic in time. He writes as though present at a conversation in Heaven, knowing what has happened, is happening and shall come, both in time and beyond it. And he moves a single image, this time the trumpet, from one stage of existence to another, pressing it forward as he sees beyond man's renovation to the ultimate end of salvation itself:

> the bright Minister that watchd . . . blew
> His Trumpet, heard in *Oreb* since perhaps
> When God descended, and perhaps once more
> To sound at general Doom.   (XI, 73–76)

While Adam and Eve attend the coming of Michael in Eden, Moses and his people attend at the bottom of Mount Sinai the coming of the Lord, and Milton and God's Englishmen expect the coming of the Son in final triumph. In this metaphorical manner, as F. T. Prince says, '*Paradise Lost* takes us from eternity to eternity, from the eternity before the universe was created to the eternity after it will be dissolved. The story which began with the revolt of the angels will end only with the Last Judgement, the end of the world as we know it'.[6]

By these opening metaphors Milton places before us the streams of time, where the consequences of the Fall spread across space and into human history. He has established Adam in the role of everyman by restoring free will and human consciousness to him. He has indicated that what will follow will be the spiritual biography of every rehabilitated man. Further, he has begun to convert scriptural history and prophecy into universal history so that the interchangeable significance of prophecy and history may emerge. The pattern or law of historical change, which emerges in the set pieces of vision and then of narrated prophecy, is the process toward greater and greater amplitude of Christian liberty in the world coupled with the necessary darkening of human affairs in politics, when individuals allow their consciences to become enslaved, whence follows their political enslavement. As the

---

[6] 'On the Last Two Books of *Paradise Lost*', *Essays and Studies*, n.s., XI (1958), 40.

liberty grows clearer, the possibility of regeneration increases. At the same time the personal choice becomes more pressing. Christ's self-sacrifice announced in the final part of Michael's prophecy is the most freeing act of all. It does not derogate from man's dignity or coerce him. Christ will mitigate man's doom by giving him a chance to realise heroic stature. Adam goes down into the world as a Christian, in his lifetime having been vouchsafed a foreknowledge of the redeemer, for Christ's redemption reopens action, makes courage, piety and self-sacrifice meaningful. Michael comes to tell Adam what will be done throughout history in order that Adam can conduct himself as a Christian, to embody as well as to inherit Christ's kingdom.

II

'Thy going is not lonely'

The brief drama which precedes Adam's vision of the future is not lightly to be passed over as an interesting preliminary. It looks forward, of course, to the scene of expulsion where Adam and Eve manifest their heroic magnitude, but in itself it indicates the reciprocal responsibilities, powers and duties of man and wife. Love itself is heavenly and the choices and decisions made in it are a profound part of man's salvation. As in Heaven the Father was laying on Michael the two charges 'Without remorse drive out the sinful Pair' and 'reveale/To *Adam* what shall come in future dayes . . . so send them forth, though sorrowing, yet in peace' (XI, 105–17), meanwhile in Eden Adam and Eve began to speak to one another of hope. Their hopes were as varied as their personalities: Adam's rational and Eve's good but delusory. In hope of his continued communion with God Adam remembered the promise that his seed should bruise the serpent, reasoned from that promise to a mediator from among his descendants who should save mankind, and greeted his consort

> Whence Haile to thee,
> *Eve* rightly calld, Mother of all Mankind,
> Mother of all things living, since by thee
> Man is to live, and all things live for Man.   (XI, 158–61)

She replied, much humbled, in the right tone of penitence but with the wrong deduction, ready to start upon the new laborious toil but in

Paradise itself: 'What can be toilsom in these pleasant Walkes?/Here let us live, though in fall'n state, content'. The sight of Nature decaying all about them disabused Eve at once. The eagle ravened, the lion pursued, clouds formed in the East, and the very descent of Michael appeared as darkness. Adam warned Eve to retire and Michael abruptly executed his first commission, 'to remove thee I am come' (XI, 260).

The command to be gone forced Adam into a swoon and Eve into lament for the walks of Paradise, the flowers she had named, too delicate to transplant, and chiefly the nuptial bower she had adorned. In her grief as compared to Adam's, Milton's concept of marriage is reflected. 'Hee for God onely, shee for God in him' (IV, 299). For as Eve sorrowed for the past marital bliss of Eden, Adam, recovering consciousness, most grieved for God's presence there. And as Michael had mildly reminded Eve that Adam would be found in exile, 'Thy going is not lonely, with thee goes/Thy Husband . . . Where he abides, think there thy native place' (XI, 290-2), so to Adam his answer is of God's omnipresence. Adam may meet God in valley and in plain, 'still compassing thee round/With goodness and paternal Love' (XI, 352-3). The restoration of free will which came to Adam and Eve in their prayers had been preceded by the restoration of amity and peace in their marriage. They had prayed as one, they have just been seen united in kindness to each other awaiting the angel and they have responded united though variously to the order to go. When Michael and Adam ascend the hill from which the vision of the future shall be seen, leaving Eve to learn in her second dream what Adam shall reason out under angelic tutelage, the marriage is a whole felt to be one, and the double mood that ended Book X—remorseful, contrite but exalted—is continued to the close between earth's loveliest pair.

The theme of matrimonial bliss, one of the most remarkable in *Paradise Lost*, transmutes into a new ideal the humanistic doctrine that love enlarges the soul with the Christian dicta of subordination and obedience in marriage. When Raphael admitted that love was the joy in the angelic state, as when the poet hymned wedded love, the truth Milton presented was that an inward relationship of close harmony and delight in an equal conversation with another is the greatest solace and fruition of the complete person. To that end in Book VIII Milton had drawn a picture of God amiably testing his perfect new creature Adam, who surveying and naming all the creatures saw none among them his fit company and feared the solitary state. 'What callst thou solitude', God had asked.

> Seem I to thee sufficiently possest
> Of happiness, or not? who am alone
> From all Eternitie . . . (VIII, 404–6)

Adam had answered then what Milton had sufficiently argued in the divorce tracts: Man although perfect in kind was made imperfect in degree, perfect except in self-sufficiency, made to be completed by society. His lack of self-sufficiency required love to make him a full person. As this was man's condition before the Fall, even more crucially it is his state after the Fall. If salvation is to come only in progressive experience, where was experience to be sought if not in marriage, experience to be had through the distinctions of roles and understandings given to Adam. Moreover if the saved were joyful, where was joy to be known but in the delight of love? To the question 'and is there marriage in heaven', Milton wholly concurs in Richard Baxter's affirmative. 'Lay by all the passionate part of love and joy, and it will be hard to have any pleasant thoughts of heaven . . . What is heaven to us if there be no love and joy'. The sorrow and solace with which Adam and Eve are sent together into the world is prepared for in this opening scene of Book XI, built upon the restoration of the first marriage.

III

'This transcient World, the Race of Time'

From the hill on which he stood, Adam's eye commanded a prospect of all time and space simultaneously present: 'destind Walls', 'where Rome was to sway', 'yet unspoild' so also spoiled Guiana (XI, 377 ff.). The first pair of visions afforded Adam are a demonstration in the theory of accommodation by way of typology. Accommodation means that revelation is a vital part of every man's knowledge of God, that Scripture is plain enough for every Christian to understand, and that it is to be read not through a multi-levelled figurative interpretation but typologically. Presented in Scripture, accommodated to man's understanding is one sense in every one place and that one sense to Milton is 'a compound of the historical and the typical'. A type is a prefiguration of something to come; the history of the world is explainable as the type of the man of faith prefigures Christ, as the old Adam prefigures the new, as the perfect life of the redeemed prefigures the perfect development of the state. The critical passage of Scripture which dictates the choice of visions to be shown to Adam is *Hebrews* 11–13. From the summary account of the achievements of men of faith in *Hebrews*, Milton makes the selection of his central typical scenes.

Michael first shows Adam a scene taken from *Hebrews* 11: 4, 'By faith Abel offered unto God a more excellent sacrifice than Cain, by which he obtained witness that he was righteous'. The first pair of visions pivot on death as the effect of Adam's crime and are aimed to show that death should be taken quietly. They prepare for the understanding that it is not purely a curse but the door of life. They are very much visual in their presentation: Adam beholds a scene called up before him and is dismayed and horrified. To his question, 'Is Pietie thus and pure Devotion paid?' comes the answer of God's approval given Abel in his martyrdom: the subsequent quick question, 'But have I now seen death?' introduces the masque of illnesses in the Lazar-house, the deformity of which Michael expounds as man's self-defilement:

> themselves they villifi'd . . .
> Disfiguring not Gods likeness, but thir own,
> Or if his likeness, by themselves defac't
> While they pervert pure Natures healthful rules (XI, 515–23)

The picture of death in the lazar-house is then mitigated by the picture of death in old age as a ripening of fruit on the vine. What is begun here to strip death of its horror is accomplished in Book XII when death becomes finally 'like sleep,/A gentle wafting to immortal Life' (434–5). The faith that recognises death as the gate of life and evil as the means toward good Adam finally, after many incomplete realisations, shall lay hold on. To this wisdom is then coupled right acts.

The second pair of episodes follows from the next verse in *Hebrews*, 'By faith Enoch was translated that he should not see death'. Here Milton shows the actions of the unrighteous in peacetime and in war, where the lives of the unrighteous invite comparison to those of the fallen angels in Books I and II as they exploit Hell's natural resources or engage in martial exercises. The ethical content touches the nature of true heroism: true and false renown are contrasted in them, might and martyrdom opposed. First Adam sees the arts of peace displayed along with the diversions of nuptial lust. Since what he sees seems natural, he approves: 'Here Nature seems fulfilld in all her ends' (XI, 602). But Nature's end is nobler than self-gratification, as Michael explains. If the proximate good of peaceful self-indulgence seemed natural to Adam, the ensuing picture of war which ends with Enoch's translation seems at once as bad as it can be. 'Adam was all in tears' at it. Michael's interpretation moves from the ethical issue of true versus apparent good to the allied political issue of what is honest and heroic in nations.

> For in those dayes Might onely shall be admir'd,
> And Valour and Heroic Vertu calld;
> To overcome in Battell, and subdue
> Nations, and bring home spoils with infinite
> Man-slaughter, shall be held the highest pitch
> Of human Glorie . . . to be stil'd great Conquerors,
> Patrons of Mankind, Gods, and Sons of Gods,
> Destroyers rightlier calld and Plagues of men.
> Thus Fame shall be achiev'd, renown on Earth,
> And what most merits fame in silence hid.   (XI, 689–99)

The last two visions take up the theme of how far the righteous man may alter the course of history and in what circumstances. They follow directly on in *Hebrews*. Their content is again both ethical and political. 'By faith Noah, being warned of God of things not seen as yet, moved with fear, prepared an ark to the saving of his house; by the which he condemned the world, and became heir of the righteousness which is by faith'. Adam nearly overlooks the lesson of temperance in the scene of Noah's disdaining of public riot and the building of the ark, because of his grief when the flood swallows up his sons. The picture of Adam's grief Milton presents in his own voice not Michael's, interrupting a narrated scene with a scene in the foreground where the audience sees itself in Adam and identifies itself with him.

> How didst thou grieve then, *Adam*, to behold
> The end of all thy Ofspring, end so sad,
> Depopulation; thee another Floud,
> Of tears and sorrow a Floud thee also drownd,
> And sunk thee as thy Sons; till gently reard
> By th'Angel, on thy feet thou stoodst at last,
> Though comfortless, as when a Father mourns
> His Children, all in view destroyd at once;
> And scarce to th'Angel utterdst thus thy plaint.   (XI, 754–62)

By that vision Michael showed Adam how in pursuit of intemperate pleasures a generation had besotted itself. His lesson, 'for th' Earth shall bear/More than anough, that temperance may be tri'd' (XI, 804–5), was personal moderation. Noah boarding the ark, Michael turned to the effect the goodness of the one upright man has upon the course of history. The flood dislodged Eden itself and spoiled it to an island salt and bare, but when it dried, another world was revealed surmounted by the rainbow which Adam needed no intermediary to interpret. The meaning of the New Covenant, that history shall go forward for the sake of the one just man it may bear, that

> Seed time and Harvest, Heat and hoary Frost
> Shall hold thir course, till fire purge all things new,
> Both Heav'n and Earth, wherein the just shall dwell.
>
> (XI, 899–901)

Adam was so swift to understand that the method of his instruction must be changed, but the point is still that the whole of history be made to serve the education of Adam and his sons. The movement of Book XI was downward in destruction, although Adam had some cause to rejoice in the prophecy of Christ's triumph as well as much cause to despair at mankind's degeneracy. But tears abounded and much grief was expressed. The movement of Book XII, however, is upward, to restoration. 'So heer th' Archangel paus'd/Betwixt the World destroyed and World restor'd' (XII, 2–3).

IV

'Depriv'd of outward libertie, thir inward lost'

Book XII drops the masque-like presentation, but not to substitute an undramatic dogmatising. Adam is put to sleep and hears what follows as in a dream, but his sleep is not so deep as to prevent him sometimes from questioning and continuing to react. Retained still, too, is the sense of suspense which both books share, as J. E. Parish has pointed out,[7] by virtue of the ambiguous oracle about Satan's bruising in the Son's sentence of judgement in Book X. As the types of the faithful man approximate more closely to Christ, the emphasis upon the bruising of the serpent becomes more insistent and finally it is climactically explained. The staged degrees allow for suspense, surprise and finally

[7] 'Milton and God's Curse on the Serpent', *Journal of English and Germanic Philology*, LVI (1959), 244 ff.

for an exceptionally strong stress upon the moral significance of the oracle, that man's choice in his own soul is the annihilation of Satan. The pace of the lessons now considerably speeds. The unremitting surge of experience has a dramatic likeness to the hasty overtaking by event in human life, for which men and women are as little prepared as is Adam. Now Michael's speech grows less and less broken, and the prophetic and historical summaries are punctuated by very brief moral lessons which cut through the histories presenting them but do not interrupt them. The intellectual unity of the last book is such that after the Nimrod episode the full stretch of summary growing ever more compressed seems organised into a great unbroken chain.

The very first episode breaks the pattern of continued reliance upon *Hebrews* to revert to *Genesis* 10 and 11, in which the settlement of Babylonia and Assyria is ascribed to the warlike hero Nimrod, whom in *Eikonoklastes* Milton had saddled with the crime of first establishing kingship, Nimrod, 'the first that hunted after faction . . . the first that founded monarchy'. The next section reverts to *Hebrews*. The reason for the interpolation is to seek in the use Milton makes of this final occasion to drive home the lesson of the interconnection between liberty and reason, between self-government and right government in nations, between the rule of Christ in the one just man and the reign of Christ upon earth in history, or equally the rejection of Christian liberty in the individual and the enslavement of nations. Adam, having heard how Nimrod

> Will arrogate Dominion undeserv'd
> Over his brethren, and quite dispossess
> Concord and law of Nature from the Earth;   (XII, 27–29)

has no difficulty in expressing the significance of the scene and execrates him as usurper. Michael needs only to explain the inner logic of tyranny and make explicit the analogy between the condition of the soul and the condition of the state:

> yet know withall,
> Since thy original lapse, true Libertie
> Is lost, which always with right Reason dwells
> Twinnd, and from her hath no dividual being.   (XII, 82–85)

The epitome of Milton's political doctrine embedded in the Nimrod episode, owing its force to his experiences before and at the Restoration, contains the reason why the Reformation is not mentioned in the darkening picture of the history of the church which Adam is shown after the Resurrection, when 'Truth shall retire/Bestuck with slandrous darts, and works of Faith/Rarely be found' (XII, 535–7). The exercise of political rights is natural to man but is dependent upon his inward understanding of the true nature of liberty. Collective spiritual progress or general political wisdom had been so little the yield of Milton's own experience of the Puritan revolution that the closest he could come toward predicting the universal realisation of liberty was to place it unassailable, tight within the soul of the upright man. Until completed, history would record the trials testing right reason. As Noah was the type of Christ, so Nimrod was the type of anti-Christ. His personal ethic was false at the core: he did not care, in his lust for fame, whether he garnered true or false renown. He dared, therefore, to pretend to divine sanction ('from Heav'n claiming second Sovrantie') like a Stuart, to enslave those ripe to lose their freedom.

In unbroken recitation after the Nimrod episode, Michael delivers the story of the faithful from Abraham to Moses, unbroken save for a single interposition from Adam asking that the Law be explained. Because of Abraham's faith and the iniquity of his times, God rejects the unregenerate mass and causes to appear in history the pattern of election by which the seed of Abraham justifies its redemption. It is in Moses that the meaning of the type elected under the Law is clearest and the deficiencies in that historical stage made most manifest. Moses in the wide wilderness is elected to establish the rule of Law,

> part such as appertaine
> To civil Justice, part religious Rites
> Of sacrifice, informing them, by types
> And shadowes, of that destind Seed to bruise
> The Serpent.   (XII, 230–4)

The Law is reported through Moses in order that the Jews be 'Instructed that to God is no access/Without Mediator' (239–40). The giving of the Law is followed by a period of consolidation and reform for several generations. It is here that half rejoicing and half puzzled Adam asks what the intention of so much law can be. He does not pick up the hints of sacrifice and mediation and ask that they be explained but rather quizzes Michael about the Law. Nonetheless in Michael's explanation the meaning of heroic martyrdom for the redemption of history is plain. Michael's lesson is that the lawgiver's role in history is negative: through the Law Moses and the Jews understand but do not inherit the promise of God's reign on earth. Mosaic Law was given so that sins might be defined and men know that they could not justify themselves by legal righteousness.

> So Law appears imperfect, and but giv'n
> With purpose to resign them in full time
> Up to a better Cov'nant, disciplind
> From shadowie Types to Truth, from Flesh to Spirit,
> From imposition of strict Laws, to free
> Acceptance of large Grace, from servil fear
> To filial, works of Law to works of Faith. (XII, 300–6)

There is no greater security in bondage to the Law, when in fear men discover their sinfulness, than in bondage to human authority. The only security lies in obedience to the dictates of reason, the conscience placed in each man which can only act in Christian liberty. The presentation of sin as the usurpation of reason by the passions, the insistence upon the connection between inward and outward liberty, the Puritan opposition of ceremonies and outer rites to conscience, all irresistibly tend to emphasise the recovery of Paradise from within: an emphasis which is Puritan, rational, and firm.

V

'The better part of Patience and Heroic Martyrdom'

With the birth of Jesus the history of the Jews ends and that of the Church begins, initiated by the predicted failure of the Law to keep God's chosen people constant. The goal of this stage of history is man's redemption. Every human actor has his part to play in it and it sums up the whole. The life of Adam is the history of Israel; he falls from his promised land into bondage like that in Egypt; the life of the new Adam is the life of the second Israel who lives in the Gospels what was prefigured in *Exodus*. To eat the apple, to call forth the flood, to seize power over men, to break the law, to crucify the redeemer is at every stage to bring into being the world, to establish the continuance of time, to give occasion for the exercise of political wisdom, to institute inner freedom in place of outer law, to transfer the struggle for good to the innermost soul of man. The completest expression of what might be called the paradox of the fortunate fall, the institution of Christian liberty, is contained in Michael's expounding of the typology of Mosaic Law. While the Law indicts him, it makes man see the reason; thus the Law which dooms, disciplines to the next stage, that of freedom given to man by the appearance of the redeemer. In obedience to Christ the law of magnanimous love, a pattern more perfect than obedience to outward form, is established. That pattern is Christian liberty, obedience only to love and right reason, the Christian being at liberty to disregard all injunctions but that of conscience.

Dramatic urgency is secured in Michael's summary of the history of the Christian church by the device which has been in use throughout the last two books, by Adam's interjection of a spontaneous and emotional response which is not perfectly correct. This time his brief glorying in the coming of the Son in triumph calls forth the account of the true meaning of bruising the serpent's head, not in war or duel or the old heroisms of knightly dragon slaying, but in a 'God-like act', one faithful loving sacrifice to self in an heroic martyrdom sufficient to extirpate the works of Satan in all who comprehend it. When Michael says:

> Dream not of thir fight,
> As of a Duel, or the local wounds
> Of head or heel: not therefore joines the Son
> Manhood to God-head, with more strength to foil
> Thy enemie; nor so is overcome
> *Satan*, whose fall from Heav'n, a deadlier bruise,
> Disabl'd not to give thee thy deaths wound:
> Which hee, who comes thy Saviour, shall recure,
> Not by destroying *Satan*, but his works
> In thee and in thy Seed: (XII, 386–95)

he speaks as though Adam had imagined some such war as John drew in *Revelations*. That would have been one sort of heroic argument enough. But that Michael brushes aside and Milton refuses to versify. He had had enough of wars, and caricatured them savagely, with the War in Heaven. In its place he gives instead the more heroic argument far, the Epistle to the Romans, the struggle of the old and new Adam in each breast. The true second coming is when God calls on the soul to believe in the Redeemer; it is the individual experience of faith, of being called. The images Milton has created throughout *Paradise Lost* are all put at the last inside man. All attention by a great introversion at the end of the poem draws down to the inner stage of the human heart, where will take place the ultimate action of the poem, the regeneration of the individual soul. All hope comes down to this, not social, economic, political or evolutionary hope, but personal rehabilitation. This is the final stage not only in the elimination of Satan as a dramatic character but in the withdrawal of all the supernatural personages so that only man is left. There is little of the Passion delivered then, for the true crucifixion of Christ is in the heart of the sinner, but more weight is given to the familiar Puritan theme of history as revelation and revelation as human history.

> All Nations they shall teach; for from that day
> Not onely to the Sons of *Abrahams* Loines
> Salvation shall be Preacht, but to the Sons
> Of *Abrahams* Faith wherever through the World;
> So in his seed all Nations shall be blest.   (XII, 446–50)

Thence until 'when the Worlds dissolution shall be ripe', it will always be so that the free man will struggle both to redeem his age and to redeem himself.

Adam's joy and wonder, the reflection of his Christian faith, yet spares a thought for the early Christian. He asks what shall befall him and hears of the trouble of the Christian church to the present day, 'Wolves shall succeed for teachers, grevious Wolves' as 'carnal power' shall presume to force conscience (XII, 508 ff.). Yet nothing for lamentation emerges, but rather occasion again for virtuous deeds, and it is a wiser quieter Adam who at last replies

> Henceforth I learne, that to obey is best,
> And love with feare the onely God, to walk
> As in his presence, ever to observe
> His providence, and on him sole depend,
> Merciful over all his works, with good
> Still overcoming evil, and by small
> Accomplishing great things, by things deemd weak
> Subverting worldly strong, and worldly wise
> By simply meek; that suffering for Truths sake
> Is fortitude to highest victorie,
> And to the faithful Death the Gate of Life;
> Taught this by his example whom I now
> Acknowledge my Redeemer ever blest.   (XII, 561–73)

In the last two books is the answer, then, to H. R. Swardson's question, 'Does Milton really think he is singing "the better fortitude of Patience and Heroic Martyrdom"? Where? What space and prominence does he give it?'[8] The better fortitude is in Adam himself, in Abel, in Enoch, in Noah, in Abraham, in Moses and in Christ; and the effect of their choices is steady and cumulative. Heroic fortitude is quite other than passive resistance, as Michael's final charge declares:

>   onely add
> Deeds to thy knowledge answerable, add Faith,
> Add Vertue, Patience, Temperance, add Love,
> By name to come calld Charitie, the soul
> Of all the rest: then wilt thou not be loath
> To leave this Paradise, but shalt possess
> A paradise within thee, happier farr.   (XII, 581-7)

They descend the hill of revelation to find Eve and with her all that chance for answerable deeds, she herself steadied and ready to go into exile in the re-establishment of their matrimonial harmony. It is not that all shall be well or even that God shall triumph in the Millennium which gives to the expulsion scene its remarkable peace. In capable and beautiful final lines, the hesitation captured in their forward movement is a willing hesitation at the very threshold of the transcient world and the race of time.

Endurance has been half the theme and love the other of the final books; man's patience half the theme, his magnanimity rooted in his sense of the divine order the other. Heroic virtue is identical with the lesson of charity which fulfils all the Christian virtues. The place of man in the universe and the place of reason in his soul have been so explained by the Angel that what most merits fame is no more in silence hid and what shall be man's probationary lot until immortality is plain. So the experience of the human pair finds them at its close 'quiet though sad', 'though sorrowing yet at peace', 'though in fallen state, content'.

Highest praise may yet be reserved now for this and now for that particular section of *Paradise Lost*, but when the poem ends with the father and mother of mankind leaving Eden on their long journey, the last words give us no image of them which the whole poem was not preparing from the beginning—a vision which all the rangings through

---

[8] *Poetry and the Fountain of Light* (London, 1962), p. 153.

time and space explained, the final focus on the state of the soul of man, where the power of light drives out the image of dark. What emerges from a reading of the last two books is, I think, the force of Milton's intellect, a revelation of the power of his mind, the greatness of his idea, the continuing tone of nobility with which he pursues his quest to establish the right manner of life and conduct. Michael's great discourse of reintegration after the Fall puts forward the paradox of increased liberty and the ideal of the paradise of the peaceful conscience; he fills the whole stage with the final purposes of God and develops before Adam's eyes a reunified universe filled throughout with the providential will of God, not coercive on the private will. As human affairs unroll and in them forms the picture of the just elect minority, the epic design stands clear. At the outer rim is the God who is all in all; at the heart, the man of upright mien.

Milton and the Theatrical Sublime

F. T. Prince

Milton's three dramatic poems contain little or nothing that can be called theatrical. In *Samson Agonistes* the only spectacular event takes place off the scene. In *Arcades* the scene and action are of the slightest. In *Comus* there are some essential but simple theatrical effects: the dance of monsters, the intervention of the Brothers to save the Lady, and the rising up of the river-goddess, for example; but the poet's chief interest and endeavour lie elsewhere.

As for *Paradise Lost*, it is generally agreed that Milton shows a liking for dramatic technique, and reveals a tendency to think in terms of drama; there are the moments of soliloquising, as if before an invisible audience, and there are some speeches which may seem to say little more than 'See where he comes' or 'Hark, I hear voices' (IV, 866–73; V, 307–13; XI, 226–37). Sometimes these dramatic devices have been considered to be a source of weakness, and sometimes explained as relics of an original draft in dramatic form, which has been imperfectly absorbed into the epic. But I hope to show that there is a far more powerful element in the poem which can well be described as *theatrical*, and that it is not irrelevant to our understanding of Milton's vision and purpose. It may indeed help us to see *Paradise Lost* in a somewhat new way; and even to look more favourably on some debatable parts of it. In the wider discussion one must naturally include the evidence of Milton's conception of drama as an instrument of religious teaching, and some consideration of the ways in which he put it into practice.

Milton's scheme for a drama on the Fall of Man, *Adam Unparadized*, is obviously relevant. Together with that other document of the 1640s, his discussion of possible forms of high poetry in *The Reason of Church-Government*, it gives us a glimpse of a form of drama combining a

Greek logic and restraint with a visionary religious splendour. Milton says that the poet for whom religion and patriotism are one, may adopt the form of either epic or drama:

> Or whether those Dramatick constitutions, wherein *Sophocles* and *Euripides* raigne shall be found more doctrinal and exemplary to a Nation, the Scripture also affords us a divine pastoral Drama in the Song of Salomon consisting of two persons and a double Chorus, as *Origen* rightly judges. And the Apocalyps of Saint *John* is the majestick image of a stately Tragedy, shutting and intermingling her solemn Scenes and Acts with a sevenfold Chorus of halleluja's and harping symphonies: and this my opinion the grave autority of *Pareus* commenting that booke is sufficient to confirm.

The reference to the Book of Revelation and the opinion of Paraeus was repeated more than twenty years later, in the preface to *Samson*. But the importance of the phrase about a Chorus of Angels becomes apparent if we look rather at *Adam Unparadiz'd* and *Paradise Lost*.

However, one should perhaps make the point now that, if *Paradise Lost* had been written as a drama, it would have been, like *Samson Agonistes*, a kind of drama for which we have no name. One cannot call it simply literary drama; it is a poem in dramatic form, not written for the stage, but for the inward eye. The possibility of stage presentation is put aside: 'to which this work never was intended', says Milton of *Samson*. Yet the drama, the poem, is shaped and visualised as for a mental stage. We should realise that we are being made to watch the scene and the action *on the page*: it is there on paper. When Milton wants us to visualise a setting, a character, or a movement, he gives us just as much indication as we need. We have the setting in the opening lines, the bank with 'choice of Sun or shade'. Samson refers to his fetters and his beggary; the Chorus on its entry describes his posture and dress,

> In slavish habit, ill-fitted weeds
> Ore worn and soild;

and so his image is fixed for the rest of the poem. The Chorus describes Manoa as he approaches

> With careful step, Locks white as doune.

Each new character as it appears is described for our inner eye; Harapha, the Philistine Officer, or the Messenger,

> one hither speeding,
> An *Ebrew*, as I guess, and of our Tribe.

The most detailed and vivid of such descriptions, commensurate with her importance in the story, is that of Dalila, as she enters:

> But who is this, what thing of Sea or Land? . . .

Even her appearance, as she prepares to address her husband, is set before us.

Thus *Samson* gives us the clearest evidence, written into the fabric of the poem, that Milton is fulfilling the demands of a special form: the drama which is complete on the page, when 'seen' by the reader. The conventions of Greek tragedy determine what he will or will not introduce on the imagined stage; but since the drama is to be read, not acted, he provides necessary aids to our imagination.

We can deduce from the MS plans that the same procedure would have been followed in *Adam Unparadiz'd*, and not only because the nakedness of unfallen man would raise a special problem. It is true that in one version the Prologue would have told the supposed audience that 'they cannot se Adam in this state of innocence by reason of thire sin'; and it is only after the action has passed its mid-point that the two main characters can appear: 'man next & Eve having by this time bin seduc't by the serpent appeares confusedly cover'd with leaves'. But the same difficulty did not deter Andreini in his *Adamo*, as it had not deterred the creators of medieval drama, in which actors had in some way represented Adam and Eve before the Fall, as after. The design for *Adam Unparadiz'd* has a Greek severity and a Puritan reserve; it offers a great contrast both with Andreini's *sacra rappresentazione* and with medieval drama. But this and other aspects and implications of Milton's proposed tragedy had better be examined later. I must first establish the quality of theatricality in the poetry of *Paradise Lost*.

I have in mind Milton's use of organised and enacted spectacle, his demonstration of the meaning of a dramatic moment; which leaves us with the impression of having witnessed a consciously complete *performance*, on the part of both the poet and his poem. One could call such poetry 'the theatrical sublime'; and one could see it as the detailed application of that power attributed to Milton by Dr Johnson: 'of displaying the vast, illuminating the splendid, enforcing the awful, darkening the gloomy, and aggravating the dreadful'.

Let me illustrate first from a passage in which Milton dramatises his Heaven—one of those Choruses 'of Heavenly Harpings and Songs between', which he seems to have thought a special resource of religious drama:

> No sooner had th' Almighty ceas't, but all
> The multitude of Angels with a shout
> Loud as from numbers without number, sweet
> As from blest voices, uttering joy, Heav'n rung
> With Jubilee, and loud Hosanna's filld
> Th' eternal Regions: lowly reverent
> Towards either Throne they bow, and to the ground
> With solemn adoration down they cast
> Thir Crowns inwove with Amarant and Gold . . .
> With these that never fade the Spirits Elect
> Bind thir resplendent locks inwreath'd with beams,
> Now in loose Garlands thick thrown off, the bright
> Pavement that like a Sea of Jasper shon
> Impurpl'd with Celestial Roses smil'd.
> Then Crownd again thir gold'n Harps they took,
> Harps ever tun'd, that glittering by thir side
> Like Quivers hung, and with Præamble sweet
> Of charming symphonie they introduce
> Thir sacred Song, and wak'n raptures high . . .   (III, 344–69)

The hymn follows, as fully developed and decorated as its prelude. The conscious lavishness, the emphatic completeness of the picture and action—the enactment of the picture: these are the qualities which I would call theatrical—'the theatrical sublime'.

The term will need some further analysis or explanation; it is but one element in the poetic synthesis. But surely such writing is found, with many variations of scale and tone, in many striking contexts in *Paradise Lost*. It is most obvious in such an extended passage as I have just quoted; but there are many similar passages which are more decisive to the action, and poetically more intense. For example, there is the grand transformation scene in Book X, when Satan and his followers receive their reward and punishment. What could be more carefully prepared and more forcibly 'staged'? Satan makes himself invisible for his return to Pandemonium, but suddenly reveals himself to his debating followers:

> Down a while
> He sate, and round about him saw unseen:
> At last as from a Cloud his fulgent head
> And shape Starr-bright appeerd, or brighter, clad
> With what permissive glory since his fall

> Was left him, or false glitter: All maz'd
> At that so sudden blaze the *Stygian* throng
> Bent thir aspect, and whom they wishd beheld,
> Thir mighty Chief returnd: (X, 447–55)

We have Satan then acclaimed by 'the great consulting Peers', and his exulting announcement of success; and we have the horrible and splendid climax, which Milton elaborates through eighty lines, until the mass of tormented serpent-angels are left compulsively gorging themselves on the Dead Sea fruit of their triumph:

> greedily they pluckd
> The Frutage fair to sight, like that which grew
> Neer that bituminous Lake where *Sodom* flam'd;
> This more delusive, not the touch, but taste
> Deceav'd; they fondly thinking to allay
> Thir appetite with gust, instead of Fruit
> Chewd bitter Ashes, which th' offended taste
> With spattering noise rejected: oft they assayd,
> Hunger and thirst constraining, drugd as oft,
> With hatefullest disrelish writh'd thir jaws
> With soot and cinders filld; (X, 560–70)

There are many other turning-points in the action to which Milton has given a similar quality: the use of gunpowder by the rebel angels, and their defeat by the Son of God; or Satan's discovery by Ithuriel, who finds him squatting in the form of a toad, by the ear of Eve:

> Him thus intent *Ithuriel* with his Spear
> Touchd lightly; for no falsehood can endure
> Touch of Celestial temper, but returns
> Of force to its own likeness: up he starts
> Discoverd and surpriz'd. As when a spark
> Lights on a heap of nitrous Powder, laid
> Fit for the Tun som Magazin to store
> Against a rumord Warr, the Smuttie grain
> With sudden blaze diffus'd, inflames the Aire:
> So started up in his own shape the Fiend.
> Back stepd those two fair Angels half amaz'd
> So sudden to behold the grieslie King; (IV, 810–21)

Demonstrative action is not confined to Milton's personages, spiritual or human: it extends to his universe, which joins in the stress laid on significant moments. Hell gates spring open,

> With impetuous recoile and jarring sound . . . (II, 880)

They will never again be shut. Nature participates in the sin of Eve:

> Earth felt the wound, and Nature from her seat
> Sighing through all her Works gave signs of woe,
> That all was lost. (IX, 782-4)

When Adam learns of the transgression, the garland he has made ready manifests the blight of innocence:

> From his slack hand the Garland wreath'd for *Eve*
> Down dropd, and all the faded Roses shed: (IX, 890-1)

These few examples, both long and short, should be enough to make plain what I mean by 'the theatrical sublime'. Indeed there is nothing abstruse or ambiguous about it, however finely or significantly it may be adjusted to the needs of the context. Its essence is to be, not subtle, but powerful. A nineteenth-century example from another art can be taken from the end of the second Act of *Parsifal*, when Klingsor hurls the sacred Lance at the young hero; Parsifal seizes it in mid air; and the whole enchanted garden of Kundry dissolves in darkness and ruins, as he holds it above his head.

But am I mistaken in thinking that the 'theatrical' in *Paradise Lost*, though more apparent in some places than others, provides a clue to the distinctive beauty of the whole poem? Milton's cosmos, we have seen, is not only a setting for the drama, but takes an active part. The quality of triumphant demonstration we find in Heaven and Hell is an ingredient in his descriptions of the Universe, Earth with its creatures, Paradise, Adam and Eve in their first innocence. We know the conflict of opinion on Milton's descriptive style. Some have called it abstract, or conceptual, bookish or artificial; some have defended it as richly sensuous. Some seem to think that when they have shown in what ways Milton uses the English language, the style stands self-condemned; others argue that such linguistic procedures are finely appropriate to his poetic task.

The notion of the 'theatrical' seems to point to the latter view. Can we not see Milton's descriptions of Nature as yet another version of this kind of dramatisation? Nature before the Fall must not only be perfect, but be seen to be perfect; to be seen as perfect, it must display itself, make an almost conscious exhibition. Natural phenomena must be *exemplary*, and therefore they must appear as they might be expected to appear; but they must also be vivid and striking. Milton's method is to show them as if for the first time, both in his description of Paradise and in his account of the Creation; but to show them displaying their quintessential qualities. Words and deeds are wedded to natural creation in a way that makes elements, plants, or animals seem conscious of doing or being just what they ought:

> From Branch to Branch the smaller Birds with song
> Solac'd the Woods, and spred thir painted wings
> Till Ev'n, nor then the solemn Nightingal
> Ceas'd warbling, but all night tun'd her soft layes:
> Others on Silver Lakes and Rivers Bath'd
> Thir downie Brest; the Swan with Arched neck
> Between her white wings mantling proudly, Rowes
> Her state with Oarie feet: (VII, 433-40)

There is no need to labour the quality of 'expectedness' here. Epithets become mere extensions of substantives. The lakes and rivers are silver, the birds' breasts are downy, the swan has proud white wings and an arched neck. What gives such poetry its life is the conviction and consistency which lie behind, not only each passage as it unfolds, but the whole epic. Here as elsewhere—as in the theological expositions or the motivations of the main characters—we have triumphant demonstration, a conscious exhibition of the true nature of things. The poet's intention reaches into every detail of the style, and transforms the Latinate neo-classical formulas by giving them a new purpose. Thus the use of terms from human art to heighten descriptions of nature helps to sustain the impression of a conscious display. The birds' wings are 'painted'; the flowers carpeting the nuptial bower,

>   with rich inlay
> Broiderd the ground, more colourd then with stone
> Of costliest Emblem: (IV, 701-3)

Literary conventions such as personification are used to imply that natural phenomena have a conscious life, a self-awareness in carrying out their allotted functions:

> Now came still Eevning on, and Twilight gray
> Had in her sober Liverie all things clad;
> Silence accompanied, . . .

When the nightingale sings,

> Silence was pleas'd: now glowd the Firmament
> With living Saphirs: *Hesperus* that led
> The starrie Host, rode brightest, till the Moon
> Rising in clouded Majestie, at length
> Apparent Queen unvaild her peerless light,
> And ore the dark her Silver Mantle threw.   (IV, 598–609)

Milton's swan, Milton's moon, are not stage properties; but they are playing their part in a great dramatic exhibition of the fitness of things, as God first ordered them. Milton's Creation is like a cosmic pageant, every creature or element 'conscious of doing what it ought'. The lion paws its way from the ground, the trees rise 'as in dance'. The waters ostentatiously obey God's command to 'let dry land appear':

> as Armies at the call
> Of Trumpet (for of Armies thou hast heard)
> Troop to thir Standard, so the watrie throng,
> Wave rouling after Wave, where way they found,
> If steep, with torrent rapture, if through Plaine,
> Soft-ebbing; nor withstood them Rock or Hill,
> But they, or under ground, or circuit wide
> With Serpent error wandring, found thir way,
> And on the washie Oose deep Channels wore;
> Easie, ere God had bid the ground be drie,
> All but within those banks, where Rivers now
> Stream, and perpetual draw thir humid traine.   (VII, 295–306)

The force which holds together all such poetic procedures, and which wields them as one poetic instrument, is Milton's didacticism. If we accept his unremitting moral purpose as the powerful poetic force which it is, and trace its working, we shall see it moulding and animating every detail, and giving the poem a unity which is not superficial but profound.

So Milton's 'theatricality' is didactic. To this end he dramatises the conventions of neo-classical poetic diction, as he dramatises epic grandeur. But should we not consider whether *Paradise Lost* does not owe a great deal to medieval religious drama as well as to classical epic? We should at least look again at his scheme for *Adam Unparadiz'd* in this connection, for it gives us a link with Andreini's *Adamo*, if not with the popular *sacre rappresentazioni*; and we should realise that those religious dramas of the seventeenth century in Italy and other Catholic countries were simply a Renaissance version of the medieval religious drama which had flourished everywhere in Europe before the Reformation.

Adam Unparadiz'd was intended to be a dramatic poem, to be seen not on the stage, but by the inward eye. In this it would have resembled Andreini's drama, and this point of resemblance is perhaps ultimately more important than the identity of subject. The *Adamo* is a literary work; Andreini subtitles it a *sacra rappresentazione*, and refers in his preface to that still flourishing tradition of popular religious drama in Italy. But both the text of his poem and the preface can only be understood if we realise that he is attempting something new: a sophisticated *literary* version of a mystery play. The work has many weaknesses, apart from its generally undistinguished poetic texture; it is too long and wordy; the design is neither clear nor coherent; there is little dramatic tension or characterisation. Yet one can see how it could have roused Milton's imagination to perceive the possibilities of both the theme and the form. The notes for *Adam Unparadiz'd* show him bringing a characteristic intellectual discipline to the shaping of the poem; but the working basis remains that of Andreini, a combination of Renaissance art and medieval religious imagination. Andreini introduces, not only the Seven Deadly Sins, but such allegorical personages as the World, the Flesh, Hunger, Labour, Despair, Death and Vainglory. Milton's drafts include a similar list—'Labour Sicknesse Discontent Ignorance Feare Death'—and add some others: Heavenly Love, Conscience, Justice, Mercy, and Wisdom, Faith, Hope, and Charity.

Milton's design has a Greek concision, as well as such obvious marks of Greek tragedy as the Chorus and the use of a messenger. In projecting in such detail a drama on the Fall, he must have become aware of the artistic problems the subject would raise, especially in this form. In its full scope the drama would have to cover the whole economy of sin and salvation, like *Paradise Lost*. Milton was forced to envisage a whole series of narratives, either by the Chorus, or by individual angels, or by such abstractions as Faith and Mercy. In the third draft, the Chorus would have concluded four of the five Acts with long descriptive narrations: 'Chorus of Angels sing a hymne of the creation'; 'Chorus sing the mariage song and describe Paradice'; 'Chorus . . . relates Lucifers rebellion and fall'. In the final draft, Adam is shown by an angel 'a mask of all the evills of this life and world', which is presumably described as it passes by; and 'at last appeares Mercy comforts him promises the Messiah'. We see how much contrivance the dramatic form would have imposed; the amount of narrative needed might be said to point directly to the epic form as more appropriate. Because of the narrations, the poet's voice would have predominated in *Adam Unparadiz'd*, though he might speak through a Prologue, a Chorus, or an Angel: why not set it free, to speak in his own person, as an epic poet?

The structure of *Paradise Lost* is itself a vindication of Milton's decision to abandon drama for epic; there is no need to cast round in search of his reasons. But it is it not possible that among them was the realisation that the subject could be treated much *more* dramatically in epic form? *Paradise Lost* contains far more action, drama projected more vividly and more immediately on the inward eye, than we can imagine being fitted into the framework of *Adam Unparadiz'd*: and if I am right, it is not only more dramatic, but more 'theatrical', than the tragedy could have been. Milton created what was in form a narrative, but in feeling and content a drama: a colossal pageant of dogma and sacred history. Among the formative influences on it was the tradition of medieval religious drama, mediated to him through Andreini's literary *sacra rappresentazione*. Milton's type of poetic drama, whether as it appears in *Paradise Lost* or in *Samson Agonistes*, may well have one of its sources in the concluding passage of the Preface to *L'Adamo* (1617). Andreini runs artlessly through the difficulties offered by his subject, and apologises for his failure to deal with them worthily. Among other things, he seeks to excuse the appearance, in human form, of God the Father and the Devil;[1] and asks the reader to look rather to the substance than to the accidents, 'seeing in the work its aim of bringing to the Theatre of the Soul the unhappiness and lamentations of Adam, and making your heart the spectator of all, to raise it from these lowly things to the grandeur of Heaven, by means of virtue and with the help of God'.[2]

Finally, if we accept *Paradise Lost* as a drama for 'the Theatre of the Soul', we might find ourselves looking with more sympathy on some of the more strictly didactic passages. Everything is enacted before us as a *lesson*; and no comment can be inept or superfluous, which makes

[1] '. . . e pur se questo è permesso, e si vede tutto giorno espresso nelle rappresentazioni sacre, perche non si hà da permettere nella presente . . .'
[2] '. . . contemplando nell' Opera il fine di portar nel Theatro dell' Anima la miseria, & il pianto d' Adamo, e farne spettatore il tuo cuore, per alzarlo da queste bassezze, alle grandezze del Cielo, co'l mezo della Virtù, e dell' aiuto di Dio . . .'

the meaning articulate. Milton's comments on the fate of Paradise after the Flood; his moralising on concord among devils and discord among men; his treatment of God in the dialogue in Heaven; and the presentation of world history to Adam (like a dumb-show, or 'a play within the play'): all these controverted features of the poem might be illuminated, might even be absorbed into an aesthetic unity, by the conception of 'the theatrical sublime'.

The Embarrassments of *Paradise Lost*

Joseph H. Summers

When I was asked to give a lecture in celebration of the tercentenary of the publication of *Paradise Lost*, I accepted immediately. A good many months after my acceptance, I began to realise that I had acted hastily. It was only six years ago that I completed the writing of a book about *Paradise Lost* which represented my reading of the poem over a period of ten years or so. What possibly could I have to say about the poem which I had not already said? I do not mean to imply that I thought I had solved all the problems of that great and complex poem; only that I had given, as nearly as I could, a general reading of it according to my lights and limitations, and it seemed absurd to repeat myself. Perhaps the wisest thing would have been for me to have sent sincere, if belated, regrets. Instead, I took the usual academic alternative, and began to read and to re-read some of the books and essays about the poem which have been published recently.

It was not difficult to come to a few conclusions. First of all, I could hardly pretend that there was any special need for me to contribute to the tercentenary celebration. With the rash of books appearing in the past few years, the poem is as generally 'celebrated' now as it ever has been in the past three hundred years. And with the recent volumes of essays collected by Arthur Barker and Louis Martz, the forthcoming volumes to be edited by C. A. Patrides, Balachandra Rajan, and Alan Rudrum, and the special lectures at York and elsewhere, hardly any student of English literature will be unconscious of the tercentenary or able to complain justly that recent and lively criticism and scholarship concerning the poem are hard to come by.

A number of these works, particularly such recent ones as Dennis Burden's *The Logical Poem* and Stanley Fish's *Surprised by Sin*, and earlier, Christopher Ricks' *Milton's Grand Style* (1963) and Helen Gardner's *A Reading of Paradise Lost* (1965), suggested also that the famous 'Milton controversy' is now over—at least in the form in which it was waged in the 'thirties and 'forties, with the exciting attacks by Eliot, Leavis, and Waldock, and the vigorous defences by C. S. Lewis, Douglas Bush, and others. This surprised me. Although I had thought the controversy more or less moribund in America, I had assumed that it was still alive in England, particularly since both Bernard Bergonzi's 'Criticism and the Milton Controversy' (published in Frank Kermode's *The Living Milton*) and John Peter's *A Critique of Paradise Lost* had made the same assumption as recently as 1960. Yet it now seems that the two latter works really did mark the end. In his book Peter echoed much of the earlier anti-Miltonic arguments, but he also found much to admire in the poem, and he ended by placing Milton, once again, firmly in the English literary pantheon as second only to Shakespeare. By distinguishing so carefully between the languages and the assumptions of the defenders and attackers of Milton and *Paradise Lost*, Bergonzi discouraged snipers on both sides: it seemed futile to keep up a simple crossfire which was guaranteed in advance to miss its targets. At any rate, within the last six years no one, so far as I know, has seriously questioned (in print at least) the greatness of *Paradise Lost*. Probably of more importance than the mere judgements of the poem's place or size, a large number of the recent studies suggest that their authors have enjoyed reading at least substantial portions of it. This would seem to support the notion that the old charge of Milton's supposed insensitivity to language is also almost dead. Concentrating particularly on passages in the poem which have been attacked as awkward or confused or inflated, Mr Ricks has demonstrated the usefulness of such attacks, since considering them often 'brings out just how good the lines are'.[1] It seems that no reader who can agree with Mr Ricks that the demand for 'colloquial ease' was 'an extraordinary critical shibboleth'[2] should now complain about the style of *Paradise Lost*.

If there is no longer a concerted attack on *Paradise Lost* as our only finished epic and as one of the two or three greatest non-dramatic poems in the English language, does this mean that we are all now in agreement about the central issues, and that we can therefore devote our time to exploring minor difficulties and developing appreciation of beautiful

[1] *Milton's Grand Style* (Oxford, 1963), p. 46.
[2] p. 75.

details in a harmonious chorus of 'prompt eloquence'? I hardly think so. If there is more or less general agreement today about the poem's stature, there is very little agreement about anything else. Some readers seem willing to grant the greatness so long as they do not have to read the poem again. Others, acknowledging its place with an 'Alas', regret either its message or its means. The mixture of love and hate in some is intense. The poem demands (and usually gets) strong responses. Those who admire it most have a tendency to become self-appointed partisans, yet their skirmishes often indicate that they are defending very different things: occasionally one partisan fails to recognise within the poem the qualities which his allies most admire. To judge by my own case, even the most committed advocates of the poem are sometimes puzzled by it or uncertain of their judgements or interpretations of it. As the English epic, *Paradise Lost* provides almost continual embarrassments. It is not, and I do not believe it ever was or could be for readers who read it closely and intelligently, a 'comfortable' poem. It is today, to use language which Milton would have understood, a scandal and a stumbling-block.

To understand why this is so we might begin with the question, What do most readers or hearers desire or expect of the great epic poem of their language? In the past one thing could usually be assumed: the heroic poems dealt with the great actions of the heroes of a tribe or nation or civilisation. In hearing or reading them, later men could feel that their heritage was both defined and glorified by the ancestral deeds: whatever his own personal habits and whatever he thought of the character of Aeneas, a Roman could admire the *Aeneid* as a glorification of Roman destiny. In the Renaissance, of course, the great national poem also became a sign of the maturation of the national ethos, the final proof that the new tongue was worthy of taking its place with the classic languages. Although some of this may sound quite alien to us today, we should recognise the modern echoes of the older ideas within, for example, the bardic efforts to define and glorify America and the 'American language' from Whitman to Hart Crane and William Carlos Williams and beyond; it seems likely, too, that other former colonial areas will experience similar phenomena as they develop a new national consciousness. But what do we find with *Paradise Lost*? The major characters of the great English poem are neither English nor, until the final books, even fully what we know as human beings. The deeds with which it is concerned are neither tribal nor national. And although the poem constantly evokes all the civilisations known to the seventeenth century, the nearest thing to specific evocations of English civilisation are unsettling references to 'evil dayes . . . and evil tongues', 'the Race/Of that wilde Rout that tore the *Thracian* Bard/In *Rhodope*' (VII, 26, 33-35), 'an age too late' (IX, 44), or the 'Sons/Of *Belial*' (I, 501-2). If this age or nation can provide 'fit audience', they will, to judge by the text, certainly be few. No heroic poem was ever less a glorification of a nation or a civilisation.

And the language? I think we will all have to agree, despite Dr Johnson, that it is English, but an English so artful, so evocative, under so much pressure that we must usually be as attentive to it as we would be to a foreign language. There *are* occasions when Milton uses the colloquial in the poem (the bickering of the fallen Adam and Eve at the end of Book IX is a fine example), but most of the time it would never occur to us to exclaim that this is the language in which we say *mamma e babbo*. Rather than seeming the elevation and crowning of 'our language', the 'purification of the dialect' of our tribe, it seems a new creation, formidable in its magnificence.

If *Paradise Lost* does not give us much satisfaction as a glorification of our ancestry or nation or civilisation or our ordinary language, can it at least serve another use to which the epics have been put in the post-classical world? Will it do as a significant text by which the young may be taught, not only some of the discipline and complexities of versification, but, more important, the approved values of our societies? The poem has certainly been taught with such general aims in mind, but one wonders with what results. (I like to think that in trying to teach at the university level, I am attempting to help adults—youthful peers—read it rather than to indoctrinate the young.) For the purpose of instructing the young in the mysteries of English versification, wouldn't we have fewer difficulties if we chose verse which was simpler, or less idiosyncratic, or at least about which there was a little more scholarly and critical agreement? One can anticipate the difficulties today in the larger aim, the inculcation of our 'approved' values, since there is so little agreement about both what they are and should be; but I think it likely that almost any state or established society would find *Paradise Lost* potentially embarrassing if not actually subversive as a text for the very young. Before going on to other discomforts, I might remark in passing that the well-established British and American tradition (which only recently shows signs of breaking down) for teaching in schools only the first two books of the poem may be related to the possibility of pedagogical embarrassment at the prospect of instructing a classroom of adolescents in the later descriptions and celebrations of sexual love. With a careful reading only of those first Books, any number of young students have decided that Satan is the true hero, the figure to be imitated. And if the teacher attempts to correct that response, he is faced with the indubitable fact that most of the heroic and civilised and official virtues are found in Hell.

Any moralist would have to recognise that the very subject of *Paradise Lost* limited its pedagogical and civic usefulness: with its action in Eden, the poem could not very well serve as a sort of *Télémaque*, a model for all the proper responses to all the occasions likely to be met in a civilised life. But surely Milton might have been expected to fulfil at least one use of the heroic poem which Renaissance readers assumed Homer and Virgil had unquestionably established: the glorification of the martial virtues as a necessary counterweight to the softness of a civilisation devoted to reading or even listening to the songs of the sirens. I should imagine that a good deal of the dissatisfaction with Books V and VI which many readers have expressed from the seventeenth century until today derives from the assumption that Milton intended (or should have intended) his account of the War in Heaven to serve that traditional epic purpose; and the adult reader who makes such an assumption can hardly find Milton's account anything but confusing, absurd, embarrassing. In so far as the poem's narration of the Great War refers to ordinary earthly wars, it implies that they do not really settle important issues ('Warr wearied hath performd what Warr can do,/And to disordered rage let loose the reines'—VI, 695–6), that heroic boasts are absurd, and that warriors in the heat of battle (including the appointed forces of good) can become so violent that they would destroy Heaven itself unless God intervened to stop them. The poem's direct references to human warfare are even more hostile. In Book XI, Adam sees the future warriors as

> Deaths Ministers, not Men, who thus deal Death
> Inhumanly to men, and multiply
> Ten-thousandfold the sin of him who slew
> His Brother; for of whom such massacher
> Make they but of thir Brethren, men of men? (676–80)

And Michael describes the creation and continued admiration of the very type of the military hero as a sign of an unnatural and degenerate age:

> For in those dayes Might onely shall be admir'd,

> And Valour and Heroic Vertu calld;
> To overcome in Battle, and subdue
> Nations, and bring home spoils with infinite
> Man-slaughter, shall be held the highest pitch
> Of human Glorie, and for Glorie done
> Of triumph, to be stil'd great Conquerours,
> Patrons of Mankind, Gods, and Sons of Gods,
> Destroyers rightlier calld and Plagues of men.
> Thus Fame shall be achiev'd, renown on Earth,
> And what most merits fame in silence hid. (XI, 689–99)

Surely *Paradise Lost* should be high on any list of books condemned as subversive by the ordinary patriotic military society.

And what about religion? Shouldn't the conservatives find the poem useful for defending the old values at least there? Probably few readers would disagree that the poem is 'pious', at least in intent, but it is a bit difficult to see how it could be comfortably used for the purposes of supporting a specific established piety. Roman Catholic and Anglican admirers have always had to make some sort of allowances or adjustments for what the poem says or implies about their churches and worship. Just how some strict Calvinists managed to read the poem with approval has been something of a mystery; probably they assumed that all the poem's insistence on the freedom of the will referred only to the condition of man before the Fall[3]—despite the obvious difficulties of such a reading. Although many religious readers of all convictions have objected to the speeches of God the Father, most Trinitarians had few difficulties with the poem's doctrine of the Godhead until after the revelation, with the publication of the *De doctrina christiana* in the nineteenth century, that Milton was a subordinationist; since then, a number claim to have had difficulties. And although Deists, Unitarians, and others approved of the heresies (while occasionally misinterpreting them), they could hardly have been happy with what the poem plainly says about the Son: the 'begetting', the Incarnation, and the rest. For the educational purposes endorsed by the modern secular state, the poem's aggressive Christianity must be something of an embarrassment. And, as William Empson's *Milton's God* (1961) has recently suggested, agnostics or atheists must make more than the usual historical allowances for this theocentric poem.

[3] See George Sensabaugh's account of George Bellamy's use of *Paradise Lost* in his sermons of the 1750s, *Milton in Early America* (Princeton, 1964), pp. 48–52.

But if we forget all about the peculiar assumptions or expectations concerning the epic or heroic poem, surely we can use *Paradise Lost*, like any other poem, as a text for the ordinary purposes of the study of English literature? Of course we can, but I think that there, too, we are likely to encounter major embarrassments—not least of which may concern the nature of those 'ordinary purposes'. Of course an intelligent student can learn a great deal from a study of the poem about the uses, persuasive and other, of language. But we should recognise that for a very long time one of the chief 'uses' of some knowledge of English literature has been as a sort of semi-hermetic lore, talismanic for determining (and for entering) the educated or ruling classes. A young man at the Court of Elizabeth or the early Stuarts found the ability to read and even to write verse most useful, if not absolutely essential, for getting ahead; and I know of one American student who was surprised when he was refused permission to enter an honours field at Harvard merely because he admitted that the reason he wished to study the history and literature of England was so that he would have something to talk about at cocktail parties with his future brokerage clients. The ordinary little jokes about *Paradise Lost* and the standard quotations often serve, I believe, as milder academic equivalents of essentially the same phenomena: the uses of literature for personal decoration and for the establishment of a certain status within a group. Behind such uses seems to lie an ideal image of the knowing consumer, the unflappable connoisseur. *Paradise Lost*, like Shakespeare's plays, has often been used in this way; but one would think that a serious effort to read the poem and to develop anything like the sort of firm and fine discriminations which the poem demands might prove most uncomfortable for readers who primarily intended such uses. Adam's speech just after he has first eaten of the fruit surely provides a crushing judgement on the fatuity of port-and-cigars connoisseurship as the major aim in life:

> *Eve,* now I see thou art exact of taste,
> And elegant, of Sapience no small part,
> Since to each meaning savour we apply,
> And Palate call judicious; I the praise
> Yeild thee, so well this day thou hast purveyd.
> Much pleasure we have lost, while we abstain
> From this delightful Fruit, nor know till now
> True relish, tasting; if such pleasure be
> In things to us forbidd'n, it might be wisht,

> For this one Tree had bin forbidden ten.
> But come, so well refresht, now let us play . . . (IX,1017–27)

A more responsible purpose for the study of English literature, one that seems to have gained strength since the nineteenth century, is its presumed usefulness in developing the qualities of a 'reasonable man', tolerant, flexible, humane—something approaching an ideal citizen, or even an ideal civil servant: responsible, a bit sceptical, able to compromise and willing to 'play the game', preferably well-mannered. Such qualities are indeed likeable and desirable in many situations, but they are probably more useful in the administration of an ongoing concern than in providing leadership during a period of revolutionary change or cataclysmic crisis; to consider them as the only qualities we need to develop is to assume that our society or civilisation will continue to run largely of its own momentum. I believe that *Paradise Lost*, with its evocation of dozens of civilisations (all fallen), should give pause to anyone who makes such an assumption. The poem's insistence on the righteous heroism of one man (or angel) alone, Abdiel or Enoch or Noah or Abraham—or Christ—against not only a legal majority but *everyone* is, if not an open encouragement to fanaticism, at least probably unhelpful in developing what we usually mean by the qualities of reasonableness:

> faithful found,
> Among the faithless, faithful onely hee;
> Among innumerable false, unmov'd,
> Unshaken, unseduc't, unterrifi'd
> His Loyaltie he kept, his Love, his Zeale;
> Nor number, nor example with him wrought
> To swerve from truth, or change his constant mind
> Though single. (V, 896–903)

And isn't the poem's hostility to the developed rituals of state and church unhelpful for a future civil servant? What about its pessimistic view of history after the death of Christ? Its view of the Apocalypse? Wouldn't Plato have found here additional grounds for banning the poets from his Republic?

If the poem seems to offer little useful support for the conventional values of the establishment, can't it then serve admirably for the propagation of a peculiarly modern sort of individualism? Doesn't it support the notion that in a time of the breaking of nations only the 'authentic self' can serve as a just criterion? that, no longer primarily concerned about how to continue or preserve the values of one civilisation, we can only build the possibilities of another upon the heroic individual's honest perceptions of his own momentary sensations, his desires—and perhaps his wounds? One can go fairly far with this, I think: among other things, *Paradise Lost* is concerned with where to start, what is worth believing or doing if an entire civilisation or even the world itself, should be about to end. But eventually the reader who tries to use the poem as a doctrinal text in support of this position, too, will probably be embarrassed. For with all the poem's celebration of the heroic individual, its only example of an individual who tries to fulfil his own will absolutely, to achieve a condition of total self-sufficiency is, of course, Satan. And although in some respects Satan seems prophetically modern, a true example of Faustian man, the poem does not view him with Goethe's, or even Marlowe's, tenderness: we see his evil and something of the process of his damnation; but what is worse, we see him damned to self-deception, ineffectuality, and silliness. Heroic individualism may be essential, but, according to the poem, it is not enough. Moreover, if the poem seems surrounded by civilisations which have fallen, it is also filled with individuals who fall. It does not provide much support for the notion than an individual or society can abolish the past within this world. Neither does it encourage the dream underlying some of the modern emphasis on 'identity' and the 'authentic self', that the only significant barriers to individual beatitude are the corruptions of civilisation. The most fatal corruptions within *Paradise Lost* begin precisely with the self and expand to the entire universe. The poem as a whole, moreover, seems a reproof to the ultimate, solipsistic individualism which insists that we can never know anything except our own, isolated perceptions: *Paradise Lost* is not an autobiography; and if we can feel Milton's presence or hear his voice within it, it is not at all because he has confined himself to what he has individually known or experienced as sensation.

If the poem is difficult if not impossible as a celebration of the nation or the language and as a pedagogical or propagandistic text for either the Establishment or the anti-Establishment, can we not develop a strictly literary appreciation of it, avoiding all those matters which are often said to be beyond the proper business of the literary critic? It is more difficult than one might suppose. Whatever his literary theories, almost any critic finds it difficult to disentangle those moral, religious, philosophical, social, and political strands which Milton has bound so firmly into *Paradise Lost*. But assuming that we can do so, can we develop an adequate treatment of the purely literary issues? It should help that we seem to have recently abandoned the notions, common among some of our best critics for about a century, that a long poem cannot be all 'poetry', and even that there can be no such thing as a long poem. It should also help us appreciate the artful subtlety of Milton's language if we have really been able to give up both Wordsworth's and Eliot's demands for colloquial language. But can we also come to agree that rational argument as well as 'sensory appeals' and 'symbolic structures' can have a major place in a great poem? Can we grant that the will may be appealed to as justly and successfully, and almost as directly, as the imagination? Can we develop other standards besides 'realistic characterisation' or 'human psychology' by which we may judge the characters in this poem, angelic, hellish, divine, or human? Can we appreciate standards for narrative other than the usual novelistic ones? Can we develop a coherent appreciation of the many ways in which the poem imitates or uses the classical epics and the extraordinary ways in which it departs from them and criticises them? Can we learn, from Isabel MacCaffrey, say, how to read the poem 'as myth',[4] and still keep in mind the warning of that arch-mythographer, Northrop Frye, that 'we are not to read the great cycle of events in *Paradise Lost* cyclically; if we do we shall be reading it fatalistically'?[5] Can we learn to respond to multiple and shifting points of view? to literary representations of objects and persons almost constantly in motion rather than composed in relatively static scenes? If we can do all this, we shall probably be most able literary critics; and then, if we are devoting our lives to the study and criticism of literature, can we make terms with an artful poem which so firmly subordinates art to devotion, literature to religion?

At this point I should have a good deal of sympathy with anyone who wished to exclaim that we should forget about epics, education, higher purposes, teaching, criticism, and the rest, and *enjoy* the poem as individual readers. It is a possible stance (although something of a question-begging one); but even an attempt at a disinterested 'private' reading of the poem is likely to encounter some difficulties. It is extremely unlikely that any living reader can assent to the religious doctrine of *Paradise Lost* in all of its details; it is also almost impossible to ignore it. And Dr Johnson indicated something of the other chief 'personal' embarrassment: 'We read Milton for instruction, retire

[4] *Paradise Lost as 'Myth'* (Harvard, 1959), *passim*.
[5] *The Return of Eden* (Toronto, 1965), p. 102.

harassed and overburdened, and look elsewhere for recreation; we desert our master, and seek for companions.'[6] I can recognise some of my own experience in that formulation. As much as I admire the poem, I cannot live with it constantly; as a non-heroic reader, I find it eventually wearing. With its complexity, its brilliance, its intensity, we cannot lean back in our chairs in its presence; and for most of us there is a limit to how long we can sit forward.

If *Paradise Lost* seems to provide a large number of embarrassments for most of the traditional uses, public and private, what then? Should we give it up? Instead, we might begin again: it is, I think, *our* great heroic poem. Perhaps some of our difficulties arise from the fact that we have seen it too exclusively as a poem which looks to the past, to an alien antiquity, and not sufficiently as one which looks also as firmly and unmistakably towards the future. Perhaps, conscious of the mistakes which the Romantics made in their reading of it, we have not boldly enough taken possession of it as our own. Surely we should have realised that a great modern poem, 'our' heroic poem, would inevitably bring not traditional comfort or simple glorification or aggrandisement, but challenges and embarrassments. Of course a great modern heroic poem would be complex rather than simple in both structure and style. Of course it would be concerned with international or universal issues rather than with national ones. Of course it would centre on the problems and struggles of maturity rather than the established doctrines suitable for the indoctrination of the young. Of course it would glorify the perfection of human sexuality. Of course it would attack war and militarism. Of course it would be continuously concerned with human freedom, political, social, and personal. Of course it would find its primary symbols of value not in scenes or images of static order (ultimately derived from the assumption that in some simpler, remote past everything was fixed, unchanging, and 'right') but in energy, change, continuous and creative movement in space and time. And of course we should have therefore expected it to be subversive of established orders—even revolutionary ones—and to be chiefly concerned with individual actions and decisions in moments of crisis and revolution rather than with the ordinary continuities. And with what we know of the literary developments of the past two hundred years, we should have realised that such a poem must in some ways be far more subjective than the ancient epics, that its primary field of action might more likely be the mind and soul of an individual

[6] *Milton Criticism*, ed. James Thorpe (New York, 1950), p. 81.

than the plains of Troy, or Hastings, or Naseby, or even Waterloo or Flanders.

I do not mean to imply that such revised expectations and recognitions will resolve or prevent our embarrassments with the poem, only that they may make them more fruitful. If we recognise *Paradise Lost* as a modern poem and not merely as a last great manifestation either of a dead classical form or an outdated religion, we will no longer be able to treat it as a 'sacred' object, one before which we occasionally give official genuflections almost in order to make sure that it is safe, that it cannot harm us or intervene directly in our lives. In that case, as William Empson has recently demonstrated, a reader's embarrassments with the poem may be more pressing—and more obvious—than ever, but at least they may be more honestly faced and profitably discussed. Empson's *Milton's God* is an important book not only because Empson has both wit and passion and is great fun to read, but also because he likes to read *Paradise Lost* and does it the courtesy of taking it seriously. Since he is convinced both of the greatness of the poem and the evil or stupidity of what he thinks is Christianity, his intellectual embarrassment is intense, and it forces him into some marvellously ingenious misreadings. But by stating openly what seem to me his misconceptions about both the nature and value of central Christian doctrines and traditions (misconceptions shared by a large number of academics), Empson has brought such matters into the open discussion of contemporary responses to the poem, and that strikes me as all to the good.

We could use more studies as bold and as personally committed as Empson's. With them, a number of things about our great modern work which we could not so easily have predicted might come, with hindsight, to seem inevitable: that along with its insistence on individual freedom it should so clearly demonstrate the reality of self-enslavement: 'Thy self not free, but to thy self enthralld' (VI, 181); that it should perceive ultimate human evil as the perversion of extraordinary natural abilities and gifts—the full potential equipment of a hero—to unnatural, destructive ends ('Save what is in destroying, other joy/To mee is lost' —IX, 478–9); that with its exploration of the subjective and the visionary it should also seem to anticipate and reject the modern notion that individual vision or 'imagination' is all that matters, that every man can create whatever world or universe he desires (underlying all its various and shifting perspectives, *Paradise Lost* assumes—one might even say demonstrates—a world and a universe larger than man, the reality of which man ignores or opposes at his peril), that, while using logic and ordinary reason to the utmost, such a poem should also insist on the limits of such logic before the paradoxes of human experience and the vital processes of growth and decay; that the ultimate import of such a poem should concern a joy on the farther side of tragedy.

We might also come to see *Paradise Lost* as at the very centre of the English literary tradition. One must be careful in using that word, *tradition*—a word, incidentally, to which Milton refused both respect and authority since he assumed that it implied accumulated error and corruption. But if we think of the literary tradition as implying not just the sort of literature we like best—or are trying to write—but the major achievements of literature in the English language from the fourteenth to the twentieth centuries, we must recognise that the most striking thing about it is its extraordinary range. Without the dubious help of an official Academy, English literature has managed to sustain over a remarkably long period various and even apparently opposing strains and characteristics, only roughly suggested by what we have come to think of as the differing values of classicism and romanticism. By definition, '*the* tradition' is infinitely larger than any one work or man or school or age or genre. But in what one work other than *Paradise Lost* can one find, marvellously together, so many of those differing and valuable qualities and effects—elegance and energy, reason and emotion, public and private speech, large architectonic structure and passages of brilliant intensity, 'decorum' and astonishing originality? And what other work so clearly unites in admiration or imitation (with however many oddities of interpretation and judgement) such grand and diverse later figures as Pope and Keats, Dr Johnson and Blake, Dryden and Wordsworth? The poem seems central, moreover, not only in its relationship to the English works which come after it, but also as it mediates between the past and the present, between the antiquities of Judea and Athens and Rome and modernities even beyond England. Where else in English is so obviously the bridge between the questing hero of Homer and the monomaniacal hero of Herman Melville and other moderns? What other work so clearly imitates and recreates the rhythms and sounds of Virgil and Ovid and also provides (along with Milton's other poems) a model and an inspiration for the experiments and aural innovations of Gerard Manley Hopkins? Where else is a more obvious link between the biblical concerns with freedom and justice and J. S. Mill's concerns? What clearer connection between the 'praises' and celebrations of the Psalms and those of Whitman? What other single, extensive, completed work so successfully uses and develops a mythology between *The Divine Comedy* and the various modern attempts?

But the game of matching roles for the continuing drama of English literature can be almost endless, and as Francis Bacon remarked (in quite another context), we should not stay too long in the theatre. I hope I have said enough to suggest that, if we can forgive Milton for not being Shakespeare and *Paradise Lost* for not being a drama, we may come to recognise the centrality of the poem for English literature as well as for ourselves.

Along the way we can make use of almost all the 'true experience' and knowledge, scholarly, critical, and personal, that we can acquire. We may find, I think, that some knowledge of Milton's own intellectual and literary development is likely to prove particularly helpful to us as we attempt to read his poem. From his youth, Milton's imagination kindled most intensely to a developing vision of a free harmony which resolved the seemingly contradictory issues of freedom and necessity, good and evil, by its movements within time. Such visionary sound (one can hardly speak of such matters without a solecism) was traditionally associated both with the Pythagorean music of the spheres and the celestial music of the Christian heavenly choirs. Milton also boldly affirmed it as characteristic of the entire providential course of human history (which it was a part of the Christian poet's duty to make audible), and as the inevitable accompaniment of creation, whether of the great or of little worlds, whether by God or man. It is within *Paradise Lost*, I believe, that Milton embodied that vision most completely. We can often glimpse some of its implications even in apparently 'neutral' passages such as the description of Adam and Eve before their morning hymn in Book V:

> Lowly they bowd adoring, and began
> Thir Orisons, each Morning duly paid
> In various stile, for neither various stile
> Nor holy rapture wanted they to praise
> Thir Maker, in fit strains pronounc't or sung
> Unmeditated, such prompt eloquence
> Flowd from thir lips, in Prose or numerous Verse,
> More tuneable than needed Lute or Harp
> To add more sweetness . . .   (144–52)

When we begin truly to 'see' and to hear that vision of a 'normal' human life as one which combines technical mastery and joy, free individual expression and unanimity or harmony with the expressions of others, variety and order, spontaneity and ritual, individual and communal creativity, our former embarrassments may come to seem as nothing compared to our newer ones: those which are caused, not by our difficulties in understanding and judging the poem, but by our more personal difficulties when we come to feel that the poem is judging us.

Paradise Lost: The Anti-Epic

T. J. B. Spencer

During the latter part of his life Milton's reputation in Europe was rather unsavoury. This was a consequence, of course, of his share in the defence of the execution of King Charles I.

But when he was a young man, on his travels, his admiring foreign friends in Florence and in Rome, with poem and panegyric, told him that Homer, Virgil, and Tasso must look to their laurels, now that this Englishman had appeared. Milton was much impressed by these foreign testimonies—as he tells us in his prose treatise, *The Reason of Church-Government*, published in 1641:

> in the privat Academies of *Italy*, whither I was favor'd to resort, perceiving that some trifles which I had in memory, compos'd at under twenty or thereabout . . . met with acceptance above what was lookt for, and other things which I had shifted in scarsity of books and conveniences to patch up amongst them, were receiv'd with written Encomiums, which the Italian is not forward to bestow on men of this side the *Alps*. . . .   (*Works*, III, 235–6)

—in consequence of all this, as well as of his interior conviction, he began to feel that he 'might perhaps leave something so written to aftertimes, as they would not willingly let it die'. He only reluctantly abandoned his hopes for the European reputation as a poet that might have come to him if he had written in Latin, the international language. We, looking back over the centuries, can see that the continuance of Latin as a language of literature in Europe was already precarious, and that its stability and universality were a delusion. The poets who wrote Latin epics—some of them men of considerable poetic distinction—are now rarely read. One can guess what would have been the fate of that *Arthuriad* in Latin which Milton, as a young man, had envisaged as the main achievement of his life, but which he abandoned for the theme of the Fall of Man. Milton said that he realised that 'it would be hard to arrive at the second rank among the Latines'. The situation was, in fact, far worse than that. To be in the second rank among the Latins, or in the first rank among the Neo-Latins, was to be nowhere at all.

> I apply'd my self [Milton continues] . . . to fix all the industry and art I could unite to the adorning of my native tongue; not to make verbal curiosities the end, that were a toylsom vanity, but to be an interpreter & relater of the best and sagest things among mine own Citizens throughout this Iland in the mother dialect . . . not caring to be once nam'd abroad, though perhaps I could attaine to that, but content with these British Ilands as my world. (*Works*, III, 236-7)

Yet Milton's melancholy words at the beginning of the ninth book of *Paradise Lost* are perhaps partly prompted by his disappointment at his failure to be a European poet. His theme, he says, is sufficient of itself to raise his name—that is, to give him poetic fame—

> unless an age too late, or cold
> Climat, or Years damp my intended wing
> Deprest; and much they may . . .   (IX, 44-46)

Nevertheless, having determined to write in his mother tongue, Milton is still out for the first prize in poetry. He is willing to take on all comers.

The literary historian can, no doubt, separate the various influences upon the form and structure of *Paradise Lost*: Greek, classical Latin, Renaissance Latin, Italian, and so on. This, however, rather obscures the important point. For Milton, the great poets of former days in Europe were not influences, but rivals; rivals to be surpassed. And the opening lines of *Paradise Lost* establish the tone of his rivalry, in a remarkably lively way. The first thing Milton has to do is to make his claim to superiority over the Greek and Roman poets. The Muses of pagan mythology, as everyone knows, inhabited alternative mountains: Mount Helicon or Mount Parnassus; they haunted various springs, notably the Castalian fountain which flowed near the temple of Apollo's oracle at Delphi. But Milton has a Heavenly Muse, the same muse that inspired the poetry of Moses as author of the Pentateuch, the lyrical poetry of King David as author of the Psalms, and the prophetic poetry of Isaiah and other writers of the Old Testament. And this Heavenly Muse igeniously has her mountains and springs, as had the Pagan ones—mountains and springs hallowed by these three genres of biblical poetry:

> Sing Heav'nly Muse, that on the secret top
> Of *Oreb*, or of *Sinai*, didst inspire
> That Shepherd, who first taught the chosen Seed,
> In the Beginning how the Heav'ns and Earth
> Rose out of *Chaos*: Or if *Sion* Hill
> Delight thee more, and *Siloa's* Brook that flowd
> Fast by the Oracle of God; I thence
> Invoke thy aid to my adventrous Song.   (I, 6–13)

Thus inspired, the poet can expect to outdo his heathen rivals: he

> with no middle flight intends to soar
> Above th' *Aonian* Mount.

It is a proud claim, I suppose; but also a display of cleverness; and the wit which Milton is exercising in this opening passage should prevent us from taking it too solemnly.

This sense of rivalry with the poets of the past, instead of a sense of merely inheriting a great tradition, was explicit in the theories of the nature of a poet's life; about what a dedicated poet should do to train himself for his craft and profession. The notion current in the sixteenth and seventeenth centuries about how the poet should live was largely derived from the example of the biography of Virgil, who passed from *Bucolics* to his *Georgics*, and thence to his *Aeneid*. The aspiring young poet of modern times should begin as Virgil did, by writing pastorals, because these concern subjects which do not demand much experience of life, themes such as love, and sheep, and the death of some other shepherd. Then, in his second phase, the poet turns to a kind of realistic poetry—the occupations of men (as in the case of Virgil's *Georgics*); or perhaps to satire. But meanwhile the poet is training himself for the third period of his life when he will produce the epic masterpiece which will place his name alongside Homer and Virgil. Milton obviously supposed his life to conform to this pattern, as Spenser did before him, and as even Pope did, a little half-heartedly, after him; although in his second phase Milton's literary energy was taken up by his extensive prose writing on the political questions of the day.

This scheme for the life of a typical poet has disappeared nowadays, having subsequently been superseded by another one: a pattern, still in three phases, but based vaguely upon the biography of Goethe (I suppose) rather than of Virgil. It came to be expected that in the first period of his life the poet was wild, licentious, and revolutionary. In the second period he reached maturity and wrote his best work. But this was followed by a third period when he became reactionary (or conservative) in politics and religion; suffered from an impoverishment of literary sensibility; and to the younger generation was a venerable, but somewhat deplorable, survivor of his own literary merits. Wordsworth, Coleridge, and many nineteenth-century poets (in England and other countries) tended to fit into this pattern.

But Milton, accepting the older notion, had in his earliest years thought of himself as an epic poet on the grand scale. In a poem written when he was nineteen, with the unpromising title of *At a Vacation Exercise in the College,* he claimed that he would like to make use of his native language for 'some graver subject':

> Such where the deep transported mind may soare
> Above the wheeling poles, and at Heav'ns dore
> Look in . . .
> Then sing of secret things that came to pass
> When Beldame Nature in her cradle was . . .

(that is, the cosmogonic or religio-philosophico-scientific epic)

> And last of Kings and Queens and *Hero's* old,
> Such as the wise *Demodocus* once told
> In solemn Songs at King *Alcinous* feast,
> While sad *Ulisses* soul and all the rest
> Are held with his melodious harmonie
> In willing chains and sweet captivitie.   (33-35, 45-52)

This was a robust ambition in a poet aged nineteen. It was an intention which essentially was fulfilled. But it was matured and radically modified as Milton grew older. The vigorous aspiration expressed in this poem *At a Vacation Exercise in the College,* and in some of his early Latin poems, leads to his bold assertion of superiority at the beginning of the ninth book of *Paradise Lost,* where he invites a self-comparison with Homer and Virgil on the one hand and with the Renaissance romantic epics on the other. The theme of *Paradise Lost* is, he asserts, a better one than those of the *Iliad,* the *Odyssey,* or the *Aeneid.* It is

> Not less but more Heroic then the wrauth
> Of stern *Achilles* on his Foe persu'd
> Thrice Fugitive about *Troy* Wall; or rage
> Of *Turnus* for *Lavinia* disespous'd,

> Or *Neptun's* ire or *Juno's*, that so long
> Perplexd the *Greek* and *Cytherea's* Son.   (IX, 14-19)

And thinking principally of the Italian *romanzi,* Milton somewhat sardonically described himself as:

> Not sedulous by Nature to indite
> Warrs, hitherto the onely Argument
> Heroic deemd, chief maistrie to dissect
> With long and tedious havoc fabl'd Knights
> In Battles feignd . . . or to describe Races and Games,
> Or tilting Furniture, emblazond Shields,
> Impreses quaint, Caparisons and Steeds;
> Bases and tinsel Trappings, gorgious Knights
> At Joust and Torneament; then marshald Feast
> Serv'd up in Hall with Sewers, and Seneshals;
> The skill of Artifice or Office mean,
> Not that which justly gives Heroic name
> To Person or to Poem. Mee of these
> Nor skilld nor studious, higher Argument
> Remaines.   (IX, 27-43)

This disclaimer (that he was 'not sedulous by nature to indite' this sort of thing) is particularly entertaining after Milton had already—in the description of the War in Heaven—provided battle-scenes which bear a kind of parody-relation to the 'long and tedious havoc' of the epic convention. Presumably those modern readers who have difficulty over the War in Heaven are failing to sense that relationship; and so they are being more solemn than Milton himself.

In fact, a preparation for this passage in the ninth book, concerning the conventional military material both of epic and of heroic romance, had already been made in the first book; a direct, devaluing comparison. The 'imbodied force' of Satan's fallen angels, 'in guise/Of Warriors old with orderd Spear and Shield', had no parallel (we are told) in the history of man, and could have none, even though one were to imagine as jointed together

> th' Heroic Race . . .
> That fought at *Theb's* and *Ilium* . . .
> . . . and what resounds
> In Fable or Romance of *Uthers* Son
> Begirt with *British* and *Armoric* Knights;

> And all who since, Baptiz'd or Infidel
> Jousted in *Aspramont* or *Montalban,*
> *Damasco,* or *Marocco,* or *Trebisond,*
> Or whom *Biserta* sent from *Afric* shore
> When *Charlemain* with all his Peerage fell
> By *Fontarabbia*. (I, 577–87)

All this (Milton says) would, if compared to Satan's forces, be merely like the pigmies—that 'small infantry', he describes them, slipping into a pun, 'warrd on by Cranes'. The Italian poets are here dealt with gently, for they were felt to be only modest rivals; but they are put firmly in their place, just the same.

These are examples of Milton's invitation to comparison between himself and his predecessors, in general terms. But in Milton's time the practical criticism of ancient authors—that is, the comparative criticism of parallel passages in Greek and Latin poets—was well developed, though unfortunately it was not much exercised with English authors, and consequently gets omitted nowadays from histories of literary criticism. Already in the first book of *Paradise Lost* Milton writes passages which bear a direct relation to some of the admired achievements of the greatest poets. He offers them as examples of his own poetic virtuosity, demonstrating his equality or superiority. The earliest Greeks, Hesiod and Homer, are soon dispatched. His readers, Milton seems to be saying, may have admired Hesiod's fall of the Titans; but so that he can be judged by *that* standard, he offers you his Fall of the Rebel Angels, whom

> the Almighty Power
> Hurld headlong flaming from th' Ethereal Skie
> With hideous ruin and combustion down
> To bottomless perdition, there to dwell
> In Adamantin Chains and penal Fire,
> Who durst defie th' Omnipotent to Arms. (I, 44–49)

Again, towards the end of the first book of the *Iliad* are some lovely and much-admired lines about the fall of Hephaestos (or Vulcan), flung by Zeus in his rage out of the Olympian court. Hephaestos says:

> On a time ere this, . . . he caught me by the foot and hurled me from the heavenly threshold; the whole day long was I borne headlong, and at the set of sun I fell in Lemnos, and but little life was in me. There did the Sintian folk make haste to tend me for my fall. (I, 590)

Towards the end of the first book of *his* epic poem (and the placing is surely significant) Milton has the temerity to offer you *his* lines on the same theme, just to show you that he can accept the challenge for the palm of poetry on ground chosen by his adversaries, inviting practical criticism. One of the fallen angels is an architect (known as Vulcan or Mulciber):

> and how he fell
> From Heav'n, they fabl'd, thrown by angry *Jove*
> Sheer ore the Crystal Battlements: from Morn
> To Noon he fell, from Noon to dewy Eve,
> A Summers day; and with the setting Sun
> Dropd from the Zenith like a falling Starr,
> On *Lemnos* th' *Ægæan* Ile.   (I, 740–6)

And having delighted you by this enchantment, Milton quietly deflates the impression:

> thus they relate,
> Erring; for hee with this rebellious rout
> Fell long before.

This is a sophisticated kind of poetic wit, which relates the poem to great traditions. But it does not use these great traditions to increase the dignity or elevation of the passage. Rather it persuades the reader to concede the new poet's superiority.

Wherever we turn in the poem we find this ironic disparagement operating. In the epic formula the inset narrative (Odysseus's tale to Alcinous, Aeneas's tale to Dido) takes place after a feast; and what feasts they were! In *Paradise Lost* Eve, like a good housewife, does her best for the sudden and uninvited guest:

> with dispatchful looks in haste
> She turns, on hospitable thoughts intent.   (V, 331 ff.)

Eden is, indeed, a paradise for vegetarian gourmets:

> What choice to chuse for delicacie best,
> What order, so contriv'd as not to mix
> Tastes, not well joind, inelegant, but bring
> Taste after taste upheld with kindliest change.

Such 'delicacy' of connoisseurship startles the reader who recalls Dido's ghastly banquet, with its finger-bowls and napkins, with its fifty waiters laying the tables, trimming the lamps, and smoothing the cushions; and its hundred waitresses who load the tables with food and wine (*qui dapibus mensas onerent et pocula ponant*—I, 706). And everybody remembers that Odysseus was a terrific eater, skilful in cutting off pork slices with (says the poet) the fat on both sides of them. The contrast with Eve's delicate gastronomy is striking:

> fruit of all kinds, in coate,
> Rough, or smooth rin'd, or bearded husk, or shell
> She gathers, Tribute large, and on the board
> Heaps with unsparing hand; for drink the Grape
> She crushes, inoffensive moust, and meathes
> From many a berrie, and from sweet kernels prest
> She tempers dulcet creams . . . (V, 341–7)

And lest the unthinking reader fails to take the point, Milton slyly introduces the names; for Eve brings

> Whatever Earth all-bearing Mother yeilds
> In *India* East or West, or middle shoare
> In *Pontus*

(these are commonplace seats of luxurious food)

> or the *Punic* Coast, or where
> *Alcinous* reignd. (V, 338–41)

But here in Paradise 'No fear lest Dinner coole' (396) and

> down they sat,
> And to thir viands fell, not seemingly
> The Angel . . . but with keen dispatch
> Of real hunger. (V, 433–7)

One of the most famous similes in the history of European poetry had been the comparison of the leaves of a tree to the generations of men. From Homer, through various intermediaries, it came to Virgil, for whom the spirits awaiting waftage to the opposite bank of the river Styx are like the leaves which fall from the trees in autumn.

> quam multa in silvis autumni frigore primo
> lapsa cadunt folia . . . (*Aeneid*, VI, 309–10)

The Italian poets had dared to imitate Virgil; but surely, after all that, a perceptive English poet could not have the rashness to try his hand and write the odious comparison? But Milton puts it into his first book (which is crammed with similar pieces of outrageous virtuosity):

> he stood, and calld
> His Legions, Angel Forms, who lay intranst
> Thick as Autumnal Leaves that strow the Brooks
> In *Vallombrosa*, where th' *Etrurian* shades
> High overarcht imbowr . . .
>   So thick bestrown,
> Abject and lost lay these, covering the Flood.   (I, 300–12)

Just so, the 'high capital' of Satan and his peers is a splendid classical temple, with its pilasters and pillars, golden architrave, cornice, and frieze. In the seventeenth century the most admired antique building was the Pantheon in Rome. (Milton could hardly have failed to visit it—consecrated as the Church of Santa Maria dei Martiri—when he was in Rome in 1638). Are we not intended to be entertained by the way in which the Pantheon becomes the *Pandaemonium* in Milton's infernal topography? C. H. Herford was surely wrong when he wrote that Milton 'with a curious blend of Hellenic enthusiasm and Puritan animus . . . made his fallen Fiends meet for debate in a Greek temple'.[1] One cannot help wondering what would have been Milton's attitude—if he could have seen them—to the neo-classical churches in London in the Greco-Roman style, with which Wren provided a pagan environment for worship in the Established Church. Or, to turn from gastronomy and architecture to philosophy, think of the splendid aphorism:

> The mind is its own place, and in it self
> Can make a Heav'n of Hell, a Hell of Heav'n.   (I, 254–5)

They are inspiring words; a quintessential expression of the stoicism that was the fine flower of Greek and Roman thought, perhaps the highest reach of the human mind before the coming of the Christian hope. With what a malicious pleasure Milton puts the words into Hell, into the mouth of Satan himself!

There is then, in *Paradise Lost*, not only a respect for the great cultural traditions of the past, but also a kind of witty devaluation of them, or inversion of them. It is not enough to say that Milton is writing under the influence of Greek, Latin, and Renaissance poetry; still less,

[1]*Bulletin of the John Rylands Library*, XI (1927), 274.

that he is 'showing off' his erudition. What Milton is 'showing off' is usually his poetical virtuosity, challenging the severest comparisons.

His attitude is, in this respect, consistent with the passage in the fourth book of *Paradise Regained* where he permits his figure of Christ to speak so slightingly of Greek poetry (IV, 330 ff.)—a passage which some critics have found disquieting, and would attribute to the increasing severity of his Puritanism.

> if I would delight my privat hours
> With Music or with Poem, where so soon
> As in our native Language can I find
> That solace? All our Law and Story strew'd
> With Hymns, our Psalms with artful terms inscrib'd,
> Our Hebrew Songs and Harps in *Babylon*,
> That pleas'd so well our Victors ear, declare
> That rather *Greece* from us these Arts deriv'd;
> Ill imitated, while they loudest sing
> The vices of their Deities, and thir own
> In Fable, Hymn, or Song, so personating
> Thir Gods ridiculous, and themselves past shame. (IV, 331-42)

Perhaps it is not easy for us to feel aware of the degree of Milton's sardonic disparagement of the classics. In a world in which the Greco-Roman tradition was the only one that seemed valid for literature—for the Hebrew-scriptural one tended to be over-worked by the parson—humility in the face of the astonishing achievements of the Greeks and the Romans was the natural reaction of a good and perceptive judge of literature. It was easy to slip into the attitude—or scale of literary and artistic values—that what the Ancients did was right and that any other method was wrong. We need not suppose that Milton's delightful ousting of the Greek and Roman classics in *Paradise Lost* indicates his ultimate critical judgement upon them. It is, rather, an attitude appropriate for the structure of the poem. But grimly sanctimonious readers who are unresponsive to *Paradise Lost* as a poem about poetry as well as a poem about man's first disobedience may mislead us. T. S. Eliot quoted, with signs of distress, part of one of Milton's 'catalogues':

> City of old or modern Fame, the Seat
> Of mightiest Empire, from the destind Walls
> Of *Cambalu*, seat of *Cathaian Can*
> And *Samarchand* by *Oxus, Temirs* Throne,

To *Paquin* of *Sinæan* Kings, and thence
To *Agra* and *Lahor* of great *Mogul*
Down to the gold'n *Chersonese*, or where
The *Persian* in *Ecbatan* sate, or since
In *Hispahan*, or where the *Russian Ksar*
In *Mosco*, or the Sultan in *Bizance*,
Turchestan-born . . .   (XI, 386–96)

—and so on. Eliot felt that 'this is not serious poetry, not poetry fully occupied about its business, but rather a solemn game'.[2] Well, I suppose that Milton thought poetry was a serious business, and not a 'solemn game'. I know that in his great treatise on *The Reason of Church-Government Urg'd against Prelaty* he had said that his ambition was to produce 'a work not to be rays'd from the heat of youth, or the vapours of wine, like that which flows at wast from the pen of some vulgar Amorist, or the trencher fury of a riming parasite' (*Works*, III, 241). But that was twenty odd years before, and in the interval Milton had grown more sensible. And somehow Eliot's reference to a 'solemn game' is too easily pejorative. This delightful passage about the Persian in Ispahan and the Russian Czar in Moscow and the Sultan in Bizance bears a clear relation to the catalogues in heroic poetry: it is so much better.

Eliot accepted the conventional critical descriptions of *Paradise Lost* and didn't like them. With very little verification of these critical descriptions from the poem itself, he yet instinctively resented the current interpretations and mistakenly supposed he was resenting the poem. In the perspective of the history of Milton criticism, Eliot can now be seen to have inherited rather conventional views of *Paradise Lost*. He censured Milton for, in this poem, what he described as 'at least an occasional levity'. One might retort that Milton's was a judicious levity, delighting the perceptive reader by its surprise, and by its appropriateness. It is a levity (if we can accept this derogatory word) which was successfully subordinated to the plan and the purpose of the poem. Milton's manoeuvring of the great poetry of the past, his placing himself alongside, or above, the great poets of the past, was not pride or pomposity, but a stroke of wit. Later Eliot exchanged the phrase 'an occasional levity' for the more ambiguous 'a kind of inspired *frivolity*', which he amplifies as 'an enjoyment by the author in the exercise of his own virtuosity, which is a mark of the first rank of

[2] 'A Note on the Verse of John Milton', in *Essays and Studies of the English Association*, XXI (1935); reprinted in *On Poetry and Poets* (1957), p. 144.

genius'.³ (These passages from the British Academy lecture of 1947 were omitted in the reprint of the lecture in *On Poetry and Poets* in 1957).⁴

Frivolity, even an 'inspired frivolity', may at first be difficult to take. Certainly Milton's sense of humour has no high reputation. Most of us, if asked to comment on it, might use words comparable to his own about the elephant's behaviour in front of Adam and Eve:

> th' unwieldy Elephant
> To make them mirth us'd all his might, and wreath'd
> His Lithe Proboscis . . .   (IV, 345–7)

But I recall that Dr Johnson said that 'The Tragedy of *Coriolanus* is one of the most amusing of our author's performances.'⁵ Charles Williams wrote of an 'element of comedy running all through *Paradist Lost*' and C. S. Lewis persuasively expounded the view that Satan was a foolish character—an inevitable inheritance from the Christian notion that 'the Devil is (in the long run) an ass'. Only those readers will fully understand *Paradise Lost*, wrote Lewis, 'who see that it might have been a comic poem'.⁶ But both Williams and Lewis were resisting the absurdities of the simple-minded view of those over-impressed by the intensity of the dramatisation of Satan, and thought that Milton was a self-deceived adherent of the Devil's party. On the contrary Milton was, of course, a great dramatist *manqué*, a born theatrical genius, as everyone knows who has seen *Samson Agonistes* performed, even if it were not obvious from reading *Paradise Lost*. His bad characters, like those of Shakespeare and of his favourite Euripides, are plausible and effective, as bad characters must be in a drama which is to create excitement. His Comus, Satan, and Dalila continue to perplex the simpleminded who would, presumably, wish those morally reprehensible characters to be shown as feeble, ineffectual, and contemptible, instead of vigorous, dynamic, and dangerous. With the temperament of a dramatist, Milton was inevitably a sophist. Enjoy, says the Lady to Comus,

> Enjoy your deer Wit, and gay Rhetorick
> That hath so well been taught her dazling fence, (*Comus*, 790–1)

---

³ *Proceedings of the British Academy* (1947), p. 76.
⁴ See Helen Gardner, *A Reading of 'Paradise Lost'* (1965), pp. 44–45.
⁵ *Johnson on Shakespeare*, ed. Sir Walter Raleigh (1908), p. 179.
⁶ Williams, 'The New Milton', *The London Mercury*, July 1937 (reprinted in *The Image of the City and other essays* [1958], p. 23); and Lewis, *A Preface to 'Paradise Lost'* (1942), p. 93.

and we say the same thing to Milton. A certain shrewdness in perceiving human motives, a sardonic inability to be 'taken in' by illusions, and a just awareness of the extent to which self-deception and self-justification can rule the conduct of human beings and fallen angels, inevitably accompany such sophistry.

Tillyard noticed the humour of *Paradise Lost*. There is (to quote Miss Helen Gardner's words) 'a good deal of satirical wit and of the sardonic in *Paradise Lost*', though she goes on to say that 'it is a minor element in the whole'. And Professor Roy Daniells has explored the comic moments in the poem, which he associates with Milton's baroque tendencies. He emphasises 'the opportunities for formal gaiety which the conventions of Renaissance art permitted'.[7] A certain amount of conscious ludicrousness has been discerned in the poem; though we need not go so far as one critic of Milton who defends the account of the War in Heaven by declaring it to be 'terribly funny'. It is (says Arnold Stein) an 'epic farce'. When by that 'jaculation dire' the 'Hills amid the Air encountered Hills/Hurld to and fro' (VI, 664–5)—here (we are told) Milton employs the comic technique of the 'custard pie'.[8]

But perhaps the gaiety I have indicated in Milton's treatment of epic traditions is more than a minor element of a baroque sparkle. I must be careful. For I would not (like Milton at the hands of T. S. Eliot) wish to be accused of levity, not even an 'occasional levity'; nor of frivolity, not even an 'inspired frivolity'. But in some respects *Paradise Lost*, like *The Rape of the Lock*, is a kind of joke against the epic. And there is something to support the view that Milton had a sardonic mind, an audacious comic sense even from a consideration of Milton's earlier works. The prose writings of Milton that we read are, naturally enough, those written in English. We remember the splendid (if slightly embarrassing) autobiographical passages: the sanctified lips; the proud realisation 'that he who would not be frustrate of his hope to write well hereafter in laudable things, ought him selfe to bee a true Poem'. But when writing for Europe, in Latin against Salmasius, another Milton appears. He adopts another *persona*; a scurrilous Milton. This Milton tends to be forgotten; Milton the wag, the verbal buffoon, the author of that laughter-provoking book the *Pro Populo Anglicano*

---

[7] Tillyard, *Studies in Milton* (1951), pp. 71 ff.; Gardner, *A Reading of 'Paradise Lost'* (1965), p. 97; and Daniells, 'Humour in *Paradise Lost*', *Dalhousie Review*, XXXIII (1953), 159–66 (reprinted in *Milton, Mannerism and Baroque* [Toronto, 1963]).

[8] Arnold Stein, *Answerable Style* (Minneapolis, 1953), pp. 20 ff.

Defensio. Dr Johnson thought it was all rather disgraceful, something *infra dig.* in the puritanical poet and the author of religious epics. 'Such is the controversial merriment of Milton', exclaims Dr Johnson.

I don't see why *we* should take this attitude to Milton's 'controversial merriment'. We appreciate *The Dunciad*, and I don't see why we shouldn't renew our acquaintance with Milton's flagellation of the 'inquisitorious and tyrannical duncery'.[9] Salmasius is not all that dignified a character. And, besides, the 'inquisitorious and tyrannical duncery' are still with us, and deserve what they get, from Milton or from us. As a controversialist, let us admit it, Milton is a *scurra*. His comic wit is fully exercised, pursued relentlessly. Presumably Milton supposes that his European audience will enjoy his ponderous 'ragging' of poor Salmasius; or his chastisement of the universities (institutions which showed a deplorable preference for the Royalist cause). The universities were 'not yet well recover'd from the Scholastick grossness of barbarous ages'; and the students there were 'mockt and deluded all this while with ragged Notions and Babblements, while they expected worthy and delightful knowledge' (*Works*, IV, 278–9). In his attack upon the Universities he particularly objects to the behaviour of young men, who while aspiring to Holy Orders, yet perform in College plays.

> in the Colleges so many of the young Divines . . . have bin seene so oft upon the Stage writhing and unboning their Clergie limmes to all the antick and dishonest gestures of Trinculo's, Buffoons, and Bawds; prostituting the shame of that ministery which either they had, or were nigh having, to the eyes of Courtiers and Court-Ladies, with their Groomes and *Madamoisellaes*.
> (*Works*, III, 300)

Dr Johnson found this 'sufficiently peevish'. But we can surely be more broadminded. While Milton is writing a vigorously controversial pamphlet, the universities were fair game for him to hunt, especially the frivolities of undergraduates who were preparing themselves for Holy Orders in the Established Church.

Need we really blind ourselves to the poet of the sonnet on his book called *Tetrachordon*?—so much misunderstood, he felt, by the idiots who attacked it:

> I did but prompt the age to quit their cloggs
> By the known rules of antient libertie,
> When strait a barbarous noise environs me
> Of Owles and Cuckoes, Asses, Apes and Doggs.

[9] *The Reason of Church-Government*, Preface to Book II (*Works*, III, 240).

> As when those Hinds that were transform'd to Froggs
>   Raild at *Latona's* twin-born progenie
>   Which after held the Sun and Moon in fee.
>   But this is got by casting Pearl to Hoggs;
> That bawle for freedom in their senseless mood,
>   And still revolt when Truth would set them free.
>   Licence they mean when they cry libertie . . .   (Sonnet XII)

The comic effect of the rhymes, *Cloggs, Doggs, Froggs, Hoggs*, is the work of no insensitive artist. Can we not respond to his tirade 'On the new forcers of Conscience under the Long Parliament'?

> But we do hope to find out all your tricks,
>   Your plots and packings wors then those of *Trent*,
>   That so the Parlament
> May with their wholsom and preventive Shears
> Clip your Phylacteries, though bauk your Ears,
>   And succour our just Fears
> When they shall read this clearly in your charge
> *New Presbyter* is but *Old Priest* writ Large.

It could be claimed, perhaps, that this last line is one of the best strokes of wit in the English language.

The devils invented gunpowder (VI, 470–520). They also invented sarcasm. For Satan secretly brings up his 'devilish Enginrie' (VI, 553) and then gives his instructions 'scoffing in ambiguous words' (568):

> Vangard, to Right and Left the Front unfould;
> That all may see who hate us, how we seek
> Peace and composure, and with op'n brest
> Stand readie to receive them, if they like
> Our overture, and turn not back perverse;
> But that I doubt, however witness Heaven,
> Heav'n witness thou anon, while we discharge
> Freely our part: yee who appointed stand
> Do as you have in charge, and briefly touch
> What we propound, and loud that all may hear.   (VI, 558–67)

After the first success of their artillery, Satan's jesting is followed by Belial 'in like gamesom mood' (620):

> Leader, the terms we sent were terms of weight,
> Of hard contents, and full of force urg'd home,

> Such as we might perceive amus'd them all,
> And stumbl'd many: who receives them right,
> Had need from head to foot well understand;
> Not understood, this gift they have besides,
> They shew us when our foes walk not upright. (VI, 621–7)

Addison thought that this sort of thing was disgraceful in an epic poem.

> Sentiments which raise Laughter, can very seldom be admitted with any Decency into an Heroic Poem, whose business it is to excite Passions of a much nobler Nature.

Addison remembered that there are comic passages in Homer, and he even remembered that there is one laugh in Virgil's *Aeneid*.

> The only Piece of Pleasantry in *Paradise Lost* [he says] is where the Evil Spirits are described as rallying the Angels upon the Success of their new invented Artillery. This Passage I look upon to be the most exceptionable in the whole Poem, as being nothing else but a String of Punns, and those too very indifferent ones. (*Spectator,* No. 279; 19 January 1712)

Personally I relish the Miltonic malice in putting the comedy into the mouths of the devils; their gleeful puns and sarcasms, their mean verbal triumphs.

God and the Messiah do not communicate by any kind of verbal ambiguity. They converse with an ostentatious lack of rhetorical devices. They have very little imagery. As a pair they have no wit, still less have they any humour—though in his dialogue with Adam, God has a certain dry good-humour. The contrast with Satan and the fallen angels is striking. Satan is, after all, a highly entertaining character, and a brilliant conversationalist. When touched by Ithuriel's spear, he is revealed and asked who he is. To this tactless question Satan replies with splendid and unforgettable wit:

> Not to know mee argues your selves unknown, (IV, 830)

—a line which has something of the tone of Congreve.

A great range of writing had preceded *Paradise Lost*, and a good deal of it can be felt behind the poem, and indeed within the poem. *Paradise Lost* is, after all, a very entertaining poem. It is surely the most entertaining of the world's epics. The *Iliad* is full of excitement; the *Odyssey* is full of marvels. Still, *Paradise Lost* has probably a greater variety of amusement. When it comes to a question of amusement, the *Aeneid* is scarcely a competitor in this respect, for all its poetical merits.

Without wishing to expose myself to the accusation of paradox, I think that there is demonstrably in *Paradise Lost*, what there demonstrably always was in Milton, throughout all his writings: a sardonic wit, a sense of the absurd, an amused contemplation of scale and perspective, a growling sense of the comic, which finds expression often in a quiet or surreptitious deflationary technique, very often about the poetry itself, about the kind of poem *Paradise Lost* is expected to be. Perhaps the qualities I have been indicating in *Paradise Lost* are a little more perceptible if it is compared with an epic poem which was quite definitely not a joke against the Epic: a religious heroic poem on the ancient model which we know that Milton read and—at least in his youth—admired: I mean the *Christiados* of Girolamo Vida. In the early ode on *The Passion* Milton refers with admiration to the other poet who had written on that subject:

> Loud o're the rest *Cremona's* Trump doth sound.   (l. 26)

The *Christiados* is odiously imitative of Virgil. It is a very serious literary achievement, exemplifying the principles expounded by Vida in his *Poetica* of 1527, the work which earned Pope's compliment in his *Essay on Criticism*:

> Immortal Vida! on whose honour'd brow
> The Poet's *Bays* and Critic's *Ivy* grow.   (705–6)

Of course, Vida had had his joke at the expense of the epic in his *Scacchia Ludus*, a mock-heroic poem on the game of chess, in which Vida supposed he was following in Homer's footsteps in his *Batrachomyomachia*. But this is quite another thing. In his *Christiados* Vida intends to please his reader by taking over, without a flicker of irony, the words and sentiments which Virgil had used in heroic contexts. Christ becomes the *dux*, *heros*, and so on; the Virgin Mary even becomes a *nympha*.

In comparison with the *Christiados*, *Paradise Lost* scintillates with wit and dazzles us with subtlety and variety. Andrew Marvell found appropriate words for the effect of *Paradist Lost* on the reader:

> At once delight and horrour on us seize,
> Thou singst with so much gravity and ease;
> And above humane flight dost soar aloft,
> With Plume so strong, so equal, and so soft.
>   (On *Paradise Lost*, 35–8)

And the interesting achievement of twentieth-century criticism of Milton is to make us perceptive of just such variations of style and sensibility in the poem. From the older critics of Milton one supposes that they found him grand but somewhat monotonous. What they admired they described eloquently. But they did not admire Milton nearly enough. We may flatter ourselves that we can take a good deal of *Paradise Lost* in a double and richer sense. We have learnt to feel that Satan is a comic figure as well as a tragic figure; that Adam and Eve are domestic characters as well as archetypal figures; that Milton responds to and understands—as surely a poet must—both rebellion and obedience; that the poem is about Providence as well as Damnation; and that it is a poem about love both human and divine; that the poem means *us*. Extreme views have been expressed about Milton. But I can think of no poet whose critics have, in the last generation, so educated and sensitised his readers.

And now by a lucky chance we are perhaps in a peculiarly happy condition for becoming close to *Paradise Lost*. Contemporary critical theory and practice have accustomed us to the notion of the 'anti-novel' and the 'anti-hero'. It is now at last obvious what *Paradise Lost* is. It is the anti-epic. Wherever we turn we find the traditional epic values inverted. It closed the history of this poetic genre in England—the epic form as understood by Petrarch, Ronsard, Vida, or (for that matter) Boileau and Dryden. It closed the history of the epic (for you will not expect me to comment on the unspeakable labours of Blakemore, Glover, and Wilkie).

Never was the death of an art form celebrated with such a magnanimous ceremony, splendid in ashes and pompous in the grave. The death of tragedy was a mere decline into a whine and a whisper. But the death of epic was, in Milton's hands, a glorious and perfectly staged suicide.

Milton's 'Mortal Voice' and his 'Omnific Word'

J. B. Broadbent

We celebrate centenaries to prove that we are here, and that our existence is legitimised by a continuous ancestry. So we celebrate not only what Milton did in 1667 but also what other ancestors, perhaps more closely related to us or more congenial, did then, and did in 1767 and 1867. It is more comfortable to remember our uncles than our great-grandfathers: uncles are jolly and human, like us, but grandfathers lead eventually to Adam and to God. Milton is not avuncular. Theologians describe him as a subordinationist because he was not convinced of the Son's equality with the Father. Milton was one of those people who disconcerts you over the telephone by declaring that he deals only with principals. It is the same with his poetry.

Surrounding *Paradise Lost* are Dryden's exotica—*The Indian Queen* and *The Indian Emperor* of Mexico, *The Maiden Queen* of Sicily—and that genial poem, of which this is also the tercentenary, *Annus Mirabilis*. You can find almost anything you're looking for in *Annus Mirabilis*. For one thing, it is a *Locksley Hall* two hundred years before: in his apostrophe to the Royal Society, Dryden, like Tennyson, prophesies a future which is our present:

> Then we upon our globe's last verge shall go
>   And view the ocean leaning on the sky:
> From thence our rolling neighbours we shall know
>   And on the lunar world securely pry.

The ambition is Milton's, and so is the language—*globe, verge, ocean, lunar* are important words for him; they have a world-constructing energy, the omnific quality that my title refers to. But Milton uses *pry* as well, a mean and mortal word, in exactly Dryden's sense. 'Our rolling neighbours' looks like Dryden's characteristic contribution, a sociable domesticating of the cosmic; but that too is available in what I call Milton's 'mortal voice': after a grandiloquent description of Satan landing on a volcano, he remarks, 'Such resting found the sole/Of unblest feet' (I, 237 f.); in the Limbo of Fools he refers to 'the backside of the World' (III, 494).

But the difference is more important than the likenesses. Although Milton was ambitious as a poet to explore the universe, he put no faith in the exploitation of human science. On the other hand, although he will sometimes write as concretely as Dryden, he did not do so in order to make anything easier. In the same passage, Dryden says to the Royal Society:

> O, truly Royal! who behold the law
>   And rule of beings in your Maker's mind,
> And thence, like limbecs, rich ideas draw
>   To fit the levelled use of human kind.

Milton did not accommodate himself to 'the levelled use of human kind'. And yet, though seeming so aloof, Milton was surely much more concerned with humankind?

> For still they knew, and ought to have still rememberd
> The high Injunction not to taste that Fruit,
> Whoever tempted;   (X, 12–14)

That lament is another example of Milton's 'mortal voice'; but then he changes to the 'omnific word':

> which they not obeying,
> Incurrd, what could they less, the penaltie,
> And manifold in sin, deserv'd to fall.

At the change of tone we reject him; not so much because he takes God's side—we will listen to God when Herbert, for example, makes him speak, in a still small voice; but because Milton seems to be presuming to speak with the very voice of God itself, not accommodated to our weakness, as God accommodated himself, but invincible and heavy with power—*incurrd, penaltie, manifold, deserv'd*. We feel this kind of language to be of the law rather than the spirit, for a good reason: it has not itself put on flesh, but remains pure logos.

That we blame Milton in this way makes him equal to Shakespeare but on the other side of the coin. We praise Shakespeare for being so much what we want ourselves to be—humane, percipient, eloquent, randy, a little bitter in middle age, ripe as a plum at fifty, joking at death. We use Milton the other way round: just as he projected onto Satan and Sin, Comus and Dalila, even the waters that drowned Lycidas, all that he feared and hated in himself, so we project onto him. He is rigid, puritanical, misogynistic, vindictive, he takes no interest in human beings, he is verbose without being witty, self-righteous yet torn by conflict, and his learning is a burden not only to him but to generations of students. Every professor must see himself in him. Like Satan gazing on Sin, 'Thy self in me thy perfect image viewing', we become enamoured with narcissistic hatred of Milton, and rape him.

Milton exposes us to conflicts. Typically, he sets up a temptation and then refuses to fall for it, or regrets that others do: 'thus they relate,/Erring' (*P.L.*, I, 746 f.); 'Thy pompous Delicacies I contemn' (*P.R.*, II, 390). As a department of this puritanism, there is a temptation-resistant habit of language. Just as Christ despises the romantic feast in *Paradise Regained*, piled with fish of

> exquisitest name, for which was drain'd
> *Pontus* and *Lucrine* Bay, and *Afric* Coast

and served by striplings of both sexes, so Milton excites but will not allow us to indulge certain linguistic appetites.

Milton's puritanism is manifest in language because his apperception was abnormally conceptual. His talent was for making words work semantically, rather than as evokers of imaginary sensations. So that even when he writes as simply and concretely as Dryden, it is often the arrangement of the words, or the single abstract word, rather than a genial run of colloquiality, that strikes us. In *Paradise Regained*, Satan muses on the possibility of being an apostle; he sees Christ's face between him and the Father's anger, as

> A shelter and a kind of shading cool
> Interposition, as a summers cloud.   (III, 221–2)

Within the hesitant colloquiality it is *interposition* that does the defining work; and the hiatus after *cool*, rather than the word's associations, that realises coolness.

The phrases in my title, 'mortal voice' and 'omnific word', both come from Book VII of *Paradise Lost*. They roughly define, and illustrate, two extremes of Milton's poetic language. In the invocation at

Book VII he says that, now he has finished the war in heaven and is about to describe the creation of the world, he will be

> Standing on earth, not rapt above the Pole,
> More safe I Sing with mortal voice . . .   (23–24)

When the Son rides out in his chariot to chaos,

> Silence, ye troubl'd waves, and thou Deep, peace,
> Said then th' Omnific Word, your discord end.   (216–17)

The mortal voice of man; the omnific word of God. We shall agree that Milton used them both.

We can see that his mortal voice can be considered in terms of colloquial rhythms and diction, or vernacular idiom, or just a prosaic plainness; I am most interested in the last, especially when it leads to a special kind of definiteness.

The omnific word is more difficult to categorise. We shall agree, though, that Milton had the world-making ambition I've already referred to, and that it was manifest in language. I suggest that the same ambition is manifest on a microcosmic scale when he indulges in empathy with very large or very powerful objects or activities such as flying angels, or the sea creatures in Book VII, 'Wallowing unweildie, enormous in thir Gate' (VII, 411). Those habits hardly need further attention, so I shall point more to what I think is another manifestation of the same drive, not world-making but word-making—word-making of a peculiar kind, certainly unShakespearean. Two obvious examples of it in Book VI are 'incentive reed . . . pernicious' (VI, 519 f.) and 'jaculation dire' (665).

Although it is in Book VII that Milton says he is going to 'sing with mortal voice', to our ears the language in which he describes the creation of the world is not much more mortal, or less omnific, than that with which he describes the war in heaven.

But in Book VII the language is in places 'mortal' in a specific sense: it delineates nature simply as it is, with that fine edge of definition which Milton's eighteenth-century followers practised so well, and which was lost in the empathy and synaesthesia of the Romantics. When Keats simply catalogues 'The vine of glossy sprout' (*Endymion*, ii, 412) he is writing in the line of 'then Pansie freakt with jeat' and Smart's 'quick peculiar quince' (*Song to David*, lix). When Keats writes of

>   the sweet buds which with a modest pride
> Pull droopingly, in slanting curve aside,
> Their scantly leav'd, and finely tapering stems   (*I stood tip-toe*, 3)

he is turning the objective personification of 'Cowslips wan that hang the pensive hed', a typical sixteenth-seventeenth-century phrase, into subjective personification, empathy: the buds are girls and he is them. When Keats describes bedclothes as 'coverlids gold-tinted like the peach' (*End.*, ii, 396), he is transferring to the textile a whole range of vegetable qualities—not just the colour of the peach's skin but also its texture, and its associations of luxury. When Milton describes the bower in the Garden of Eden he transfers in the opposite direction, from manufacture ('art') to nature, as was normal in the Renaissance:

>   underfoot the Violet,
> Crocus, and Hyacinth with rich inlay
> Broidered the ground, more colourd then with stone
> Of costliest Emblem: (IV, 700–3)

Yet the appeal is not to sensation but to intellect—the phenomenon of colour in vegetables and minerals, the theory that nature is the art of God. The flowers are unaltered: they remain distinct, as they are named, violet, crocus, hyacinth.

Two phrases on the sixth day, when the animals rose out of the earth, exemplify Milton's habit of delineation. One of them, describing the insects, is 'smallest Lineaments exact' (VII, 477). The other, a whole line between colons, is 'The Cattel in the Fields and Meddowes green' (VII, 460).

The phrase 'smallest Lineaments exact' offers little in the way of imaginable substance; yet it seems to me an almost complete statement of insectness—as experienced from outside. Milton is hardly ever inward with small things. Who in the seventeenth century is? Flowers, dewdrops, insects, were charged with emblematic significance—the prudent crane, the parsimonious emmet—so that they did not need, or have room for, occupation by a poet. The larger mansions of the Romantic poets—clouds, winds, oceans—were still inhabited by deities.

This phrase presents first the most obvious external characteristic of an insect, smallness; then *lineaments* as it were details that smallness; *exact* completes it abruptly. The effect comes from the word *lineaments* being contained so firmly by *smallest* and *exact*, as the invisible details of an insect are contained in tiny integrity by its visibility as a singular object. *Lineaments* is semantically complex. In 1667 it could mean features, especially the face; but also rudiments or elements; and outline or pattern; and the last two meanings could both be paraphrased as *trace*, meaning a trace of something, a little particle; and the trace of an outline. To recognise these meanings is an intellectual effort, not an experiential one. If we do recognise them we may in some sense 'see' the insect—but in an unusually intellectual sense: we are less likely to see its face in our mind's eye than to be aware of the mind's own action in tracing round the curious diagram of the word *lineaments* as if it were the insect's face. There is no mimesis of the insect, only perhaps of the mind's act in conceiving of it. Milton does not, as we say, create an insect; he stimulates our minds to consider insect nature. Of course this is how more directly mimetic language actually works. Some poets effect the illusion of mimesis, but it is only an illusion: they manipulate language to give the impression that it is behaving like a substance, a sensory stimulus; but language cannot really imitate anything except other kinds of language. Milton accepts that limitation and uses language as language. His words are not substitutes for stuff but signs for ideas.

We might call this an absolutist or *a priori* way of writing, as opposed to an empirical one. That is what we would expect of Milton; it is what his ethic demands. He believed—to use Descartes' words for it—that 'God has endowed each of us with some light of reason by which to distinguish truth from error' (*Discourse on Method*, part 3). He writes also as if, at the mere words, we were able to distinguish insect from whale, field from meadow, and the three meanings of *lineaments*. He relies on some kind of rational faculty, which I suppose is related to the final authority of right reason, to get the reader's co-operation; and he expects it to be conceptual rather than sensory. He could not agree with Hobbes that the origin of every thought

> is that which we call 'sense', for there is no conception in a man's mind that hath not at first, totally or by parts, been begotten upon the organs of sense.
> (*Leviathan*, Ch. I)

Milton writes the other way round. Correspondingly, of course, he could not agree with Hobbes about the relativity of ethical concepts:

> these words of good, evil, and contemptible, are ever used with relation to the person that useth them, there being nothing simply and absolutely so. (Ch. VI)

For Milton, everything is simply and absolutely so. That is another reason for blaming him: we do not like to be restricted. The question is whether, in spite of this absolutism, his language offers any opportunities for freer exercise of the reader's mind?

'The Cattel in the Fields and Meddowes green': there are not many poets who would leave that as a single line, isolated by punctuation. It is offensive to grammarians for it claims to be a sentence yet has no verb. Certainly Milton himself exercises freedom. But there is a sort of verb, though the grammarian might overlook it for it exists if at all only in his own mind, and disguised as an adjective. Because Milton often puts the verb at the end of the line, we half expect *green* to be a verb. It is an adjective; yet to make it work as an adjective our minds have to move back over the line colouring the fields and meadows: the action, the verb, is in our mind. Milton writes in such a way as to prompt the reading mind to act, to think. In this case, the action is not so simple as it looks. There is a conceptual distinction between fields, which may be hilly, dry and stubbled, and meadows which must be flat, watered and green.

Milton often made that kind of distinction between functional parts of nature—most notably in Book VII between the *nutriment* of molluscs and the *food* of carnivorous crustaceans at line 407:

> Or in thir Pearlie shells at ease, attend
> Moist nutriment, or under Rocks thir food
> In jointed Armour watch . . .

This is the functionalism the Augustans were to follow. If you search for metaphors you find a merely amusing lobster in armour; if you search for concepts you find not only nutriment and food but also a distinction between different kinds of shell. Metaphor is synthetic, establishing the previously unapprehended relations between things; Milton's method—the eighteenth-century method—is analytic, remarking distinctions. Milton had a categorising mind; and such freedom as he offers comes from playing categories against each other. We are not accustomed to that. We are trained to regard the associative syncretic method, rather than the analytic categorising one, as the essentially poetic. We know that Shakespeare writes in a highly associative way, mimetic of the continuum of consciousness, so that it is often impossible to analyse his syntax. For example, Antony at IV, xii:

> the hearts
> That spanielled me at heels, to whom I gave

> Their wishes, do discandy, melt their sweets
> On blossoming Caesar; and this pine is barked,
> That overtopped them all.

The peculiarity of this speech is that, as in expressive conversation, Antony jumps from concept to concept—hearts, spaniels, sweets, blossom, pine—by a special, a highly individuated, route. The route is not signposted by that degree of objectivity which we normally expect in a simple concept such as spaniel or blossom. So far as words serve to communicate roughly agreed and therefore limited concepts, hearts cannot spaniel—indeed *spaniel* cannot be a verb, as the First Folio knew when it printed 'pannelled'; nor is it characteristic of hearts or spaniels or their sweets to melt on Caesar, or for him to come out in blossom. Of course we know what it all means; we see that the associations run something like: fawning hearts . . . fawning spaniels . . . spaniels drooling sweet saliva as they're fed under the table with melting sugarplums. Editors have made much of their insight here, though it's obvious. At *blossoming*, however, our associations check, and the editors keep quiet. Is the blossom transferred from the crystallised fruit fed to the dogs? or from some other set of images in the play? or is it reached through dogs urinating on flowers and trees? Then it becomes easy again—short but flowering fruit-tree apposed to tall but barked pine-tree (perhaps via sweets and the tapping of canes for sugar, or pines for gum). Now to read like this gives us a wonderful sense of freedom. We are set a puzzle, we tighten our faculties, then we realise that in order to solve it we should relax and free-associate. Tension sets up only when we run out of associations, as with *blossoming*; and even then we do not feel angry with Shakespeare, for we count it as a sign that his mind is as muddled as ours, though here his tangle takes a different loop. It is very liberating. But from the linguistic point of view, it's noticeable that the words don't matter. The same general impression could have been gained from other stimuli and other routes of association.

With Milton, the words do matter; and the structure is not associative but syntactical. This makes us feel constricted; but some of the freedom and energy which Shakespeare offers in his associative routes, Milton offers in alternative syntactical routes. We are not invited to associate from the cattle and fields and meadows—the words operate as strictly limited concepts, permitting only what is generally agreed to be their qualities; but we are expected to shuffle their places in the sentence, and encouraged to do it by the peculiarity of *green*. In this way perhaps we call up a richer experience than the plain words alone suggest. Here are the options which are left open by the apparently rigid structure of the statement:

A   cattle in green fields and in green meadows
B   cattle in fields and in green meadows

The next alternative takes the caesura as breaking the line into two separate concepts:

C   cattle in fields   green meadows

The fourth uses *green* as both a verb for the cattle to act and an adjective for us to colour the land with:

D   cattle green (= graze? in fields and meadows, which become green as we make them so

This is very primitive linguistic analysis, and the statement is a simple one; but it is characteristic of Milton to direct us as much to the linguistic possibilities of what he is saying as to the experiential referents.

The main point to make about this line is the original one, that it is so blank, almost blatant a statement—an articulation of certain concepts, simple, undecorated. In short, Milton's style is not all 'gigantic loftiness'; sometimes he speaks in a distinctly mortal voice. But when he does, the effect is often highly intellectual even so.

There are of course cases where the effect is not intellectual, but representative of common experience—the clay showing through the diction in pastoral. A good example is a line which might come from anybody's conversation—'The leaf was darkish, and had prickles on it'—but which actually comes from *Comus* (631). This colloquiality is strong in the prose, particularly in contexts of polemical anger:

And it is still *Æpiscopacie* that before all our eyes worsens and sluggs the most learned, and seeming religious of our *Ministers*, who no sooner advanc't to it, but like a seething pot set to coole, sensibly exhale and reake out the greatest part of that zeale, and those Gifts which were formerly in them, settling in a skinny congealment of ease and sloth at the top: and if they keep their Learning by some potent sway of Nature, 'tis a rare chance; but their *devotion* most commonly comes to that queazy temper of luke-warmnesse, that gives a Vomit to GOD himselfe.   (*Of Reformation*, in *Works*, III, 11-12)

The colloquiality here involves associative imagery of the Shakespearean kind: in Milton's prose there is a series of references to congealing skin, and scabs, and eruptions, which recurs in some of the angrier contexts of *Paradise Lost*—the scenery of hell in particular. It is a pity that this kind of language should be restricted to such areas; it suggests that for Milton, immediate sensory experience, and spontaneous assocation, could be discharged only in aggression.

Colloquial diction and rhythms increase towards the end of *Paradise Lost* as we move down into the fallen world. It is appropriate, but even here the context is often aggressive. At XI, 632, Adam, having been shown a scene of debauchery, remarks,

> But still I see the tenor of Mans woe
> Holds on the same, from Woman to begin.
> From Mans effeminate slackness it begins,
> Said th' Angel . . .

Michael retorts again in the last book when Adam asks whether the Christians will not be persecuted: 'Be sure they will, said th' Angel' (XII, 485). Milton himself uses the tone to describe parts of the vision of the future—'Smote him into the Midriff with a stone' (XI, 445, about Cain and Abel), 'Botches and blaines' (XII, 180, about the plagues of Egypt). In *Paradise Regained*, Satan makes a speech comparing a thunderstorm to a sneeze, and threatening Christ:

> So talkd he, while the Son of God went on
> And staid not, but in brief him answerd thus.
> Mee worse then wet thou find'st not.   (*P.R.*, IV, 484–6)

When Satan first returned after the storm to look for Christ,

> Him walking on a Sunny hill he found,
> Backt on the North and West by a thick wood.   (IV, 447–8)

This is Wordsworthian in its insistence on the prosaic. Here, and at places in *Samson* and the last books of *Paradise Lost*, it seems to me that we are dealing with the first modern poet, or at any rate the first nineteenth-century one (Arnold, who of all nineteenth-century poets wrote in a style close to our own half-contemptuous diagnostic flatness, thought highly of *Paradise Regained*).

But Milton's rhythms and idiom are not prevailingly colloquial. More important is the effect that his merely flat and simple words gain from an elevated and complicated context. There is a simile for Satan coming to tempt Eve like a town cad bringing corruption into the country:

> As one who long in populous City pent,
> Where Houses thick and Sewers annoy the Aire,
> Forth issuing on a Summers Morn to breathe
> Among the pleasant Villages and Farmes
> Adjoind, from each thing met conceaves delight,
> The smell of Grain, or tedded Grass, or Kine,
> Or Dairie, each rural sight, each rural sound . . . (IX, 445–51)

It's a familiar passage, and we know that the function of the simple rural diction is to domesticate the Fall, to present it as in some sort an actual event composed of our own experiences. The point I want to stress is Milton's ability to use, in these simple contexts, words which when you isolate them look unassimilable to poetry. Since Baudelaire at least we can understand a poet incorporating sewers because they have a strong negative symbolic force; but *dairy* is more difficult. Milk is symbolic, milkmaids are picturesque; but a dairy is just a dairy. I suggest that Milton is able to incorporate it in his epic, without making it either portentous or ridiculous, because his prevailing tone is not simple and idiomatic. The form implies a control which keeps *dairy* exactly in its place. In fact its place here is kept by the mild formality of the list before it—gain, tedded grass, kine—and of the generalisation and abstraction after it, 'each rural sight, each rural sound'. This of course suggests, as the insect phrase did, a particular way of handling physical experience: it suggests an intellectual control of, in this passage, the physical pleasures of smell and sight and hearing, an ordering and defining of experience by the mind. We may very well object to that kind of behaviour; but we should not transfer our ethical objection onto the language without declaring our prejudice.

The most general effect of Milton's mortal voice is one of definition; and sometimes the definition is less limiting than it looks. To go back to *dairy* again. It is just possible that Milton was using it in its rarer sense, not the place where they make butter and cream, but the milch-cows which produce it. If so, we should have the series grain or grass, oxen or milch-cows. This would not lessen the weight that falls on *dairy* at the end of the series and the beginning of a new line; and it would follow a typical Miltonic pattern of words in which the objects are linked not by aesthetic or by associative qualities but by functional or behavioural ones—grain for human food, hay for animal food; oxen for work, cows for milk. It is slightly more likely, however, that Milton was referring to a dairy-house; if so, the very bareness of his statement forces us to deposit the little building in the landscape; it is defined by its own simplicity; yet it also sets up a shift in the series—cereals and animals as the natural materials of agriculture; now a human building designed to exploit both for food.

Another case of definition: when Adam describes in Book VIII how he first saw Eve in his sleep, while God was still fashioning her, he uses a phrase which is not remarkable for colloquiality or even simplicity but has this defining force: 'Under his forming hands a Creature grew,/Manlike, but different sex' (VIII, 470 f.). In this sense, *manlike* was a fairly recent and uncommon word. It throws all the weight onto man as a creature among other creatures, a species; but also offers a male human, upright on two legs, looking masculine. Then the phrase 'but different sex'. This does three things. Firstly, its compact simplicity represents the way a child makes distinctions—a child who, seeing a lynx, might say 'Like a cat but different ears'; this is appropriate to the newly-created Adam, but also to the primitive shock we get from the opposite sex. Secondly, the word *different* was stronger then than it is now: it meant significantly different, distinct, defined by that difference, rather than just 'a bit different'; the difference signalled a distinction, as in heraldry. Thirdly, *sex* defines the difference. It seems obvious, but there are not many literary definitions of men and women; and it is a familiar curiosity that when we see men and women in the street we tell them apart by various externals such as hair and clothes and size; we don't usually think much about the fundamental differences, except how to exploit them. Indeed, the important differences, inherent and biological, tend to be forgotten or hidden under the superficial ones of dress, colour, attractiveness, social role and so on. What Milton has done here is to throw us back on the rudimentary, the defining difference. It is not clear how much he means by the word *sex*—certainly gender, probably genitals as well. But exactly what we may see in the mind's eye does not matter much: he has made what seems to be a bald statement, but the statement includes a question, What is the difference between men and women? and an answer, Sex; and the answer takes us back to the question again. His simplicity prompts us to think, even if only in a circle.

The invocation at Book III of *Paradise Lost* includes both the pastoral plainness of the dairy passage, and the defining force of the others:

> Thus with the Year
> Seasons return, but not to mee returns

Day, or the sweet approach of Ev'n or Morn,
Or sight of vernal bloom, or Summers Rose,
Or flocks, or herds, or human face divine . . .   (III, 40–44)

The rhetoric is striking. It enforces a cycle of time—the repeated *return* reminds us that time is measured by the earth's movements. Then it breaks the cycle down, from year to seasons, from day to morning and evening; and then lists objects peculiar to those times and seasons. At the shift from seasons to days, the negative comes in, his blindness: 'but not to me returns/Day'. He can sense the seasons but cannot see the days, or what lives in them. (This is highly characteristic of Milton, that an important point is made by implication of syntax.) The careful ordering goes on, the objects of sight, which he cannot see, are dealt with in an intellectual order—in fact the order of creation: bright light, gentle light; coloured light of vegetables; animals; men, and so back to the original brightness with *divine*. 'Vernal bloom, or Summers rose' looks verbose; but it carries on from the seasons, distinguishing spring flowers from summer roses. The slow unqualified list, 'Or flocks, or herds', drives our minds to consider language—the function of generic nouns—as a means to considering what these nouns represent, sheep and cattle, anonymous gregarious creatures opposed to the individuality of man. Once again, Milton is using words as words, rather than as things. Finally, the phrase 'or human face divine' takes us right up the scale of nature, through men to God, yet holds our experience of both man and God down to the face which Milton cannot see.

Milton's omnific word is a secondary interest for me on this occasion, so I shall be rather dogmatic. I believe it is at its best when acting most freely and in terms of physical existence or action—when Milton is exercising heroic games, playing in fact with his power. Quite often he expresses aggression in this way—the descriptions of the fall of the rebel angels, the anti-creation when Sin and Death build their causeway—'Death with his Mace petrific . . . by wondrous Art/Pontifical' (X, 294–312)—the phrases such as 'from one entire globose/Stretcht into Longitude' (V, 753 f.). The context is often, like the prose, polemical, as in the flyting between Satan and Abdiel—'Precipitate thee with augmented paine' (VI, 280). But even here there are two difficulties. The first is that we feel the aggression is being discharged in a false context. It is natural for us to attack our inner foes, but it seems presumptuous to do it so often in a divine epic; it seems to be projecting one's conflicts too confidently onto a cosmic scale. It is not the conflicts we object to—how could we?—or the power, for these lines have an eccentric energy which the eighteenth century admired when they so often called Milton 'amazing'. It is rather that the power seems to be raising quite ordinary human motives to a pitch where they have no place. When Lear uses omnific—or, in this case, omni-destructive—language, and cries, 'And thou, all-shaking thunder, Strike flat the thick rotundity o' the world!' (III, ii), he calls on God and nature to co-operate with him; but he remains a man, helpless, and mad. As an undergraduate, Milton said that he wanted to use language in such a way that

> the deep transported mind may soare
> Above the wheeling poles, and at Heav'ns dore
> Look in, and see each blissful Deitie
> How he before the thunderous throne doth lie, . . .
> Then passing through the Spheres of watchful fire,
> And mistie Regions of wide air next under,
> And hills of Snow and lofts of piled Thunder,
> May tell at length how green-ey'd *Neptune* raves,
> In Heav'ns defiance mustering all his waves . . .
>
> (*At a Vacation Exercise*, 33–43)

He fulfilled this ambition exactly. But it is a hubristic ambition; and in fulfilling it he had not only to describe the cosmos objectively, but dramatise the voice of God itself. He went further: there are places where he writes as though he were God, the coeternal Logos, author of all concepts, who by uttering a word could call into being the reality it named. It is here that we reach the second difficulty with his omnific language. If the first is that in concrete situations the motive for it may be inadequate to its power, the second is that the language itself may, especially in more abstract contexts, appear as another and less satisfactory kind of world-making, a conjuring of concepts *ex nihilo*.

Like all renaissance poets, Milton experimented with recent adaptations from Latin. Many of them he tried only once—*conflagrant*, for example (*P.L.*, XII, 548), *interlunar* (*S.A.*, 89). Some of these experimental words were unlucky in the evolution of language, though Milton's own preference was reasonable: for his purposes *disordinate* (*S.A.*, 701) was better than *inordinate* because of its suggestion of disorder; *illaudable* contained a useful pun and was more economical than *unpraiseworthy*. Many of Shakespeare's choices from recent Latin adaptations were discarded too—*continuate* (*Timon*, I, i), *intrinsicate* (*Antony*, V, ii), *undividable* (*Errors*, II, ii). Indeed, Shakespeare invented more words for himself, and many of them were learned-looking Latinate formations of the kind we associate with Milton: *dispropertied* (*Coriolanus*, III, i), *immoment* (*Antony*, V, ii), *imperceiverant* (*Cymbeline*, IV, i), *incarnadine* (*Macbeth* II, ii). On the other hand, Shakespeare's unique or peculiar words do strike us as having been made up in the heat of the moment to articulate a single and intensely local idea; they belong to their immediate occasion. The reason for this is that they are being used to express. When Cleopatra says, 'Say, good Caesar, That I some lady trifles have reserved, immoment toys, things of such dignity as we greet modern friends withal', the function of the phrase 'immoment toys' is not to define what she has kept back—'lady trifles' has done that already—but, mainly, to emphasise the attitude she is taking to Caesar: it provides the boy or actress with a pouting, deprecating appeal to femininity. Milton very occasionally uses language in this expressive way: when Eve, having eaten the apple, comes to tempt Adam, she wheedles, claiming to have fallen for his sake:

> For bliss, as thou hast part, to mee is bliss,
> Tedious, unshar'd with thee, and odious soon.   (IX, 879–80)

Tedious and *odious* carry no particular conceptual meaning; they are there for a tonal function, to characterise Eve with the vocabulary of the heroine of a Restoration comedy of manners.

To put it epigrammatically, we might say that whereas Shakespeare's peculiar words tend to come to him, and live in his mouth, Milton's come from something, and live in his head. Sometimes they have no life except in his head. In *Paradise Lost,* X, the angels sing a hymn to God:

> Just are thy ways,
> Righteous are thy Decrees on all thy Works;
> Who can extenuat thee . . .   (643–5)

Extenuate is puzzling: why should God need extenuation? Milton of course is using it in the Latin sense of make thin, diminish, slight. This was a possible usage in the seventeenth century but it was not common even then. The special sense of diminished guilt or mitigated punishment was the usual one, both in Shakespeare (*Troilus*, II ii; *Antony*, V, ii) and in Milton himself: Dalila says, 'not that I endeavour/To less'n or extenuate my offence' (*Samson*, 767 f.), and there *lessen* provides a clue as well. What is happening in the angels' hymn then? That Milton should have chosen an unpopular word doesn't matter—we don't expect angels to speak with the tongues of men. But the word is not drawn from any religious context that I know of: it is a word of Milton's, rather than of God's. This is where we begin to feel angry, at the arrogance. And we go on feeling angry because the context gives us no help. The word does not express anything; its meaning lies in itself alone; to understand it we must know the word; but our knowledge of it cannot be experiential; so we cannot respond, we are frustrated.

Are we justified in our anger? Or would we be justified in our delight, if it pleased us to construe the word? This is after all the major characteristic of Milton's special diction. All sixteenth- and seventeenth-century writers used Latinate words, like adolescents exercising an expanding vocabulary. Milton, more than most, used Latinate words in both the original Latin and the modified English senses at once; and sometimes in the Latin sense alone. This is why I said 'construe': you are forced to recollect the Latin and so to introduce into your response a conscious act of construing. Here are some cases in which only the Latin meaning makes sense: the *fervid* chariot-wheels, meaning red-hot (VII, 224); *frequent* as an adjective, crowded (I, 797); *in procinct*, a translation of *in procinctu* so literal that it has to be further translated in the mind as 'stood to arms' (VI, 19); *inhabit lax* which might mean 'take your ease' but more likely the Roman military command, *habitare laxe*, spread out in open order (VII, 162); *succinct* meaning girt up, *succinctus* (III, 643). Most of these extraordinary games are played in military contexts; it is one of Milton's ways of being heroic in the most obvious and conventional way; and no doubt he is quite often being ironic, as if to say (as he does explicitly from Book VII onwards and in *Paradise Regained*), This is what your Roman virtue looks like when the scale is magnified—vain-glorious and clumsy. One of the most penetrating comments on *Paradise Lost* as a satire is Eliot's in *Gerontion*:

> Unnatural vices
> Are fathered by our heroism. Virtues
> Are forced upon us by our impudent crimes.

Some of the rejections of human power are themselves 'mortal', such as 'that cumbersome Luggage of war' (*P.R.*, III, 400). They are more convincing than the 'omnific' parodies. That is to say, the vainglory is also Milton's own; and it may also be ours.

It is usual to discuss our response to language in aesthetic terms: we refer to sensibility, sensitivity, precision, feeling, sincerity and so on. By sleight of hand, we often transfer our response to the poem, or even the poet himself. If *Lycidas* does not evoke much feeling in us, Milton is unfeeling, quite possibly frigid-hearted. Milton, especially when his more omnific language is in question, loses most of these games; or, if he wins, we suspect the winner of being on his side anyway. It might help if we more openly regarded reading as a game, in the sense of interpersonal transactions or group dynamics. (To do so might, apart from Milton, begin to rescue critical theory from the primitive state it regressed into, in this country, during the war.) In *The Games People Play*, Dr Berne suggests that we play games as parents, as adults, or as children; so do the other players. Using those terms, we can abandon the aesthetic or linguistic objections to Milton's omnific style, and that is just as well, for there are so many ways of defending it that the argument just heaves to and fro. Instead, the objection becomes that, to write omnifically, with such world- or word-creating authority, is to assume a parental role. Milton's learned vocabulary, with its demand for conscious construing, and his distant perspectives, represents the authoritative unintelligibility of the parents' speech as heard by a child. (The visual metaphors applied to Milton are often parental—gigantic loftiness, stilts, spectacles.) But it is not enough to object that he assumes a parental role; the question is, with what role do we respond? For it is the conjunction of his role with ours that constitutes the game. We may meet him in the same role, by pitting our learning against his, by cherishing the ancient infant prodigy with our own footnotes, the assertion of our own paternalism. Alternatively we may throw a tantrum and try to dislodge him by hammering on his knees, or by insults and mockery, or (a particularly common reaction) by rejoicing to find that he has dozed off—there is an inconsistency in the time sequence of *Paradise Lost*, or a word has been used in the wrong sense. One of the subtlest of the infantile reactions is to claim for his work an interest or a significance more acute than is reasonable. The occasion demands that we should put ourselves in danger of doing that now. We want the world to know what a wonderful man he is. The third reaction, the adult one, would by definition be the critically proper one. It is difficult to define because you would have to be very sure of your own identity as an adult for Milton's strongly parental writing to elicit it. Presumably one would be unflustered by the scale and noise and knowledge of his language; one would recognise the game Milton is playing, the authoritarian personality's need to protect his own childish fears by grandiloquence, by pretending to be the father whom he could not meet on equal terms; but one would not judge; one might just walk away. One would react rather in the way that the last two books of *Paradise Lost* in general react to the tragedy of human existence, with a slightly mournful down-to-earthness, a wary energy and determination to go on living. You can hear that adult quality in Adam and Eve's response to their fate: 'the bitterness of death/Is past, and we shall live' (X, 157 f.); 'And thus with words not sad she him receav'd' (XII, 609); and in the way Christ meets Satan's stormy violence in *Paradise Regained*: he is 'unappalld' (IV, 425).

That language is itself not parental but adult; mortal rather than omnific. Of course in making these distinctions and equations I am pursuing anxieties of my own; the question is whether they gain any agreement? I should like to conclude with some lines which are gentler than usual in Milton, and almost characterless. In Book XI, the Flood is complete,

>   and in thir Palaces
> Where luxurie late reignd, Sea-monsters whelpd
> And stabl'd; of Mankind, so numerous late,
> All left, in one small bottom swum imbarkt.
> How didst thou grieve then, *Adam*, to behold
> The end of all thy Ofspring, end so sad,
> Depopulation . . .   (750–6)

The first lines evoked from Gustave Doré one of that Victorian illustrator's most Gothic fantasies, of monsters in the primeval slime—an interesting case of infantile response. Presumably the line 'All left, in one small bottom swum imbarkt', might move us to postulate a concealed allusion to Moses in the bulrushes; I think then we might be playing the parental game ourselves, invoking an authority more august than the situation requires. What interests me is the last line, 'The end of all thy Ofspring, end so sad,/Depopulation'. At first sight *depopulation*, for all the metrical weight falling on it, seems a disconcertingly abstract noun for the event; it is as though Milton were playing word-games with the death of the human race. It certainly is what I would call an omnific word: it makes a concept out of nothing but syllables, and on the largest possible scale. Yet as I look at it I feel it belongs more with those exact defining habits of his mortal voice. It is as if Milton were saying, 'Here are some of the experiential facts—

the flood, the monsters, the ark; and here is the simple statement of emotion—'end so sad'; now finally here is the word which comprehends them all—*depopulation*. Look on this word, abstract as it is, and consider what it means.' This is to control and categorise experience, to comprehend it intellectually. It is not, in this case, to run away from it; but rather to use the concept as a telescope through which to see what the event that it names might mean. A more romantic poet would have used a phrase more directly evocative—'the unpeopling of a world'. Reading that, we might say, like Eliot, 'We had the experience but missed the meaning' (*Dry Salvages*, ii). Milton leaves us mostly with the meaning;

> And approach to the meaning restores the experience
> In a different form, beyond any meaning
> We can assign to happiness.

'That Soft Seducer, Love': Dryden's *The State of Innocence and Fall of Man*

Bernard Harris

Artistic and dramatic survival—no less than human survival—may be a matter of successful adaptation to changed circumstance and need. Imaginative criticism, when dealing with texts of seventeenth- and eighteenth-century adaptations of the work of Shakespeare and his contemporaries, acknowledges the fact. But severe problems are raised by a dramatic adaptation of a work never intended for theatrical presentation: and grievous difficulties of appreciation are posed by an adaptation which seems never to have been staged, nor to have demanded such performance. Of this unusual sort is Dryden's 'version' of *Paradise Lost*, licensed in 1674 as an 'Heroick Opera' to be called *The Fall of Angels and Man in Innocence*—a title preserved in the manuscript texts—but printed in 1677 as *The State of Innocence, and Fall of Man: An Opera*.[1]

It is difficult to judge confidently Dryden's artistic intentions at the time of composition or his motivation at the date of publication, mainly because critical reception of the work was bedevilled by local literary partisanship operating at the level of simple prejudice. Indeed, notorious early references offer us only vague gossip and ready ridicule.

Thus Aubrey tells us that Dryden knew and admired Milton, and that Milton gave Dryden leave 'to tagge his verses'.[2] Marvell, another of Milton's 'familiar learned acquaintance', in commendatory verses before the second edition of *Paradise Lost* in 1674—the year of Milton's death—turned from the genial mockery of his blind friend's triumph to

---

[1] It was reprinted in 1678, 1684 (thrice), 1690, 1692, 1695 (twice) and 1703.
[2] *Brief Lives and Other Selected Writings by John Aubrey*, ed. A. Powell (1949), p. 72.

the yet more welcome task of demolishing, in advance, the prospective tribute of his more immediate rival:

> Yet as I read, soon growing less severe,
> I lik'd his Project, the success did fear;
> Through that wide field how he his way should find
> O're which lame Faith leads Understanding blind;
> Lest he perplex'd the things he would explain,
> And what was easie he should render vain.
> Or if a Work so infinite he spann'd,
> Jealous I was that some less skilful hand
> (Such as disquiet always what is well,
> And by ill imitating would excell)
> Might hence presume the whole Creations day
> To change in scenes, and show it in a Play.

And later in his eulogy Marvell revived the old argument of whether or not Milton should have rhymed:

> Well mightst thou scorn thy Readers to allure
> With tinkling Rhime, of thy own sense secure;
> While the Town-Bayes writes all the while and spells,
> And like a Pack-horse tires without his Bells:
> Their Fancies like our Bushy-points appear,
> The Poets tag them, we for fashion wear.[3]

Such powerful hostility was long effective. Johnson, for instance, was content to deny that *The State of Innocence* could be considered an opera ('it is rather a tragedy in heroick rhyme, but of which the personages are such as cannot be decently exhibited on the stage'), to invoke Marvell's direct dismissal of the work's feasibility, and to add his own verdict, 'It is another of his hasty productions; for the heat of his imagination raised it in a month'. Johnson then turned to more congenial matter for comment, such as the 'strain of flattery which disgraces genius' in the language of Dryden's dedication of the opera to the Duchess of York, the summary rejection of the prefatory argument for heroic verse, and the allegation of falsehood in Dryden's claim that the circulation of 'many hundred copies . . . every one gathering new faults' in manuscript necessitated an authorised edition ('he lived in an

[3] *The Poems and Letters of Andrew Marvell*, ed. H. M. Margoliouth (2nd edition, 1952), p. 260.

age very unlike ours, if many hundred copies of fourteen hundred lines were likely to be transcribed').[4]

Johnson's feigned ignorance of customary publishing lies is perhaps less notable than the fact that scholarly inspection of the five surviving manuscript copies of *The State of Innocence* has confirmed that the first printed edition had the authority Dryden claimed for it.[5]

Elsewhere modern scholarship has found little time to deal with the more essential critical problems occasioned by the work; thus Hugh Macdonald notes:

> There is no doubt of Dryden's appreciation of *Paradise Lost*, whatever we may think of *The State of Innocence*, and we may suspect that the drubbing Marvell gave him in his verses before the second edition (1674) was not entirely prompted by literary considerations.[6]

Since Marvell, at the time of his comment, is unlikely to have seen the text of *The State of Innocence* it is doubtful if any of his remarks could have been prompted by literary considerations; and until very recently such considerations have been lacking.

Yet what was the nature of Dryden's appreciation of *Paradise Lost*? And what may we think, all non-literary passion spent, of *The State of Innocence*?

Saintsbury, and he was not alone, felt that the answer to the first question was quite simple:

> it is sufficient to say that, with his unfailing recognition of good work, Dryden undoubtedly appreciated Milton to the full long before Addison, as it is vulgarly held, taught the British public to admire him. As for *The State of Innocence* itself, the conception of such an opera has sometimes been derided as preposterous—a derision which seems to overlook the fact that Milton was himself, in some degree, indebted to an Italian dramatic original.[7]

More recently, and more positively, Alan Roper, in a study of admirable range and proper ambition, has claimed that

> Dryden himself was the first writer of importance to appreciate the practical use of the large poetic resources of *Paradise Lost*: within seven years of its publication he had turned it into an opera (which was never staged), and seven

---

[4] *Johnson's Lives of the Poets,* ed. M. Arnold (1881), 'Life of Dryden', pp. 142–3.

[5] Marion H. Hamilton, 'The Manuscripts of Dryden's *The State of Innocence* and the relation of the Harvard MS to the First Quarto', in *Studies in Bibliography,* ed. Fredson Bowers (Charlottesville, Va., 1953), pp. 237–46.

[6] Hugh Macdonald, 'The Attacks on Dryden', in *Essential Articles for the Study of John Dryden,* ed. H. T. Swedenberg, Jr. (Hamden, Conn., 1966), p. 32.

[7] G. Saintsbury, *Dryden* (1881), p. 56.

years later in *Absalom and Achitophel* and *The Medal* (a year after the first edition of *Patriarcha*) he made the first important entries in the long schedule of allusions to *Paradise Lost*.[8]

Such an account recognises the originality of Dryden's conception, but relegates the opera to the status of an experiment, since 'the matter of Eden makes significant appearance only in the mature poetry from 1680 onwards'. So that even in the light of the positive testimony of Saintsbury and Roper *The State of Innocence* occupies an ambiguous position. One sees it as performing what Milton refrained from doing, namely, the ordering of his material in a specifically dramatic mode; the other views the work's significance as primarily of concern for our understanding of the development of Dryden's art. Just so Havens argued that *The State of Innocence* was an experimental drama, written for Dryden's private instruction, and to test his theory that 'an heroic play ought to be an imitation, in little, of an heroic poem'.[9]

Such an opinion certainly appears to rest upon Dryden's own authority; but the neatness of the remark disguises, perhaps, the difficulty of the conception and the scale of the achievement, so that it seems worth recalling here the caution uttered by Dobrée about our general attitude to Dryden's work as an adapter:

> it does not follow that because he altered *Troilus,* and *The Tempest,* and *Antony and Cleopatra,* that he produced inferior Shakespeare plays; he made something different because he wanted another thing.[10]

Indeed, it is fundamentally uncritical to separate what Dryden was attempting in his various adaptations from what he was engaged in with his other dramas. Yet accounts of that activity sometimes seem as ungenerous in their concept of the nature of the heroic drama as that long ago proposed by Collins:

> Carefully selecting such material as would be most appropriate for rhetorical treatment and most remote from ordinary life, he drew sometimes on the Heroic French Romance, as in *The Maiden Queen,* which is derived from *The Grand Cyrus,* and in *The Conquest of Granada,* which is based on the *Almahide* of Madame Scuderi; sometimes on the exotic fictions of Spanish, Portuguese, or Eastern legend, as in *The Indian Emperor* and *Aurengzabe*; or on the misty annals of early Christian martyrology, as in *The Royal Martyr*; or on the dreamland of poets, as in *The State of Innocence*. All is false and unreal.[11]

[8] A. Roper, *Dryden's Poetic Kingdoms* (1965), p. 111.
[9] P. S. Havens, in *Essays in Dramatic Literature: The Parrott Presentation Volume* (Princeton, 1935).
[10] B. Dobrée, *Restoration Comedy* (1924), p. 105.
[11] J. C. Collins, *The Satires of Dryden* (1936), p. xviii.

Such a reductive and dismissive view of what Dryden was endeavouring to encompass in his exploitation of the heroic potentialities of other literatures seems unacceptably limited in view of Dryden's own concept of the nature of heroic drama:

> The first rule which Bossu prescribes to the writer of an Heroic Poem, and which holds too by the same reason in all Dramatic Poetry, is to make the moral of the work; that is, to lay down to yourself what that precept of morality shall be which you would insinuate into the people; as, namely, Homer's (which I have copied in my *Conquest of Granada*) was, that union preserves a commonwealth and discord destroys it; Sophocles, in his *Oedipus*, that no man is to be accounted happy before his death. 'Tis the moral that directs the whole action of the play to one center; and that action or fable is the example built upon the moral, which confirms the truth of it to our experience: when the fable is designed, then, and not before, the persons are to be introduced, with their manners, characters, and passions.[12]

We are to ask, then, what moral has *The State of Innocence*, and what justification had Dryden in selecting the action of *Paradise Lost* to confirm the truth of that moral to our experience? And we might begin by inspecting the commendatory poem which Lee (Dryden's collaborator in *Oedipus*) provided for the printed text, 'To Mr Dryden, on his Poem of Paradise'. This procedure allows us to admit a favourable contemporary witness to Dryden's purpose. Moreover, Lee's argument might be said to have developed in response to the demands of the poem and the context of its full occasion, and hence may suggest to us what those demands and interests might be; Lee's case, in fact, should be inspected at length; even, its own length:

> Forgive me, awful Poet, if a Muse,
> Whom artless Nature did for Plainness chuse,
> In loose Attire presents her humble Thought,
> Of this best Poem, that you ever wrought.
> This fairest Labour of your teeming Brain
> I wou'd embrace, but not with Flatt'ry stain:
> Something I wou'd to your vast Virtue raise,
> But scorn to daub it with a fulsome Praise;
> That wou'd but blot the Work I wou'd commend,
> And shew a Court-Admirer, not a Friend.
> To the dead Bard your Fame a little owes,
> For Milton did the wealthy Mine disclose,
> And rudely cast what you cou'd well despose:

---

[12] Preface to *Troilus and Cressida* (1679).

He roughly drew, on an old-fashion'd Ground,
A Chaos, for no perfect World was found,
Till through the Heap your mighty Genius shin'd;
He was the Golden Ore which you refin'd.
He first beheld the beautious rustic Maid,
And to a Place of Strength the Prize convey'd;
You took her thence; To Court this Virgin brought,
Drest her with Gemmes, new weav'd her hard-spun Thought,
And softest Language, sweetest Manners taught:
Till from a Comet she a Star did rise,
Not to affright, but please our wond'ring Eyes.
Betwixt ye both is fram'd a nobler Piece,
Then e'er was drawn in Italy or Greece.
Thou from his Source of Thoughts ev'n Souls dost bring,
As smiling Gods from sullen Saturn spring.
When Night's dull Mask the Face of Heav'n does wear
'Tis doubtful Light, but here and there a Star,
Which serves the dreadful Shadows to display,
That vanish at the rising of the Day:
But then bright Robes the Meadows all adorn,
And the World looks as it were newly born.
So when your Sense his mystick Reason clear'd,
The melancholy Scene all gay appear'd;
New Light leapt up, and a new Glory smil'd,
And all throughout was mighty, all was mild.
Before this Palace which thy Wit did build,
Which various Fancy did so gawdy gild,
And Judgment has with solid Riches fill'd,
My humbler Muse begs she may Centry stand,
Amongst the rest that guard this Eden Land.
But there's no need, for ev'n thy Foes conspire
Thy Praise, and hating thee, thy Works admire.
On then, O mightiest of th'inspired Men,
Monarch of Verse; new Themes employ thy Pen.
The Troubles of Majestick Charles set down:
Not David vanquish'd more to reach a Crown:
Praise him, as Cowley did that Hebrew King,
Thy Theme's as great, do thou as greatly sing.
Then thou mayst boldly to his Favour rise,
Look down, and the base Serpent's Hiss despise,

> From thund'ring Envy safe in Lawrel sit,
> While clam'rous Criticks their vile Heads submit,
> Condemn'd for Treason at the Bar of Wit.[13]

Dryden had sufficient shame to feign embarrassment of the sort we probably exhibit more instinctively at such hyperbole. His account of the relationship which he would prefer us to perceive between his work and Milton's is notably temperate:

> I cannot, without Injury to the deceas'd Author of *Paradise Lost*, but acknowledge that this Poem has receiv'd its intire Foundation, part of the Design, and many of the Ornaments from him. What I have borrow'd, will be so easily discern'd from my mean Productions, that I shall not need to point the Reader to the Places: And truly, I should be sorry, for my own sake, that any one should take the pains to compare them together, the Original being undoubtedly one of the greatest, most noble, and most sublime Poems, which either this Age or Nation has produc'd. And tho' I could not refuse the Partiality of my Friend, who is pleas'd to commend me in his Verses, I hope they will rather be esteem'd the Effect of his Love to me, than of his deliberate and sober Judgment: His Genius is able to make beautiful what he pleases: Yet, as he has been too favourable to me, I doubt not but he will hear of his kindness from many of our Contemporaries: For we are fallen into an Age of Illiterate, Censorious, and Detracting People; who, thus qualify'd, set up for Criticks.[14]

In the spirit of this sane disclaimer of poetic rivalry Lee's verses are no more than an antidote against prejudice, which Dryden is well capable of rebuking himself ('they wholly mistake the nature of Criticism who think its Business is principally to find Fault'). Yet Lee does offer us some local and topical directions for our understanding. His series of similitudes are concerned with transformation and refinement, for which subordinate images employ terms of purifying the dross, refining the ore, and presenting the product to the sophisticated gaze and literary taste of the court. Dryden is seen as throwing light upon dark places, of identifying an essential, central feminine figure, and of introducing this ideal concept to mundane social life; indeed, Dryden is alleged to have penetrated arguments conveyed in obscure metaphors and translated them into sensible, tangible, concrete, and above all reasonable language; he has turned a melancholy message into a hopeful one; by his acknowledged wit he has effected a more balanced mode of argument, and made possible a new evaluation of the

---

[13] *The Comedies, Tragedies, and Operas, Written by John Dryden, Esq.*, 1701; Vol. I, pp. 586–7.

[14] *op. cit.* p. 590.

immediate significance for man of his fall. Dryden has made reasonable what Milton offered to our faith. Lee offers himself as a guardian both of the activity and of the achievement.

Lee's understanding of *Paradise Lost* is plainly incorrigibly defective, yet his interest in Dryden's *The State of Innocence* may be perceptive of its aims in a way that the court recognised them and that later criticism has naturally found difficult to credit. At the level of literal significance which Lee was most fitted to convey he saw that Dryden was engaged in the high conceit of shaping a marriage offering. In 1673 James, Duke of York, had taken as his second wife Mary Beatrice, Princess of Modena. There was consequently fresh assurance for those of his party for the prospect of a future dynasty, and the matter of the fall and redemption could be displayed, in the thinking then capable of being indulged, in terms of political as well as moral panegyric. Towards the conclusion of his epistle dedicatory 'To Her Royal Highness the Dutchess' Dryden rises to his theme of secular and sacred prophecy:

> if I could find in my self the Power to leave this Argument of Your Incomparable Beauty, I might turn to one which would equally oppress me with its Greatness. For Your Conjugal Virtues have deserv'd to be set as an Example to a less degenerate, less tainted Age. They approach so near to Singularity in ours, that I can scarcely make a Panegyrick to Your Royal Highess, without a Satyr on many others: But your Person is a Paradice, and your Soul a Cherubin within to Guard it.[15]

The grossness of such flattery, and the extravagance of its idealisation of a human being, would be merely offensive if it were idly declared; but the conceit is insidiously and beguilingly purposeful. Indeed, it has the accents of that other persuasion to an individual consciousness to know her perfectibility:

> So gloz'd the Tempter, and his Proem tun'd   (*P.L.*, IX, 549)

And when we take up the argument of Dryden's text it is to find that though he has adopted the 'intire Foundation' of his moral from Milton he has so altered its essential action that the design is subverted. The state of innocence which is Dryden's concern is not alone that literal state enjoyed by man before the invasion of created death; it is also the desired and achievable state of experience which is the contrary state of the soul.

So stated Dryden's attitude towards his subject must be suspected of

[15] *op. cit.* p. 588–9.

'THAT SOFT SEDUCER, LOVE'

perverse pleading, and the major critical problem of *The State of Innocence* remains the fullness or otherwise of our response to the language of temptation, and our willingness to hear its arguments presented merely through the stage dialogue of human discourse, unsupported and unadorned by descriptive and meditative poetry of the controlling narrative voice. Here the choice of operatic form works unexpectedly in favour of the drama's compression. For though the machinery of operatic devices necessarily provides the spectacle, Dryden does not permit the spectacle to obtrude upon the interplay of characters. More importantly, the operatic form enables the full range of celestial and earthly events to be suggested to the mind, and leaves the task of revelation to be partly understood in the language of the educated theatre eye:

> the whole Creations day
> To change in scenes,

gives opportunity for visual wit as well as grandeur, and enables Dryden to assert the contemporaneity of some of his visions.

Thus, even in reading, we become aware of a visual dialectic. The opening stage direction is the fullest, and most mockingly heroic:

> Represents a Chaos, or a confused Mass of Matter; the stage is almost wholly dark: A symphony of warlike Music is heard for some time; then from the Heavens (which are opened) fall the rebellious Angels, wheeling in Air, and seeming transfixed with Thunderbolts: The bottom of the Stage being opened, receives the Angels, who fall out of sight. Tunes of Victory are played, and an Hymn sung; Angels discovered, brandishing their Swords: The Music ceasing, and the Heavens being closed, the Scene shifts, and on a sudden represents Hell; Part of the Scene is a Lake of Brimstone, or rolling Fire; the Earth of a burnt Colour: The fallen Angels appear on the Lake, lying prostrate; a Tune of Horror and Lamentation is heard.

The last vision is simply an ordered use of the stage heavens to proffer to the departing Adam and Eve a regainable Paradise:

> Here a Heaven descends, full of Angels and blessed Spirits, with soft Music, a Song and Chorus. (V, sc. i)

Paradise itself is a landscape of familiar intimacy:

> Trees cut out on each side, with several Fruits upon them: a Fountain in the midst: At the far end the prospect terminates in Walks. (II, sc. ii)

But though some predictable scenes are evoked with a nonchalant use of the stage possibilities, as in

> A Night-piece of a pleasant Bower: Adam and Eve asleep in it. (III, sc. i)

the simplicity of the symbolism maintains a strict propriety followed by a contrasted levity equally appropriate in the central episode of Eve's temptation. We are given first

> The middle part of the Garden is represented, where four Rivers meet: On the right side of the Scene is placed the Tree of Life; on the left, the Tree of Knowledge. (IV, sc. i)

Lucifer enters in his human disguise, takes in the scene of beauty which he is about to destroy, and retires at Eve's arrival. Then

> A Serpent enters on the Stage, and makes directly to the Tree of Knowledge, on which winding himself, he plucks an Apple; then descends, and carries it away.

The ludicrous indignity of this enactment is impudently designed by Dryden so that Lucifer's reappearance in human shape will seem to Eve's astonished eyes a proof of the fruit's transforming powers.

The delight in the balancing feats made available by stage machinery is a proper exploitation of the literal possibilities of the action, and reveal the extent to which Dryden's dramatic intentions could happily co-operate with the illusionist world of lifts, traps and flying machines. Thus Adam, newly created, found lying among moss and flowers in 'A Champaign Country', is visited by Raphael and told of his higher home, after which

> They ascend to soft music, and a song is sung (II, sc. i)

Inevitably Lucifer, in the moment of his triumph, is startled by God's thunderclaps, and makes a conventional villain's exit:

> I'll dive below his wrath, into the deep,
> And waste that empire, which I cannot keep
> (Sinks down) (V, sc. i)

In spectacular sequence we are invited to contemplate 'a Sun gloriously rising and moving orbicularly', to be eclipsed by a black cloud bearing Lucifer, but soon to be followed in the sky progress by the horse-drawn chariot of Uriel, Regent of the Sun and restorer of his light (II, sc. i).

It becomes clear that so far from adopting operatic form as a means of indulging the vulgarities of theatrical display, Dryden is using the form to control Milton's larger world by the principle of 'imitation, in little'. The most convincing demonstration of this is the penultimate vision, granted by Raphael in response to Eve's question

> But what is death?

Raphael: In vision thou shalt see his grisly face,
   The king of terrors, raging in thy race.
   That, while in future fate thou shar'st thy part,
   A kind remorse, for sin, may seize thy heart.

   The scene shifts, and discovers deaths of several sorts. A Battle at Land, and a Naval Fight.

Adam: O wretched offspring! O unhappy state
   Of all mankind, by me betrayed to fate!
   Born, through my crime, to be offenders first;
   And, for those sins they could not shun, accurst.

Eve: Why is life forced on man, who, might he choose,
   Would not accept what he with pain must lose?
   Unknowing, he receives it; and when, known,
   He thinks it his, and values it, 'tis gone.

Raphael: Behold of every age; ripe manhood see,
   Decrepit years, and helpless infancy:
   Those who, by lingering sickness, lose their breath;
   And those who, by despair, suborn their death:
   See yon mad fools, who for some trivial right,
   For love, or for mistaken honour, fight:
   See those, more mad, who throw their lives away
   In needless wars; the stakes which monarchs lay,
   When for each other's provinces they play.
   Then, as if earth too narrow were for fate,
   On open seas their quarrels they debate:
   In hollow wood they floating armies bear;
   And force imprisoned winds to bring them near.

Eve: Who would the miseries of man foreknow?
   Not knowing, we but share our part of woe:
   Now, we the fate of future ages bear,
   And, ere their birth, behold our dead appear.

Adam: The deaths, thou show'st, are forced and full of strife,
   Cast headlong from the precipice of life.
   Is their no smooth descent? no painless way
   Of kindly mixing with our native clay?

Raphael: There is; but rarely shall that path be trod,
   Which, without horror, leads to death's abode.

> Some few, by temperance taught, approaching slow,
> To distant fate by easy journeys go;
> Gently they lay them down, as evening sheep
> On their own woolly fleeces softly sleep.
>
> *Adam:* So noiseless would I live, such death to find;
> Like timely fruit, not shaken by the wind,
> But ripely dropping from the sapless bough,
> And, dying, nothing to myself would owe.
>
> *Eve:* Thus, daily changing, with a duller taste
> Of lessening joys, I, by degrees, would waste:
> Still quitting ground, by unperceived decay,
> And steal myself from life, and melt away.
>
> *Raphael:* Death you have seen: Now see your race revive,
> How happy in the deathless pleasures live;
> Far more than I can show, or you can see,
> Shall crown the blest with immortality.

Adam and Eve are then granted their glimpse of paradise before Dryden takes up the muted cadences of the close of *Paradise Lost*. Comparison of the passage quoted with the long revelations of Michael to Adam in Book XI only confirms that this is the deliberately diminished achievement to which Dryden skilfully moves. The great vision of the future history of man has been sacrificed for a pageant of contemporary war so present to the mind of the time that it is instantly and simply oppressive to the spirit. But the sense of the immediacy of the events is not handled with the explicit application of that later invocation of man's political fate, in the Prologue to *The Unhappy Favourite* (1682):

> Our Land's an *Eden* and the Main's our Fence,
> While we preserve our State of Innocence:
> That lost, then Beasts their Bruital Force employ,
> And first their Lord and then themselves destroy.
> What Civil Broils have cost we knew too well;
> Oh! let it be enough that once we fell.

And still less is the application of the moral discovery in *The State of Innocence* managed in the convention of that tawdry topicality that afflicts *King Arthur*; where we find as the penultimate vision, this:

> After the Dialogue, a Warlike Consort: The Scene opens above, and discovers the Order of the Garter.   (V, sc. i)

By contrast the stage mechanics of *The State of Innocence* function with a sensitive efficiency that reflects the extent to which Dryden has organised his design upon principles of mechanistic thinking.

Bredvold long ago pointed out 'the most surprising expression of determinism' to be found in *The State of Innocence*, which he called 'a philosophical perversion of the epic'.[16] He noted, too, that the newly-created Adam discovers his conscious state in Cartesian terminology, and that the arguments employed by Gabriel and Raphael to expound the doctrine of the freedom of the 'will read like a brief summary of the famous Bramhall-Hobbes controversy, with Adam, despite his innocence, taking the part of Hobbes'. But Bredvold cautioned against a possible assumption that Dryden was a disciple of Hobbes or Descartes, arguing that Dryden

> must have been interested in necessitarianism, speculated on its implications, and enjoyed testing out its argumentative strength in verse. Sympathetic intellectual curiosity is one of Dryden's marked characteristics. But this very suppleness of his mind served also to liberate him from the dogmatism and egotism of Hobbes.

This favourable view of Dryden's 'suppleness' may suggest that we should look upon *The State of Innocence* with something of the detached pleasure that Dryden wishes us to take in the construction of his *Essay of Dramatic Poesy*:

> You see it is a dialogue sustained by persons of several opinions, all of them left doubtful, to be determined by the readers in general.[17]

Bruce King, however, in the most detailed critical study of the intellectual bakcground of *The State of Innocence*, has argued for a conclusion. After summarising the basic dispute between Hobbes and Bramhall over the range of philosophical attitudes to be derived from rival theories of causation, King observes:

> Dryden was attracted to this controversy which summarized so many of the intellectual and moral problems of his time, and which had a direct bearing on social and political movements. If Hobbes were right, then it was necessary to conclude that man was fated to exist within all the sad variety of hell, seeking ever further ends to feed his insatiable appetites. However, if Hobbes were wrong, and Bramhall right, then what could man do to escape sin? As we examine *The State of Innocence* we shall see that Dryden accepted Bramhall's

---

[16] L. I. Bredvold, 'Dryden, Hobbes, and The Royal Society', in *Essential Articles for the Study of John Dryden*, p. 328.
[17] *op. cit.*, p. 332.

answers to Hobbes, and that his conclusion gives a new and brilliant meaning to Milton's wonderful phrase 'Paradise within'.[18]

He makes a convincing study of the degree to which Dryden assimilated the details of the debate into the play's structure of argument, though the identification of Dryden's views as Bramhall's depends, as one might have to accept of Dryden's manoeuvres, upon the recognition that 'the weight and tone of the argument consistently go against Adam'.

We may assent, too, to the demonstration of 'a new and personal meaning' which Dryden has provided for his final scene:

> The war of nature is his version of man's degeneration into the Hobbist universe of appetites, conquests, and fear. Paradise within has come to represent those virtues of temperance and self-regulation that Dryden felt were necessary if man was to avoid life's unrest.

The close of *The State of Innocence*, from the entrance of Raphael to his concluding words of admonition and advice, seems to offer a double resolution to what has been a continual debate. The doom displayed first by Raphael is a presentation of the inevitability of that violent death which Hobbes calls the only adequate promoter of self-consciousness, which Adam and Eve no sooner acquire than they find its pressure overwhelmingly destructive; their submission is to nature's right as Hobbes declared it:

> The Right of Nature, whereby God reigneth over men; and punishes those that break his Lawes, is to be derived not from his creating them, as if he required obedience, as of Gratitude for his benefits; but from his Irresistible Power.[19]

They are restored by a heavenly display of 'goodness infinite', without reference to the second Adam or the second Eve, but to a secular confidence to be derived from their mutual profit in repentance.

What is perhaps most notably asserted by Dryden in this double conclusion is the balanced relationship of Adam and Eve; they speak with equal force and spirit as they have done all through the drama. In part, and especially in those scenes managed with the comic debating skills of Restoration comedy, such as Eve's persuasion of Adam to permit her 'my little trial to endure' (IV, sc. i), or the marital quarrel after the fall (V, sc. i), this is a necessary adaptation of an epic relationship to the terms of an intelligibly human one.

[18] *Dryden's Major Plays* (1966), p. 99.
[19] *Leviathan*, ch. 31, 'Of the Kingdom of God by Nature'.

But we can scarcely avoid recognising that the dignity of Adam and Eve at the end of the drama has been established by Dryden's additional emphasis upon the transforming power of love. The first literal transformation scene is found in the spectacle of Eve's dream before the fall:

> A Vision, where a tree rises laden with fruits; four Spirits rise with it, and draw a canopy out of the tree; other Spirits dance about the tree in deformed shapes; after the dance an Angel enters, with a Woman, habited like Eve. (III, sc. i)

When an angel feeds the deformed spirits with the fruit they too become angels and fly away. The dream-figure of Eve mourns the fact that she has deferred her content, and an angel sings to her:

> Now wiser experience has taught you to prove,
> What a folly it is,
> Out of fear to shun bliss.
> To the joy that's forbidden we eagerly move;
> It enhances the price, and increases the love.

Two other angels then descend and carry the woman aloft with them. She has not tasted, presumably because the second transformation scene of the stage-serpent into Lucifer would lose some of its effectiveness if Eve had already consented in dream. But though the vision is merely an indulgent fancy of simple wish-fulfilment, which the court would grasp more readily than Adam does Eve's infinitely more powerful presentiment in *Paradise Lost*, V, Dryden has reserved his poetic strength for the moment when Eve comes to her waking trial and stands before the forbidden tree:

> *Eve:* Thus far, at least, with leave; nor can it be
>   A sin to look on this celestial tree:
>   I would not more; to touch a crime may prove:
>   Touching is a remoter taste in love.
>   Death may be there, or poison in the smell,
>   (If death in anything so fair can dwell:)
>   But Heaven forbids: I could be satisfied,
>   Were every tree but this, but this denied. (IV, sc. i)

The enchantment occurs in these lines. Eve's words reveal an insight into the true nature of what she contemplates. It is here too that Dryden's wit reaches furthest. For Eve's knowledge of the meaning of the tree rebukes Hobbes's knowledge of the priority of touch in the order of the senses:

> The cause of sense is the external body, or object, which presseth the organ proper to each sense, either immediately, as in the taste and touch, or mediately, as in seeing, hearing and smelling.[20]

This is the order of experience which Adam proposes to Eve at their first meeting:

> *Adam:* What more I shall desire, I know not yet.
>   First let us locked in close embraces be,
>   Thence I, perhaps, may teach myself and thee.
>
> *Eve:* Somewhat forbids me, which I cannot name;
>   For, ignorant of guilt, I fear not shame:
>   But some restraining thought, I know not why,
>   Tells me, you long should beg, I long deny.   (II, sc. ii)

This is near to the profane wit with which Rochester sang of the state of innocence in 'The Fall':

> How blest was the Created State
> Of Man and Woman, e're they fell,
> Compar'd to our unhappy Fate,
> We need not fear another Hell!
>
> Naked, beneath cool Shades, they lay,
> Enjoyment waited on Desire:
> Each Member did their Wills obey,
> Nor could a Wish set Pleasure higher.
>
> But we, poor Slaves to Hope and Fear,
> Are never of our Joys secure:
> They lessen still as they draw near,
> And none but dull Delights endure.
>
> Then, Chloris, while I Duty pay,
> The Nobler Tribute of my Heart,
> Be not You so severe to say,
> You love me for a frailer Part.[21]

---

[20] *Leviathan*, ch. I, 'Of Sense'.
[21] *Poems by John Wilmot, Earl of Rochester*, ed. V. de Sola Pinto (1953), pp. 23–24.

Rochester's defeated cynicism, that 'Nobler Tribute of my Heart', is Dryden's heroic ideal. For when Eve finally consents to pluck and eat her thoughts go instantly to Adam:

> To my dear lord the lovely fruit I'll bear;
> He, to partake my bliss, my crime shall share. (IV, sc. i)

Lucifer regrets that she flew too hastily to thank him, but concedes that what has been set literally in motion no longer needs his aid·

> My work is done, or much the greater part;
> She's now the tempter to ensnare his heart.
> He, whose firm faith no reason could remove,
> Will melt before that soft seducer, love.

Dryden has deliberately transposed Earth's wound and Nature's sigh to provide Lucifer's final speech after Adam too has fallen. This means that Eve's swift flight to Adam preserves her as a romantic heroine. She is not Milton's greedy Eve 'ingorg'd without restraint', or 'height'nd as with Wine, jocond and boon', but one who can say

> I walk in air, and scorn this earthly seat;
> Heaven is my palace; this my base retreat. (V, sc. i)

Again Eve is spared the full sententious rigour of Milton's treatment of her by Adam, and the persuasion to eat is treated with a readier acceptance; the seduction is not effected by wiles but by a frank exchange of pointed and exploratory sentiments:

Adam: Must I without you, then, in wild woods dwell?
Think, and but think, of what I loved so well?
Condemned to live with subjects ever mute;
A savage prince, unpleased, though absolute?

Eve: Please then yourself with me, and freely taste,
Lest I, without you, should to godhead haste:
Lest, differing in degree, you claim too late
Unequal love, when 'tis denied by fate.

Adam: Cheat not yourself with dreams of deity;
Too well, but yet too late, your crime I see:
Nor think the fruit your knowledge does improve;
But you have beauty still, and I have love.

>   Not cozened, I with choice my life resign:
>   Imprudence was your fault, but love was mine.
>   (Takes the fruit and eats it)
>
> *Eve:* O wondrous power of matchless love exprest!
>   Why was this trial thine, of loving best?
>   I envy thee that lot; and could it be,
>   Would venture something more than death for thee.
>   Not that I fear the death the event can prove;
>   W'are both immortal, while we so can love.   (V, sc. i)

The heroically human is a difficult posture to sustain. Dryden knew as well as anyone how it might be toppled. Indeed, he provided his own parody of this romantic stoicism in a reference back from *King Arthur*:

> *Arthur:* By thy leave, Reason, here I throw thee off,
>   Thou load of Life: If thou wert made for Souls,
>   Then Souls shou'd have been made without their Bodies.
>   If, falling for the first Created Fair,
>   Was *Adam's* Fault, great Grandsire I forgive thee,
>   *Eden* was lost, as all thy Sons wou'd lose it.
>   (*Going towards* Emmeline, *and pulling off his Gantlet*)
>
>   *Enter* Philidel *running*.
>
> *Philidel:* Hold, poor deluded Mortal, hold thy Hand;
>   Which if thou giv'st, is plighted to a Fiend.
>   For proof, behold the Vertue of this Wand;
>   Th'Infernal Paint shall vanish from her Face,
>   And Hell shall stand Reveal'd.   (IV, sc. i)

The State of Innocence is the work of a sceptical intelligence, not wholly exonerable from a general charge made by Hobbes, that

> it is many times with a fraudulent design that men stick their corrupt doctrine with the cloves of other men's wit.

Yet Dryden pleads so humanly at the bar of wit and in the court of love, that even the hostile reader might find it necessary to extend to him Hobbes's own pardon, for

> if it be well considered, the praise of ancient authors proceeds not from the reverence of the dead, but from the competition and mutual envy of the living.[22]

---

[22] *Leviathan*, 'A Review and Conclusion'.

'Not Without Song':
Milton and the Composers

Brian Morris

MRS DELANY TO MRS DEWES
Clarges Street, March 10 1743-4
... and how do you think I have lately been employed? Why, I have made a drama for an oratorio, out of Milton's Paradise Lost, to give Mr Handel to compose to; it has cost me a great deal of thought and contrivance; ... I begin with Satan's threatenings to seduce the woman, her being seduced follows, and it ends with the man's yielding to the temptation; I would not have a word or a thought of Milton's altered; and I hope to prevail with Handel to set it without having any of the lines put into verse, for that will take from its dignity. This, and painting three pictures, have been my chief morning employment since I came to town.[1]

She did not prevail. Handel was nearly sixty, a respected London resident for more than thirty years, and his oratorios were becoming almost annual events. By 1744 he had completed some of the greatest of them: *Saul, Samson, Semele,* and *Joseph* had all been written in the previous five years; they were all performed at Covent Garden in the 1744 season, and when Mrs Delany wrote to her sister *Messiah* was nearly three years old. Why did the great master of the English Oratorio refuse to engage with the great master of the English Epic?

On lesser issues Handel and Milton had already met successfully. In 1740 Handel had set Charles Jennens' libretto 'altered and adapted from Milton's *L'Allegro* and *Il Penseroso*', and three years later he took Newburgh Hamilton's richer and subtler text, adapted from *Samson*

---

[1] Quoted in O. E. Deutsch, *Handel. A Documentary Biography* (1955), pp. 587-8. I quote Addison from *The Spectator*, ed. G. Gregory Smith (1898); Newton and his co-editors from *Paradise Lost, with Notes of Various Authors* (1749); and Richard Jago from *Poems, Moral and Descriptive. By the late Richard Jago* (1784).

Agonistes, as the basis for *Samson*.² *Samson* illustrates the genius Handel had displayed in setting the English language, and, especially, the deep inwardness he had with Milton's mind. There is a moment in the treatment of Samson's suffering in Act I where Handel's refusal to allow the music to enact the conventional gestures of grief makes a fine dramatic point through austerity and restraint. Samson's words:

> My genial Spirits droop, my Hopes are flat;
> Nature in me seems weary of herself;³

are set, in this recitative, to a monotone B flat, which *rises* a minor third on the word 'weary'; the continuo emphasises the solitariness, offering only a distant support as it wanders out to the remote key of A flat minor:

---

² Both works are discussed at length, though without attention to the music, in R. M. Myers, *Handel, Dryden, and Milton* (1956).

³ Milton had written:
> So much I feel my genial spirits droop,
> My hopes all flat, nature within me seems
> In all her functions weary of herself:

Hamilton's version represents a tightening of Milton's rhythms, while Handel's setting recreates the original flaccidity and exhaustion.

There are many such moments. Handel's exploration of the nature of suffering in *Samson* is unsurpassed, and it represents an experience of Milton which goes far deeper than the felicitous matching of word and phrase. Yet even if Handel's imagination had been attracted to *Paradise Lost* it seems unlikely that he would have found Mrs Delany's selection a congenial one. She proposes only some five hundred lines from Book IX, the account of the Fall itself, where the principal theme is Temptation, a subject which Handel seldom touches, and never, in the oratorios, dramatises at length. Indeed, in *Samson* he conspicuously avoids it.

To open a wider perspective, it is difficult to imagine that in the 1740s there could possibly have been any fertile union between the forms of oratorio and heroic poem. They appealed to sharply contrasted facets of the Georgian sensibility. English oratorio, as Winton Dean points out, was not 'a consciously evolved art-form', it was 'a supreme fluke'.[4] It has its origins in the patronage of English peers—the Burlington and Chandos circles, where Handel met Arbuthnot, and Pope, and Gay—circles which were serious, civilised, but only sparingly interested in the possible profundities of the religious life, and generally shy towards enthusiastic flights of piety. It took its form by sheer compulsion. Handel's dogged devotion to Italian opera, in the teeth of financial disaster, was only diverted when the Bishop of London's edict compelled performance without benefit of costume or action. Its subjects were largely enforced by the middle-class demand for a theatre art which could improve rather than debase the sensitive conscience. Miss Talbot writes about her first experience of oratorio (27 December 1743):

> I really cannot help thinking this kind of entertainment must necessarily have some effect in correcting or moderating at least the levity of the age; and let an audience be ever so thoughtless, they can scarcely come away, I should think, without being the better for an evening so spent.[5]

But hers was not the only voice. By 1740 the Puritan anti-theatrical movement was in full cry. William Law's *Absolute Unlawfulness of Stage Entertainment Fully Demonstrated* (1726) had been followed by Dr Gibson's ban on the public performance of *Esther* in 1732, and the stringent Licensing Act of 1737. The effect of this opposition, and of the whole debate as to whether the theatres were fit places for sacred

---

[4] *Handel's Dramatic Oratorios and Masques* (1959), p. 35.
[5] ibid., pp. 136-7.

representations like oratorios, was to drive Handel towards a new conception of music drama. When spectacle and action and all the devices of theatre were denied him he was forced to express the drama of his subjects through the music itself, and through the music alone. It is this compression and redirection of the dramatic impulse which brings about such triumphs of organised intense feeling as the aria 'A Serpent, in my bosom warm'd' in *Saul*, or the judgement scene in *Solomon*, or 'Deeper and deeper still' in *Jephtha*. This rich, new apprehension of the dramatic extends to the characters—transformed out of the stylised gesticulators of the operas into credible exemplars of the passions. All human life is here: hero, sufferer, pagan, Jew, Christian, the weak and the powerful, loving and hating; and this great pageant viewed with an inclusive sympathy that clearly took as much delight in conceiving an Iago as an Imogen.

Paradise Lost, in its after-life of Augustan reputation, goes the clean contrary way. The qualities which the Augustans saw and celebrated in Milton's poem were not the dramatic ones, not the unpredictable and expressive human movements, but the massive strategy, the architectonics, the monumental yet comforting solidities. And the general line of their criticism is less exploratory than evaluative; they strive to make the 'placing' judgement. Addison's critique is crucial, not only for its judicial completeness, but because it set out criteria for appraisal which lesser critics were content to accept for more than half a century after 1712. Addison is in no doubt about the 'placing' of *Paradise Lost*:

> It will be sufficient to its Perfection, if it has in it all the Beauties of the highest Kind of Poetry; and as for those who alledge it is not an Heroic Poem, they advance no more to the Diminution of it, than if they should say *Adam* is not *Aeneas*, nor *Eve Helen*.
>
> I shall therefore examine it by the Rules of Epic Poetry, and see whether it falls short of the *Iliad* or *Aeneid*, in the Beauties which are essential to that Kind of Writing (No. 267, 5 January 1712).

The examination is formal, the verdict favourable, the judgement generous. Such lapses as he censures are still 'infinitely preferable to the works of an inferior kind of author, which are scrupulously exact and conformable to all the rules of correct writing'. Later critics concur. 'Simplicity and grandeur' were the qualities Bentley sought to rescue from the ruins; the elder Richardson, speaking of 'the peculiar language of poetry', says 'Milton has Apply'd it to that sublimity of Subject in which he perpetually Engages his Readers', a judgement echoed by Newton, who describes *Paradise Lost* as 'the flower of epic poetry, and the noblest effort of genius'. Although the editors and commentators dispute endlessly the details of Milton's text, and argue the nice placing of the stops, they all know where the poem belongs: it is 'sublime', it is full of 'grandeur', above all it is 'epic', and so it must stand with Homer, and Virgil, and Tasso, and Spenser. And it has neither part nor interest with the acutely human situations and the vivid dramatic life of Handelian oratorio. Yet the Miltonic music is seductive. All the Augustan commentators investigate Milton's 'numbers', verse patterns, and sweet cadence.[6] Francis Peck, in his *New Memoirs of the Life and Poetical Works of Mr John Milton* (1740), is convinced of the influence of Milton's own musicianship on his process of composition: 'it may be premised, that he fetches more flights & beautiful images from that science than any other *English* poet whatsoever'. Peck sees the description of a fugue in *L'Allegro* (135 ff.), and the reference to an organ at *Paradise Lost*, I, 708 ff. convinces him of Milton's ability to take that instrument 'to pieces, & clean it, & put it together again, without any other person to help him'. And several of the minor poems had, of course, already been set: *Comus* three times, by Lawes, Purcell, and Arne; *L'Allegro* and *Il Penseroso* by Handel; the *Song on May Morning* by Michael Festing (1740); and *The Arcades* and even *Lycidas* followed soon after. And yet the great epic remained inviolate, unattempted; its status, its size, and its sublimity deterred even the most robust of Augustan composers.

Yet this is not wholly true. Some sixteen years before, in or about 1728, part of *Paradise Lost* had been set by the almost unknown composer John Ernest Galliard. Galliard's solution to the problem had been to ignore the grand design of the epic and to concentrate on one of its local beauties, the Morning Hymn of Adam and Eve in Book V. In a way it was an obvious choice; the passage is self-contained, it is typical of the strain of paradisal praise that runs through the central books of the poem, and it is announced as a Hymn by Milton himself. Yet we may pause to note that this first attempt to set *Paradise Lost* to music declines a number of other obvious possibilities: the Hymn to Light at the beginning of Book III, or the Angelic chorus later in the same book, the Garden of Eden in Book IV, the Triumph Song at the end of Book VII, Eve's Lamentation in Book XI, or any of the celestial or angelic conversations. And it is not the Satanic voice, so seductive to later critics, that attracts Galliard. His choice is a hymn, and a hymn of

[6] They are discussed in Ants Oras, *Milton's Editors and Commentators from Patrick Hume to Henry John Todd* (1931).

praise, and a human hymn, and a hymn sung in innocence and bliss, and, above all, in perfect domesticity. It is the recognition of the domestic strain in the epic ('our Wives read Milton' said Pope, at about the same time) that was one of the means by which the Augustan sensibility came to terms with *Paradise Lost*.

Galliard sets fifty-six lines from Book V (153–208) and omits or alters nothing that Milton wrote. He seems to have been properly attentive to the implicit instructions which Milton provides for the inner ear in the lines immediately preceding:

> . . . Lowly they bowd adoring, and began
> Thir Orisons, each Morning duly paid
> In various stile, for neither various stile
> Nor holy rapture wanted they to praise
> Thir Maker, in fit strains pronounc't or sung
> Unmeditated, such prompt eloquence
> Flowd from thir lips, in Prose or numerous Verse,
> More tuneable then needed Lute or Harp
> To add more sweetness . . .

There are only two singers and a continuo, but the 'various styles' are displayed in recitative, arias of varying lengths and kinds, and duets of differing complexity. 'Praise', of course, is the key word for the whole setting, and the hint about 'fit strains' is taken up by the intensely expressive quality of the music, which takes every opportunity to enact words like 'climb'st', 'fall'st', 'resound' and 'wave'. But what lies behind the whole Hymn, as Galliard sets it, is the sense conveyed by Milton's 'Unmeditated', and 'prompt eloquence'. The fluidity and continuity of the music, its ease, its lack of powerful contrasts, communicate an impression of uninhibited innocence, a fresh and delighted response to stimuli, which do not have to be strenuously accommodated into an existing pattern of experience. This 'promptness' of response is asserted immediately. There is no ritornello, no preparation; Adam sees, and he praises:

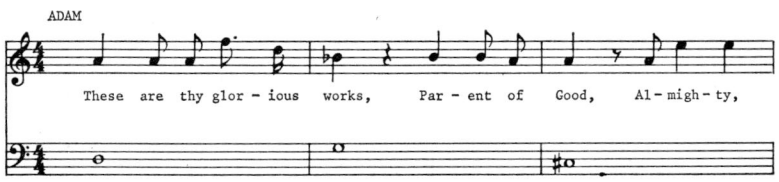

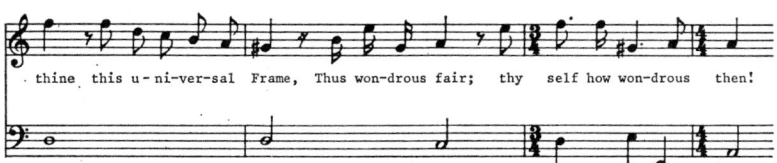

Promptly, Eve takes up the recitative and with one word, 'unspeakable', announces Milton's (and Galliard's) artistic problem— that no eloquence is sufficient, no strains fit, to praise their Maker. They must invoke angelic voices, and Nature's tongues to speak for them:

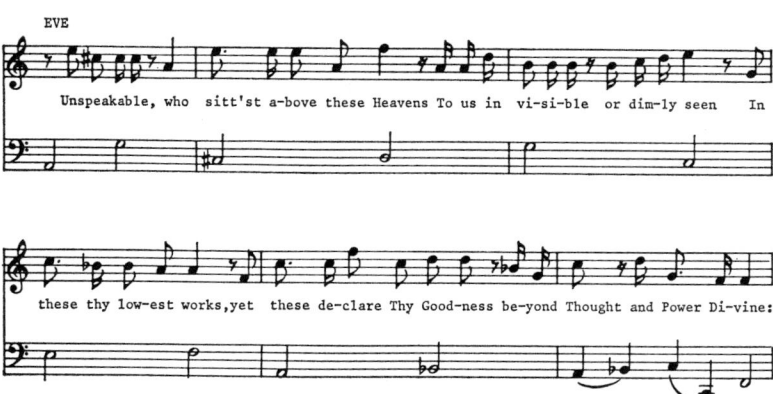

Adam takes this up, in 3/2 time and with longer rhythms, in the words 'and with songs And choral symphonies, Day without Night, Circle his Throne rejoycing'. His entry is matched a bar later by the continuo, which offers, briefly, a canon at the octave, then subsides into dialogue, until Adam creates a long, wandering division on the word 'rejoycing' which the continuo makes no attempt to match:

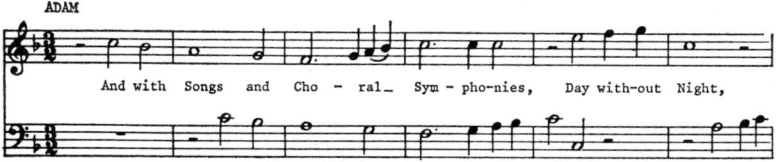

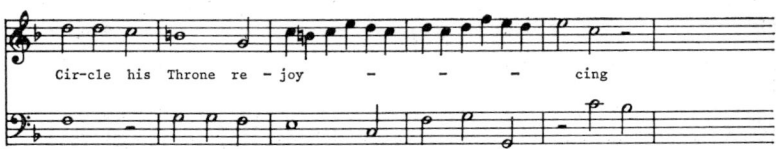

And then, responsive to the words 'join all ye Creatures to extoll', Eve enters and the duet flows limpidly along, establishing the musical delights of dialogue and word-play, and expanding to a pleasantly obvious effect in the setting of the words 'and without end':

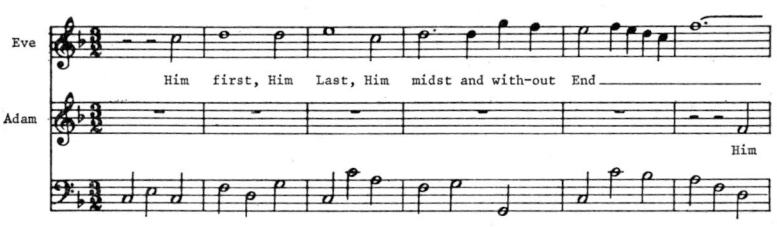

The tones proper to prelapsarian praise have been set, and the dominant quality is ease; the extended phraseology in recitative, harmonic progressions which are reassuringly predictable, civilised, responsive dialogue in duet, all these enforce the directive to 'prompt eloquence', they appear to be 'Unmeditated', they 'flow'. But domesticity is dangerous, and the perils of easy routine performance and boredom are close. Milton, working to an epic scale, can allow a tone to develop slowly, and to hold a level for fifty or a hundred lines, but song makes a swifter impact and Galliard's problem is to vary and diversify what in Milton's verse is very much a sustained performance. Part of his answer lies in a closer attention to verbal detail, and a more overtly mimetic technique. Adam's aria 'sound his praise In thy eternal course' establishes for the first time in the Hymn an extended phrase in dotted rhythm for the setting of the word 'sound', and the effect of this is to give a new note of confident formality to the utterance. This confidence asserts itself as the aria openly mimics its words—'climb'st', 'fall'st', 'and when high Noon hast gaind'. Art is imitating Nature.:

The whole Hymn is built around a sensitive apprehension of Milton's syntax. His structure is based on a repeated pattern of invocation and imperative: 'yee in Heav'n . . . join all', 'Fairest of Starrs . . . praise him in thy Spheare', 'Thou Sun . . . sound his praise', 'Aire, and ye Elements . . . let your ceaseless change Varie', and this dictates the musical form. Invocations are made in recitative, imperatives are enforced in aria. In responding musically to this structure Galliard is acknowledging precisely the insight which Addison had into the passage in one of the *Spectator* essays:

> The Morning Hymn is written in Imitation of one of those Psalms, where, in the Overflowings of Gratitude and Praise, the Psalmist calls not only upon the Angels, but upon the most conspicuous Parts of the inanimate Creation, to join with him in extolling their Common Maker. Invocations of this Nature fill the Mind with glorious Ideas of God's Works, and awaken that divine Enthusiasm, which is so natural to Devotion (No. 327, 15 March 1712).

Newton, in his edition of 1749, is even more specific in his annotations on the passage. He quotes Addison, and goes on:

> It is an imitation, or rather a sort of paraphrase of the 148th Psalm, and (of what is a paraphrase upon that) the Canticle placed after *Te Deum* in the Liturgy, *O all ye works of the Lord, bless ye the Lord* &c. which is the song of the three children in the Apocrypha.

The closeness of verbal parallel between Milton and the Canticle need not concern us, because the point about tone and structure is so obviously right. What is happening is this: Galliard is taking words which clearly declare their origin in a liturgical impulse, and enacting them in the standard, stylised gestures of polite, eighteenth-century concert music. He is domesticating the Psalmist; yet what is distilled through this process is a sense of the innocence, the security, the ease, of prelapsarian worship.

The process of imitation even turns in to regard itself. Eve's aria 'resound His praise' echoes precisely the dotted rhythms of Adam's previous area 'sound His praise', making the proper gestures of female subservience, but, like Milton's Eve, going off her own way as soon as she is ready. The climax of the Hymn comes in the setting of the last twelve lines as a prolonged duet in which the 'various stile' of three contrasting miniature movements is displayed. Our first parents begin in cheerful consort, firmly settled in D major and an untroubled 4/4 time:

The second section—slower, more meditative—invokes all Nature to continue the act of perpetual witness. God's glory must be eternally sung, and human voices are only a part of the cosmic chorus. The rhythms broaden out into a more contemplative, sonorous 3/2 time, the dialogue becomes antiphonal, and the harmonies begin to explore the officially related keys. The effect is serious and plain:

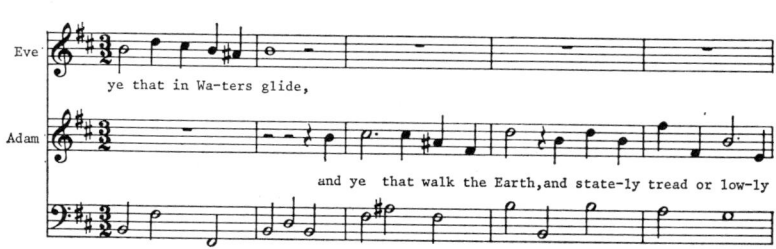

In the final movement the note of simple optimism is reasserted. Milton's 'Hail universal Lord, be bounteous still To give us onely good' gets its full Augustan due. To compare this movement with Handel's setting of Pope's line 'Whatever is, is right' in *Jephtha* would be to establish the opposite poles of the eighteenth century's little world of Man. Handel moves through the agonised meditation of Jephtha's 'Deeper and deeper still' to the perilous adventure of the chorus 'How dark, O Lord, are thy decrees', which ends with this call upon Pope's *Essay on Man* as the only palliative to a staring fatalism. Galliard's music, on the other hand, has just proved by praise that the Universe is orderly, reasonable, and beautiful, and he lays down his pen in the sure and certain hope that if 'the night Have gatherd aught of evil or conceald' God's light will disperse it as briskly as a woman sweeps a room:

This is not operatic, not theatre music, it is music for the select concert audience; it is polite and private rather than public and declamatory. Nathaniel Lee said that in *The State of Innocence* Dryden had brought Milton's virgin to Court; Galliard, in this fluent, easy setting, has introduced her, and made her very much at home, in the drawing-room. Henry Carey, in a commendatory poem, wrote more aptly than he knew, and certainly more shrewdly than he intended:

> Galliard, each note that flows from thee
> Is like thyself, polite and free.
> Thy genius, generous and gay,
> Warms like July, and blooms like May.
> Thou hast new-plum'd our Milton's wings,
> Who now not only soars, but sings.

It was more than thirty years later, and nearly a century after the publication of the first edition, that *Paradise Lost* again attracted the attention of a composer. And this second encounter would appear to be on a much more pretentious scale. Benjamin Stillingfleet's libretto, published in 1760, announces bravely on its title-page 'Paradise Lost. An Oratorio. As it is Performed at the Theatre-Royal in Covent-Garden. Altered and adapted to the Stage from Milton. Set to Music by Mr Smith.' John Christopher Smith had written music for the theatre, with a certain modest success, for some time before he turned his attention to Milton, but he is best known not as a composer, but as the amanuensis of Handel in Handel's later years. William Coxe, in his *Anecdotes of Handel and Smith* (1799) tells us that Smith was a pupil of Handel from the age of thirteen, but that Handel did not teach him composition—for that he went to Pepusch and Rosengrave. In 1732 he collaborated with Henry Carey in the opera *Teraminta*, and then spent several years in France, during which time he met Stillingfleet at Geneva. Smith returned to England when Handel became blind, and wrote out scores for him while working on his own behalf in the theatre, in close association with David Garrick. He eventually retired honourably to Bath, and died at the age of eighty, in 1795. Coxe also provides the information that Smith's setting of *Paradise Lost* was begun on 1 December 1757 and finished in the following July.

Stillingfleet's libretto, as a libretto, lives up to the ambitions of its title-page. It is very long. But on the recto of the proud title-page there is a sad, reductive 'Advertisement':

As the oratorio was found to take up too much time at the rehearsal, the lines marked thus ' are not performed.

And this immediately reduces the libretto by nearly twenty per cent. *Paradise Lost*, however, is seventeen and a half times as long as Stillingfleet's complete libretto, and in the Preface, addressed to Mrs Montagu, he shows himself conscious of the comparison:

> . . . my greatest difficulty has been to bring the materials furnished by Milton into so small a compass, and at the same time to preserve some idea of the original plan. . . . Almost all the recitative is word for word taken out of my author; and as to the songs, they are in general so much his, that i have tryed to compose them chiefly from the sentiments which i found in him, and as often as i was able to preserve his very words.

This claim is interesting in the light of what he did, in fact, do. The libretto is divided into three Acts, the first covering the latter part of Milton's Book IV, showing Adam and Eve in Paradise; the second brings together the Morning Hymn from Book V, the discussion about divided labours in Book IX, and the temptation of Adam from the same Book; the third relates the judgement of God and the dismissal from Paradise, using widely separated parts of Books X, XI, and XII. The three Acts are really organised round three themes: Obedience, Temptation, and Repentance. They represent a very clever patchwork of Milton, and they provide a satisfying shape. The Songs and Choruses are by Stillingfleet. Some are evocative echoes of Milton's rhythms and phrases, others are Augustan simplicity at its most banal. One Song, for example, at the end of Act II, comments of the Fall of Adam with gnomic complacency:

> Too, too sure the deed is done,
> Man is ruin'd, sin's begun.

Most of it is better, and chiefly to be praised is Stillingfleet's principle of selection. By neglecting Satan altogether he can focus attention on the acutely human moments in the epic, and by stressing, through the whole of the first act, that 'Truest bliss is to obey', and that:

> Thy commands well understood
> Lead us to our greatest good.

he is touching a string to which the civilised men of the eighteenth century were accustomed to respond.

We can have only a limited idea of what the oratorio was like in performance, because only the music for the Songs was ever printed. There were two performances at Covent Garden, and I take it that these were performances of the full oratorio, but the printed score gives the music only for the twenty-five songs (all of them short, and most of them simple). The recitatives and choruses, if there ever were any, seem to have perished everlastingly.

There is a brief, workmanlike overture, after which the first song is a setting of Stillingfleet's words:

> Would we hold dominion given,
> We must keep the laws of heaven:
> Wisdom thus has all things plan'd;
> Who submits shall have command.

Milton had come a long and delicate way to make this point about

> The onely sign of our obedience left
> Among so many signes of power and rule

but Stillingfleet's firm generalisation on the theme is akin to Johnson's confident analysis of moral structure:

His purpose was the most useful and the most arduous; *to vindicate the ways of God to man*; to shew the reasonableness of religion, and the necessity of obedience to the Divine Law.[7]

Smith achieves this security of judgement by setting the words in the rhythm of a grave and stately dance; it is plain, firmly set in G major, and the melody is contrived mainly by breaking up the tonic chord. The accompaniment provides a delicate, conversational commentary, and the effect is one of civilised talk on a socially acceptable moral topic:

[7] *Life of Milton* (1779).

The whole of the first act develops this tone, with celebrations of 'Bounteous Providence divine', and unexceptionable statements like 'Sweet is the Breath of Morn' and 'Thou didst also make the Night'. The difference of this from Galliard is clear, but not easy to formulate. Smith's paradisal music is less richly aware of the diversities of Eden, his celebration is simpler, more a public rejoicing than a private party. But the general unanimity of tone in his first act, is a necessary part of his strategy; the oratorio is built upon a pattern of strong contrasts; it is a much more resolutely dramatic work.

The temptation of Adam, in Act II, calls up all the resources of the theatre and the opera. The unusual feature of the song 'Thrilling horrors chills my veins' is that it is oddly reminiscent of Mozartian opera. The surge and impetus of the leaping melody, the chattering speed of the accompaniment take the song into a realm of musical experience which Handel's pupil and associate could hardly have been expected to explore:

The song is Stillingfleet's epitome of Adam's long speech in Book IX, 'O fairest of Creation, last and best', on which the contemporary critics are curiously silent. Addison ignores it, and so do Bentley and Richardson—and this is surprising when we recall the importance of the theme of Temptation to Milton; *Comus, Paradise Lost, Paradise Regained*, and *Samson Agonistes* are all deeply concerned with it. Only Thyer, in Newton's edition of 1749, seems to find this passage worth comment:

How vastly expressive are these words of Adam's tenderness and affection for

Eve, as they imply that the mere imagination of losing her had already converted the sweets of Paradise into the horrors of a desolate wilderness!

It is the 'horrors' that attract Smith, but in his hands they become the horrors not of Temptation in the primal man, but the heroic horrors of the operatic lover, publicly rending his heroic garments. The song ends with fine exhibitionism, wringing the last drop of dramatic effect out of the words 'the desperate deed'. It is interesting, in several ways, to remind ourselves that when these notes were first sung Mozart was four years old.

The third Act reverts to the softer passions. It begins with angelic admonition:

> Fond man, forbear thy maker to accuse,
> What cou'd he more, and not thy will enthral?

and drifts back to a concern with the painful realisations which fallen man must make: the perils of loneliness:

> My only strength! my only stay,
> Forlorn of thee where shall i go?

the possibility of death:

> It comes! it comes! it must be death!
> My eye-sight fails,—my limbs grow weak,—

and (most sharply realised) the pain of loss. In what is undoubtedly the finest of the songs Smith turns to the moment in Book XI when Eve realises that she must leave the garden, the 'happie Walks and Shades', and, above all, the 'nuptial Bowre' which she has adorned. She has set her heart, over-fondly, on what is no longer hers, and Milton makes this a sharply poignant moment in *Paradise Lost*. Here, and perhaps here only, Smith comes close to translating Milton's meaning. And it seems that nearly all the eighteenth-century critics of Milton found this moment deeply moving. Addison, whose critical control of sentiment was exact, says of it:

Eve's Complaint upon hearing that she was to be removed from the Garden of *Paradise* is wonderfully Beautiful: the Sentiments are not only proper to the Subject, but have something in them particularly soft and Womanish.

(No. 363, 26 April 1712)

Todd praises Milton's creative fancy, and compares the passage to the farewell in Euripides' *Alcestis*, which, he says, Milton has 'adorned with new graces'. And Newton's edition comments:

How naturally and justly does Milton here describe the different effects of grief upon our first parents!

Smith responds to the poignancy by setting the words very simply, virtually without ornament. He begins very openly in D minor, and modulates slowly and expectedly to A major after the second phrase. Then on the words 'must I then quit thee' he produces a marvellously plaintive falling phrase in F major, to evoke the utter blankness of Eve's moment of realisation. He sets the word 'comfort' on a rising minor sixth, which makes all comfort comfortless, and the song goes slowly on through a series of short sequences, first in rising keys, then in falling keys, and behind this melodic and harmonic progression there is a creeping, chromatic accompaniment in broken groups of quavers, which almost enacts a distant wailing:

The oratorio ends with a brisk reminder, in an A minor Allegro, that the 'gloomy Prince of Air shall by God's permission share power if not repulsed by Man'—a salutary moral warning which Milton unfortunately forgot to make at the end of Book XII.

Smith's work is called an oratorio, but it isn't really one. Oratorio form is indefinable, but it can be pointed to very easily. It is what Handel did in the 1740s: something intensely dramatic, yet without action; sharply concerned with the conflict of character, and the clash of personalities; heroic, yet having to do with inner and spiritual conflicts as well; elevated without being technically 'sublime'; and, with all this, perfectly at home on the Covent Garden stage. Smith's suite of songs, built though it is around the three evocations of Obedience, Temptation, and Regret, has no claim to the kind of attentiveness we must give to *Jephtha* or *Samson*. Smith's response to Milton is too simple, his eloquence is too prompt. He had the experience, but he missed the meaning.

While Stillingfleet was adapting Milton in Mitcham, the same labour was being undertaken in the village of Snitterfield, near Stratford-upon-Avon in Warwickshire, by the Vicar, the Reverend Richard Jago. The Vicar finds a modest place in the more pedestrian literary histories as the author of one of the more extensive 'loco-descriptive' poems, on the subject of Edgehill; it is in four relentless books, and has the leisure to observe that the British merchant ship can make the treasures of each clime her own:

> By gainful commerce of her woolly vests,
> Wrought by the spiky comb;

He was unfortunate with the oratorio too. It was published in the posthumous edition of his *Poems* in 1784, and the author's advertisement to the libretto contains these words:

> So far was written after the following piece was entirely finish'd', and at a time when the compiler thought that no one had engaged in the same design. In this however he finds he was mistaken, and can truly say, that had he been so much conversant in the musical world as to have known more early that a person of Mr STILLINGFLEET's merit, and abilities had undertaken this work, he would certainly have declined it.

He published it nevertheless, though with the further sad reminder that he has not succeeded in persuading any composer to undertake the music for it. Comparison of Jago's libretto with Stillingfleet's is remarkable. Both writers, apparently quite independently, ignore the first three books completely; both set the entire action in Paradise, both use Books IV, V, and IX–XII, and no other (many of the passages chosen from these books are common to both writers); both so organise matters that the Morning Hymn in Book V and the 'divided labours' speeches in Book IX appear consecutive parts of the same action. There are many other coincidences, but these are enough to suggest either surreptitious collusion or divine guidance. Such charges may be fanciful, but the similarities between the libretti point to a remarkable unanimity of critical opinion in the mid-eighteenth century as to what was significant and valuable in Milton's epic. Jago says he has attempted to unite the passages he selected into a regular and compendious form adapted to public representation, and he has done so:

> . . . by confining himself to those passages which have a more immediate reference to the principal story, and omitting what was more remote, and digressive.

The 'principal story' was the human one, the contrast between prelapsarian and fallen man, between the State of Innocence and the State of Sin. In comparison with these issues Heaven and Hell, God the Father, God the Son, Satan and the fallen angels, were 'remote' and 'digressive'. And yet the Vicar of Snitterfield seems to have felt no shadow of heresy. Perhaps the attitude of mind which he brought to Milton's epic can be indicated by one minor detail at the very end of the libretto. Jago selects very radically from Books X–XII, and in his last speech he takes the last twenty-four lines of Book XII and compresses them into nine. The two texts come together at the end, and both read:

> Som natural tears they dropd, but wip'd them soon;
> The World was all before them, where to choose
> Thir place of rest, and Providence thir guide:

but there Jago stops; that is the end of his oratorio—the human grief, the human prospect, and 'Providence'. Milton, however, added the two lines which cost Bentley all that pain:

> They hand in hand with wandring steps and slow,
> Through *Eden* took thir solitarie way.

I think Jago omitted those lines not because they were 'remote, and digressive' but because they enforce unbearably the estrangement of Man from God:

> Now alienated, distance and distaste,
> Anger and just rebuke, and judgement giv'n.

His view, like Stillingfleet's, was optimistic in spite of everything.

In a postscript to the text Jago appends some advice 'To the Composer'—in the unlikely event of one ever being found. Two points are perhaps worth notice. He says that the Recitative is of two kinds, narrative, and interlocutory, and the narrative itself is either descriptive, or introductory to the dialogue. He finds these distinctions important enough to warrant a simile:

The Composer will do well to have an eye to these distinctions, as mere *description,* or the *introductory narrative* will admit of a different kind of Recitative from the *conversation part*; the one being like *painting* in *still-life*, the other resembling the *portraits* of *living manners*.

A few lines later he meets the putative objection that there might be too much recitative and too little aria in his text, by saying that such was his intention:

And if there is less opportunity for flourishes, and repetitions, there is more room for spirited, and sensible expression, to assist the effect of the Dialogue upon the passions of the hearers. . . .

These two hints provide us with a lively idea of those pitfalls into which it seemed to Jago that a contemporary composer would be most likely to fall: banality in recitative, and garishness in the aria—and when we consider the oratorios by followers of Handel in the 1760s his warnings are shrewd.

The last musical descendant of *Paradise Lost* is incomparably the greatest, though (paradoxically) it is also the least interesting because the most remote: Haydn's *The Creation*. It was first performed publicly in Vienna, on 19 March 1799, and the whole audience was deeply impressed, though no one more so than its composer. 'One moment' he said, 'I was as cold as ice, the next I was on fire. More than once I was afraid I should have a stroke.' Its immediate reception in England was perhaps less wholly rapturous, if Anna Seward's reaction to the performance at the Birmingham Festival of 1802 is typical:

> It is little wonder that the words translated from the German almost literally into English, should be neither sense nor grammar, nor that they should make wicked work with Milton. . . .[8]

The provenance of Haydn's libretto is mysterious. Georg August Griesinger, in the *Allgemeine Musikalische Zeitung* (1809) says that Haydn told him that the text was translated from an original by someone called 'Linley'; the actual translator himself, Gottfried van Sweiten, calls the original anonymous. Donald Francis Tovey thought that the 'Linley' could have been Thomas Linley, a singing-master and concert-promoter of the period, and Edward J. Dent came forward with the ingenious theory that the word-book was the very one which Mrs Delany submitted to Handel, and he suggests that 'Linley' was the nearest that German scholarship could approximate to 'Delany'. If true, this would be marvellously convenient, but it is probably important to notice that Mrs Delany's book opens with Satan tempting Eve in Book IX, and Haydn's oratorio opens with God creating the world out of chaos, and (understandably) never gets as far as the Fall.

The Creation is partly based on *Paradise Lost*, with recitatives added from the Bible. The points of contact with Milton are naturally few, but they are interesting as an almost 'romantic' comment on Milton's themes. Some insights survive unscathed. The creation of Man as 'a living soul' is described in a pianissimo angelic recitative, and it is followed by the aria 'In native worth'. Here Haydn accompanies a simple, upright, pure melody in C major with plain, foursquare, diatonic harmonies, and matches precisely the tone of Milton's words:

> Two of farr nobler shape erect and tall,
> Godlike erect, with native Honour clad
> In naked Majestie seemd Lords of all.

---

[8] Quoted by Myers, p. 47.

But Haydn's setting of the Morning Hymn (Book V) is much less simple. It involves a duet for Adam and Eve, interset with passages of fortissimo praise for full chorus. Where Milton's characters call upon all Nature to resound God's praise, Haydn is content with nothing less than all Nature's answer. This inevitably reduces the stature of Adam and Eve, though the music Haydn provides for them could assert the point well enough:

Temptation and the Fall, with loss of Paradise, are no part of Haydn's concern, and here he parts company with Milton. Yet he cannot leave Paradise without pointing to what is to come, and he does so in a brief recitative for Uriel, in which he mutes Man's first disobedience into a euphemistic generalisation:

But the warning note is quickly drowned in a paean of praise, 'Sing the Lord, ye voices all' and a rousing 'Amen' to round off the performance. The contact between Haydn and Milton is slight, because Haydn is concerned to explore and represent the process of Creation itself. Man is no longer pre-eminent; he has receded into his natural setting, so that *The Creation* looks forward to the Romantics, rather than back to the period in which Pope could say without fear of successful contradiction:

> Know then thyself, presume not God to scan;
> The proper study of Mankind is Man.

The answer to the question of why Handel and *Paradise Lost* could not meet emerges at last as a fairly simple one. Augustan society, to come to terms with Milton's epic, found it necessary to humanise it, to reduce the proportions of its cosmic vision, to domesticate it. *The Tatler* tells us that Milton's lines on wedded love were quoted at a Wedding Breakfast, and such a sense of aptitude speaks for itself. Whatever else Handel was, he was never domestic. Let the last word be with Mrs Delany, still gossiping on, in 1751:

> Did you hear that poor Handel has lost the sight of one of his eyes? I am sure you (who so truly taste his merit) will lament it: so much for England!

Milton, Andreini, and Galileo:
SOME CONSIDERATIONS ON THE MANNER
AND FORM OF *PARADISE LOST*

John Arthos

Paradise Lost is the embodiment of a Christian view that enlarges the perspectives the *Divine Comedy* gives us. Both works extend our imaginings of truth as we refer the dogmas of faith to what we know and think of history and of the present. This is a service that poetry commonly performs, defining and picturing our thoughts in the light of our commitments and engagements. When the poetry is doctrinal and philosophical it aims to be definitive, to identify the life of the imagination with the life of faith and of reason. And if we were to suppose, as we sometimes do, that these two works supplement each other, and that they do not distract us into controversy, rather that they are enriching our understanding of the relevance of Christian beliefs to the conditions of life, I think we will agree that Dante's poem concentrates our attention upon the very immediacy of experience and Milton's upon the long view of the journey through yet undetermined tracts of time.

Dante's poem leads us into something like the intensity he speaks of as the nature of the love of God, and in our attention to the narrative we are led at almost all points to the sustained concentration on the meaning of each incident and circumstance. Milton's work, in contrast, however commonly spoken of as dramatic, is inherently less dramatic than Dante's, leading us less to the focused attention upon incidents and acts and much more quietly into religiousness and reflection. Our imaginings are not so much concentrated as they are diffused, and we are more taken with the idea of a panorama than of immediacy. One of the great advantages of Milton's manner is that it largely frees the Christian view from the limited contexts of contemporary society and

and draws us instead to think of Adam and Eve as ourselves at any moment in history and at any place entering upon an unknown life.

Yet, although Dante's poem is called a comedy, it is Milton's that is perhaps more frequently spoken of as dramatic. Dante's poem on the face of it is a succession of scenes and dialogues that ask to be thought of as dramatic scenes, but the simplicity and power of the narrative is such that one is hardly ever led to speak of the whole as other than a narrative. Paradoxically, Milton's poem, concerned so much with measureless panoramas, is spoken of as if dramatic were a more useful term for its characterisation than narrative.

Miss Helen Gardner has been one of many who have written of *Paradise Lost* in this way. She remarked on Milton's sketches of dramas to be based on Biblical stories and on several plans for a tragedy on the Fall of Man. And while she agreed that the form of 'Heroic Song' assimilated these initial plans for dramatic work, she nevertheless believed that genuinely dramatic qualities controlled important features of the work. She regarded the characterisation of God as a person with unlimited will as the determining feature of the action of the poem. She took the central event to be the action of God in exalting His Son, startling the universe with a deed as astonishing in itself as in its meaning. Miss Gardner regarded the other episodes as rather directly centring upon this, and the poem itself, as a consequence, possessed a simpler character than the classical and romantic epics which presented a great variety of actions. The simplicity of Milton's epic she thought to be the simplicity of the dramas he had at first thought he would be writing. 'It is essentially a dramatic action expanded.'[1]

Then, too, a more sophisticated use of the terms of drama has come into recent criticism where there is an effort to place Milton's work in the history of baroque and mannerist art. The baroque especially, in architecture and painting and sculpture, exploits effects that are almost literally theatrical. Contrasts are self-consciously represented as on a stage, persons apparently in motion are represented against a background that resembles the plazas and streets and alleys of a Palladian theatre. In churches altars and altar-pieces become the stage for dramatised performances. So it is argued, by extension, that *Paradise Lost* through the instrument of words is exhibiting a sense of the dramatic and of the theatre very much as do the church interiors of Bernini and Borromini. In this view of Milton's conception the dramatic emphasis is related more to his management of scene and the treatment of space

[1] *A Reading of Paradise Lost* (Oxford, 1965), pp. 32–3.

than it is to his characterisation.² The view is in part sustained by the scholarship that has made so much of the effect of developments in astronomy in the seventeenth century. Milton is able to represent events of universal importance as he does because the advances of science have enriched his understanding of the cosmos. The scientific exploration of undreamed distances extends the devices the baroque artists developed for imagining the grand and the vast. So it is that Professor Curry can speak of the action of Milton's poem as a cosmic action represented in the theatre of the universe, a theatre constructed more in Galileo's than in Bernini's terms:

> Now Milton has apparently completed a stage of sufficient immensity upon which he is enabled to present a sublime action asserting divine providence and purposing to justify the ways of God to men. As ontologist he has approached the Being of Divinity and defined his essential properties together with the qualities of the Son and Holy Spirit; he has analysed the essences of angels, of human beings, and of all created things, showing relationships of all secondary natures to each other and to God. As cosmogonist he has derived formless matter—the substrate of all creatures—from God who prepares it into a tumultuous chaos endowed with an appetite for forms. And as physicist Milton, a sort of atomist, has revealed in some detail the genesis of the World and all other creatures out of the prepared matter of chaos. Though the stage as thus conceived and executed is situated within the limits of total space, still it is not yet finished and will not be complete until vital alterations shall have been accomplished in the World's structure.³

But, in general, however useful theatrical terms may be to characterise *Paradise Lost*, the application of the idea to the action of the poem must be strictly limited, for the obviously controlling conception of the poem is in the presentation of a narrative and an argument. All is presented to us in the light of what the narrator is making of sacred history, and whatever the work may be thought to be as dramatising is clearly secondary. That there is here the material for drama, and even that from time to time scenes are presented to us as conceivably to be staged, this is obvious enough from Dryden's adaptation, and there is no doubt that more could have been made of the matter than his opera did. It is clear also that Milton was strongly drawn to composing for performance. *Samson Agonistes* was written with many of the conven-

---

² This line of criticism is elaborately worked out by Roy Daniells, *Milton, Mannerism and Baroque* (Toronto, 1963).

³ W. C. Curry, *Milton's Ontology, Cosmogony and Physics* (Lexington, Kentucky, 1957), p. 183. Mr Curry develops the metaphor of the stage more elaborately on p. 21.

tions of the stage in mind. *Comus*, however undramatic it is nowadays thought to be, was plainly written for an elaborate production. Yet dialogue, controversy, and crises do not make drama unless they are specially controlled. In *Paradise Lost* the fullness of argument and the flow of the verse quite subordinate when they do not suppress any stirrings that call for presentation by actors, and although a particular scene may seem to call for dramatisation, sooner or later we find it leading us into ratiocination as drama never does. This is Milton's habitual, perhaps his single mode, to debate vigorously and elaborately and to define his characters so sharply that they appear to be present to us, and all the while he is bent on enlarging the burden of the words and episodes so that our attention is led away from them as far as our reason can take us. What for a while might appear to approach the immediacy of drama is absorbed in the vistas that religiousness and argument open up.

If we take our cue from *Samson Agonistes*, we may judge that for Milton the effects of drama as drama that are within his range are limited ones. The arrangement of scenes in that play is devised more to represent the progress of the life within the soul of Samson than to imitate action. As the speeches proceed—normally long, explicit statements—we come to sense the nature of the forces that have brought Samson to his inert state and that are coming to be re-ordered as he prepares himself to become again a fit instrument of God's will. Our interest in the revolution in his spirit is intensified and made more comprehending by the depth of reasoning in one debate after another and in the choruses. The absence of action, the simplicity in the succession of suppliants and antagonists, and the concentration on what is happening in the passing of a day's time, all these limitations upon the scope of drama are characteristic of the limits Milton will always set—he directs drama more towards the sustaining of thought than of awe.

Samson Agonistes ends as *Paradise Lost* does in a departure. There is to the play of course a coda, the narration of what happened finally, and the account of Samson's final action and his death brings out to some degree the wonder characteristic of tragedy. But the effect of the conclusion is more subdued than in many tragedies, for one reason, I think, because the death of the protagonist by his own hand diminishes our sense of external powers at work, and indeed the account of the pulling down of the temple returns us more feelingly than before to our involvement in the state of Samson's mind and spirit. We end in contemplating not the deed but those last moments in which some rousing power was taking hold of him, and we are charmed with the idea that his thoughts were finally overcome by the sense of heavenly purpose.

An Italian of Milton's acquaintance characterised a certain sort of drama as 'sacred tragedy', 'inculcating a holy fear and a charitable compassion'.[4] This is a very different effect from the one which Aristotle spoke of, and I think the words serve better than Aristotle's to characterise Milton's play because they point more to an effect of sympathy than of purgation. And it has this effect, I think, largely because Milton has so strictly directed our attention to what is at work within Samson and he has so little turned our attention to the forces acting in the larger world and in the universe.

If we wish to call *Samson Agonistes* a drama we do so because Christianity has taught us to use the term as a paradox in contemplating the inner life. Just as elsewhere Milton can speak of the Paradise within, and of Satan himself as Hell, so here he can present the growth of purpose in Samson in the form of a tragic drama, controverting the classical idea of tragedy as the imitation of an action. On the other hand, he does wish to preserve some of the effects drama obtains through limiting the scene and concentrating such action as there is within the limits of an imagined theatre.

The consolation we feel at the end of *Paradise Lost* in visualising our first parents as they begin their long journey is also largely formed by our sympathy with what we so perfectly understand of their thoughts and their feelings. So much of our attitude is determined by what we have been weighing all along, the suggestion of the struggle between good and evil in Eve's dream, the resolution of the issues in Adam's decision to stand by Eve and to retreat from God, and so on. Much of the ending effect is determined by our sense of the growing trouble these two have accepted as their joy. But in *Paradise Lost* differently than in *Samson Agonistes* Milton does not so strictly confine the struggle and the issues. God is so much more the subject of the poem, and Sin and Death have come into the world through more than one rebellion. In the poem the world outside the self, and most especially Heaven, plays a much larger part, and there are many and tremendous actions. But here instead of working towards the peculiarly tragic effect, the representation of external powers in action negates even more forcefully the potentiality for drama. *Samson Agonistes* possesses a semblance of dramatic power by virtue of its dependence upon a single scene, but in

[4] *Tragedie di Cirolamo Bartolomei, Già Smeducci,* Impressione Seconda (Rome, 1655), sigs. e2^v–e3^r.

Paradise Lost there is anything but such a concentration. The convention not merely of a single setting but even of an imagined theatre would be wholly contrary to the purposes of the epic. Here Milton was presenting a variety of actions with different protagonists, and what he would represent takes place in realms of radically different nature. He wishes to show how the stories of the angels and of God's actions and of the Fall of Man bear upon each other but he needs to show quite as clearly how differently events take place with God and in the world of necessity. He wishes us to understand that the actions of heavenly beings have consequences for mortals, that on occasion what is represented in the lives of angels is analogous to what takes place in the lives of mortals. At the same time he wishes to show that but for God's free intervention man would have gone unminded and Heaven would have still been Heaven. When Milton would have us believe that there are true correspondences between the careers of angels and of men, for example between the Fall of Satan and of Adam, he will instruct us by appeals to sacred writings and not, as he does in *Comus* and *Lycidas*, through the explanations of philosophy. In *Paradise Lost* in certain essential respects he keeps the worlds apart and this is as necessary for him for reasons of theology as it is for the form of his work. Questions must remain unanswered as we look last at Adam and Eve.

In *Comus* there is an intermingling of the worlds of nature and heaven as the Neoplatonists think of it, so that in one realm of being the Attendant Spirit could intervene in the affairs of men exactly as the images of white-handed Hope and Faith and Chastity direct the Lady's thoughts. In *Samson Agonistes*, on the other hand, Milton provides no such intervention as the Attendant Spirit's just as he does not provide notice of a particular vision taking form in Samson's mind. He leaves us with the mere supposition of a relation between the world of spirit and the human understanding. In their diverse ways both conceptions of heavenly influence call for at least partly dramatic representation, in the objectification of the influence. And it is the difference in the conception of the ways of God in *Paradise Lost* that calls for narrative and exposition rather than for drama. Arguments are to move Adam and Eve, not presences and not invasions.

The very stuff of *Paradise Lost* is the representation of two different realms of being, and the relation to each other is extremely complex. It is not to be thought of in terms of the relationship of the eternal ideas to the world of matter as it is in *Comus*, nor is it to be reduced to the humanism of *Samson Agonistes*. Physically, both worlds appear of like constitution, but one we are to accept as the world our senses certify, the other as a world only barely conceivable. Although we fall back upon reason and analogy to support us in our imagining of Heaven and Hell, we know that we are only scantily comprehending the reality. Angels travel between the worlds, and there is reason to support the idea that souls may also move from one to the other. But neither Milton's materialism nor his doctrine of God's creativity nor of the inspiring power of the Holy Spirit leads to a certain affirmation of a principle of unity in all being. In the end reason does help faith to assert that the two worlds treat with each other but it equally asserts the possibility of their alienation. Indeed, in that very mysterious doctrine, Hell is outside the Universe.

It seems to me, then, that Milton's understanding of the substantial differences in the nature of the various realms as in the differences in God's nature and deeds and in men's, made it impossible for him to keep to the idea of classical drama as the form he required.

This is where a contrast with Andreini's *L'Adamo* can be serviceable. For Andreini a certain doctrine is that there is indeed a single principle co-ordinating all being, a certain idea of the Incarnation. This is at the centre of his thought and of his play, and in *L'Adamo*, although he modified the classical idea of unity, he was able to present the story of the Fall of Man in the light of a union between God and Man that testified to God's immanence everywhere.

This *sacra rappresentazione*—a musical drama of a strongly allegorical cast—was meant for an elaborate stage production with astonishing scenic effects, and it included singing and dancing. The single performance I have seen an account of—in the Palazzo Ducale in Milan in 1613—would have taken place in a theatre like the Farnesina in Parma or the Barberini in Rome.[5] There would have been great clouds descending from on high with choirs of angels, barks crossing the rivers of Hell bearing troops of devils, and of course some magnificent representation of God Himself enthroned. The major part of the work presents some such account of the Fall as Milton's but the latter part becomes predominantly a drama of allegorical persons—the Flesh, the World, Death, Famine, Despair, Toil—treating with Adam and Eve and Lucifer. It appears that the work now becomes as much ballet as opera, and indeed, reading it, one can imagine that these last acts would end the work in an increasingly entrancing spectacle.

There can be no doubt that what the critics of Milton call the stages

[5] *Enciclopedia della Spettacolo*, VII, 551.

of the universe here find themselves confined to a particular theatre, and what is interesting is that this is precisely a key idea in Andreini's conception of what he is about—he is composing a theatrical work for us to see what we can hardly see in any other way, the scope of his story. What his story tells us of, he says, is the drama in the lives of men. The representation upon the stage is only a reflection of what goes on within the soul, and it is also only a reflection of the energies at play in the universe. And each mirrors the other. In short, the audience is observing an imaginative similitude of what is itself never visible, whether within the life of the soul or in Heaven. We are no more to misconceive the materiality of Heaven and Hell than we are to misconceive their theatrical representations, but these images bear a relationship to truth and they are an embodiment of truth as the things of the Creation themselves continue to manifest the presence of their Creator.

> Let [my work] be surveyed, therefore, with an eye of indulgence, and blame not the poverty of style, the want of dignity in the conduct of the circumstances, sterility of conceits, weakness of spirit, insipid jokes, and extravagant episodes, to mention (without speaking of an infinitude of other things,) that the world, the flesh, and the devil, present themselves in human shapes to tempt Adam, since there was then in the universe no other man or woman, and the serpent discovered himself to Eve with a human similitude; moreover this is done, that the subject may be comprehended by the understanding through the medium of the senses: since the great temptations that Adam and Eve at once sustained, were indeed in the interior of their own mind, but could not be so comprehended by the spectator; nor is it to be believed that the serpent held a long dispute with Eve, since he tempted her rather by a suggestion to her mind than by the conference, saying these words, *'nequaquam moriemini, et eritis sicut Dii scientes bonum et malum'*,—[you shall by no means die, but you will be like gods, knowing good and evil]—and yet it will be necessary, in order to express those internal contentions, to find some expedient to give them an outward representation. But, if it is permitted to the painter, who is a dumb poet, to express by colours God the Father under the person of a man silvered by age, and to describe under the image of a white dove the purity of the Spirit, and to figure the divine messengers or Angels, in the shape of winged youths; why is it not permitted to the poet, who is a speaking painter, to represent in his theatrical production another man and woman besides Adam and Eve, and to represent their internal conflicts through the medium of images and voices entirely human? [Here, of course, one notices the special problem for Andreini who is thinking of a theatrical production even while he is also speaking of the conflict within the minds of the Adam and Eve of history as an internal one,] not to mention that it appears more allowable to introduce in this work the Devil under a human shape, than it is to introduce into it the Eternal Father, and even an angel; and if this is permitted, and seen every day exhibited in sacred representations, why should it not be allowed in the present, where, if the

greater evil is allowable, surely the lesser should be allowed? Attend therefore, gentle reader, more to the substance than to the accident, considering in the work the great end of introducing into the theatre of the soul the misery and lamentation of Adam, to make your heart a spectator of them in order to raise it from these dregs of earth, to the magnificence of heaven, through the medium of virtue and assistance of God.[6]

Andreini means us to think of his work as presented simultaneously upon a real stage and an imagined one. Whatever the resources of baroque settings and machinery, he says he wants his audience never to forget that no theatre in the world could provide a vast enough setting for the actions of his drama.[7] The hosts in the choruses, the great clouds unfolding to reveal now angels, now demons, the perspectives and vistas upon the abysses of Tartarus and the reaches of Heaven, all are but tokens of what really is. So, I suppose, with the original flight of Adam and Eve:

Adam Ah, what rebellowing sounds I hear above!
    Perchance with such a voice
Offended Heaven now drives us from the world,
And sends us banish'd to the gulfs below!
What shafts, how numberless
Strike down the woods and groves! with what wild force
The raging winds contend!
    Now rushes from the sky
Water congeal'd to forceful globes of hail!

Eve Alas! how from on high
    The swelling waters pour,
    That rising o'er their banks,
    The proud o'erflowing rivers
    Now put the beasts to flight,
    And in the groves and woods
Precipitately drive the fish to dwell.

Adam Fly! let us haste to fly

---

[6] *Adam: A Sacred Drama, Preface,* translated by William Cowper, in *Life and Works,* ed. Robert Southey (London, 1837), X, 242–3.

[7]   Above the universe himself he raised,
    Yet he behind it rests;
  The whole he now encircles, now pervades,
    Now dwells apart from all,
    So great, the universe
  To comprehend him fails.   (Cowper, X, 278–9; ll. 1012–17)

> Up to those lofty mountains,
> Where heaven now seems at last
> Satiate with ceaseless thundering to repose!
> (Cowper, X, 342; ll. 2920–40)

Andreini, as any composer of opera, and perhaps especially in his time, is in love with the particular and the concrete, the very scenery, the bodies, the voices. Yet he means to exploit the sense of the unconfined, and he means somehow to impress us with the conviction of the vastnesses that exist within the soul as within the universe. For him there are indeed wars in Heaven, great powers oppose each other there and everywhere, we see their representatives armed upon a stage, we hear thunder and the roaring of floods, and we hear words that explain the meaning of what is entertaining our senses. Even as we attend to what is before us he says we are never to forget that what we are wondering at as a man-shaped god upon a throne is truly the immeasurable God in limitless space, that those thunders are the formless, voiceless powers of the infinite, of the one power everywhere:

> Behold this ample cavern of the earth;
> Lo, it was made for love; whate'er it holds
> Within its spacious circuit,
> Of love perceives the fire.
> Love rules the earth, the sea, the air, and fire,
> With endless love a hundred genial stars,
> Not moving from their sphere,
> Scatter their flames through heaven;
> And other wandering planets
> Through those exalted regions
> Direct their golden steps.
> What river, fount, or stream,
> Unconscious flows and destitute of love?
> What frozen sea does love not penetrate
> With his imperious ardour?
> What glowing ocean does not oft discover
> A visage pale and wan,
> As if infirm with love? . . .
> And thou unmelting soul! wilt thou alone,
> Wilt thou disdain to feel
> That which all creatures prove?
> (Cowper, X, 348 and 350; ll. 3093–110, 3150–2)

This is spoken not by God or an angel but by *Carne*, the Body, an abstraction, and probably the shift in the last acts from immortals and mortals to personifications is a way of pointing to what Andreini understands of the nature of reality, and to emancipate our imaginings from the limitations of excessively personal characterisations. The language that has come down from Tasso, with the overtones of yearning and pathos, the exaggerations of the Petrarchists, and above all a conventionalised ardour—these all provide the assurance the whole work depends on, the assurance of the profundity and vitality of orthodoxy. War in Heaven never raises the doubt of eternal confusion that underlies and sustains the power of Milton's reasoning as well as of his faith. In quite other ways than in the universe of *Comus* or of *Samson Agonistes*, and of course than of *The Tempest*, this is indeed one universe with a single governing life. And this becomes an important reason why it is possible to apply Miss Gardner's idea of 'a single dramatic action expanded' to *L'Adamo* as I think one ought not to apply it to *Paradise Lost*.

As for the mingling of worlds, in contrast to Milton, this is represented according to various ideas of the nature of reality. God speaks once in this way:

> Let each spectator of these works sublime
> Behold, with meek devotion,
> Earth into flesh transform'd, and clay to man,
> Man to a sovereign lord,
> And souls to Seraphim.   (Cowper, X, 247; ll. 63–67)

At another time the unity of the great and little worlds comes about through understanding and love:

> Adam, arise, since I to thee impart
> A spirit warm from my benignant breath;
> Arise, arise, first man,
> And joyous let the world
> Embrace its living miniature in thee!
>   (Cowper, X, 248; ll. 97–101)

Again and again there is the notice that God as the Word is incarnate in Christ, and it is Satan who more than any other puts it in these terms:

> In evil hour the Word
> Will wear the sinner's form.   (Cowper, X, 263; ll. 97–101)

But I think it is in his imagery that Andreini most consistently reveals the character of this theology in which the particular and the concrete are always potentially to be transformed into the Divine. Andreini may say that all is to be thought of as an image of the inexpressible, yet his central doctrine is in fact so stamping his language that the theatre he speaks of, the setting, the actors, like the sinner, seem to be 'wearing the form of the Word'.

Andreini's readers have not commonly thought that he has achieved a great success although I am sure Ettore Allodolì was right and that the work has genuine distinction. Some who question Milton's achievement do so with criticisms that are also applied to the Italian's work—the divine figures are too particularly characterised, the action is more astonishing than credible, the religion is monstrous. With Andreini the faults are generally thought to be those of an intrinsically rhetorical Catholicism. The cult of the theatre turns out to be the cult of the spectacular.

Such a judgement is not adequate but it points to what is central in Milton's excellence. Every convention of his work and above all else the heroic manner serve the principal undertaking—the honouring of God through the narrative, and the presentation of the argument. The poet offers the argument in the light he himself is able to bring to it, and every episode in the story, every sequence, every scene-setting, serves the poet in showing how the argument deserves assimilation. Milton says Revelation has been his guide, and to the reader it seems appropriate to think of Revelation as indeed the impresario. Even so, each work bears the tone of the richest, most responsible consideration. Andreini may appear entangled in hyperbole, expressing superlatives without communicating the conviction that they are called for, and the very passions may be thought to be second-hand, but in Milton the witty elaborations in the discourses of diabolical giants, the clashing of arms in Heaven whose reverbations stir worlds extending beyond the sight—the magnification—all this we accept as bearing upon the evils and fears knowable to any human heart. Andreini's work may be governed by the requirements of a certain sort of theatre, Milton's are impressed with what the mind requires of words when it is weighing the import of its own life, and that weighing is unsupported by any doctrine of unity in the creation of the kind the dogma of the Incarnation allows. However comprehensive Milton's materialism he still suffers from the Platonist's puzzlement over the relation of the divine to the particular.

'The true ring' of Milton's mind sets not merely the tone, it establishes the form of *Paradise Lost* for another reason also partially related to theological considerations. When we comprehend that Milton is presenting the tremendous argument as his own weighing of doctrine, we understand how little the new astronomy contributed to his inspiration; and, accordingly, how small an influence this must have had in dictating anything like a dramatic forming to the episodes. Certainly the idea of the vastness of Heaven and Hell is integral to the poet's ambition to tell what never yet was told, but Milton's imaginings are as free from confinement to a particular theory of the heavens as they are to the idea of a cosmic theatre. He accordingly offers us scene after scene according to the Ptolemaic picturing and then he has Raphael undermine the authority of that picture. He can describe Pandemonium as a vast amphitheatre and then tell us that Hell is outside the universe. He can lavish his descriptions of the earth and what grows upon it with detail after detail, and then in the very language so generalise the sense that far from being able to count the streaks upon the lily we can hardly remember that we are being told about flowers:

> He scarce had said, when the bare Earth, till then
> Desert and bare, unsightly, unadornd,
> Brought forth the tender Grass, whose verdure clad
> Her Universal Face with pleasant green,
> Then Herbs of every leaf, that sudden flourd
> Op'ning thir various colours, and made gay
> Her bosom swelling sweet.   (VII, 313–19)

A certain indeterminacy in the physics, a certain indeterminacy in the theology, the generalising of description, these all serve the purpose of individual praise and the individually weighed doctrine—the delimiting of what would be too confining a view for Milton's purpose. Milton's language is as unlike Andreini's as his idea of the disparate realms of Heaven and Earth is unlike Andreini's idea of the macrocosm embracing the microcosm, or of man and wife growing together as the branches of a single plant:

> Ye lilies, and ye shrubs of snowy hue,
> Jasmine as ivory pure,
> Ye spotless graces of the shining field;
> And thou most lovely rose
> Of tint most delicate,

> Fair consort of the morn,
> Delighted to imbibe
> The genial dew of Heaven,
> Rich vegetation's vermil-tinctured gem,
> April's enchanting herald,
> Thou flower supremely blest,
> And queen of all the flowers,
> Thou form'st around my locks
> A garland of such fragrance,
> That up to Heaven itself
> Thy balmy sweets ascend,
> Let us in pure embraces
> So twine ourselves, my love,
> That we may seem united,
> One well-compact, and intricate acanthus.
>
> (Cowper, X, 276–7; ll. 942–61)

Miss Gardner spoke of Milton's alternating between the precise and the vague, between the particular and the limitless in the cosmography of the poem.[8] The observation can be extended, I believe, to characterise the conception of the poem in which the elements of the theatrical, what remains of the original idea of a tragic drama, as well as the manner of prolusion and debate, are all absorbed in argument and reflection in which much is demonstrated and much is unresolved.

Milton does indeed impress upon us his notion that human affairs are part of a vast activity, but he is not founding his sense of the grandeur of things in a view of physical nature any more than in a view of Incarnation. All centres obviously in an idea of God's magnificence and in the magnificence of His creation. But whatever praise we are to give this, our greatest praise is for His granting freedom to men and our greatest wonder is at the power that is conferred upon us whereby our acts have such consequence even for the universe. All this of course is obvious, his emphasis upon the place of free will in the divine scheme, but one needs to remark on it in order to modify any extreme claim that the new astronomy has a vital bearing upon the conception of the poem.

And all this is relevant to the idea that the poem presents a cosmic drama with cosmic forces concentrating upon the story of the Fall, for if this were a proper emphasis, according to modern ideas of the cosmos,

---

[8] *Op. cit.*, pp. 40–43.

then Adam's understanding of these forces would be a significant factor in the drama. But the characterisation of Adam does not support this view of the action.

In this respect it is important to remind ourselves of Adam's place in the hierarchy of being that ascends to the perfection of Deity. Adam has been endowed, as the humanists from Pico della Mirandola on had eloquently said, with powers that were godlike:

> God on thee
> Abundantly his gifts hath also pourd
> Inward and outward both, his image faire:
> Speaking or mute all comliness and grace
> Attends thee, and each word, each motion formes.
> Not less think wee in Heav'n of thee on Earth
> Then of our fellow servant, and inquire
> Gladly into the wayes of God with Man:
> For God we see hath honourd thee, and set
> On Man his equal Love. (VIII, 219–28)

Yet the very faculty of reason that ennobled him was strictly circumscribed:

> the rest
> From Man or Angel the great Architect
> Did wisely to conceal, and not divulge
> His secrets to be scannd by them who ought
> Rather admire; or if they list to try
> Conjecture, he his Fabric of the Heav'ns
> Hath left to thir disputes, perhaps to move
> His laughter at thir quaint Opinions wide . . . (VIII, 71–78)

Milton's qualifications here may even demean Adam below Andreini's conception:

I seemed to behold the first man Adam, a creature dear to God, the friend of Angels, the heir of heaven, familiar with the stars, a compendium of all created things, the ornament of all, the miracle of nature, the lord of the animals, the only inhabitant of the universe, and enjoyer of a scene so wonderfully grand.[9]

It is certain that Milton's Adam does not possess the power that enables man in Galileo's view to comprehend the real vastness of the physical universe and that enables him to know God perfectly:

[9] From the Preface to *L'Adamo* (Cowper, X, 240).

I have often considered with myself how great the wit of man is; and while I run through such and so many admirable inventions found out by him, in the arts as well as in the sciences, and again reflecting upon my own wit, which is so far from promising me the discovery of anything new that I despair of comprehending what is already discovered, I stand here confounded with wonder and surprised with desperation, and account myself little less than miserable.[10]

I do not believe that Milton indicates anywhere that he any more than Adam is looking at Nature as Galileo does. He speaks of 'the Book of Knowledge fair' (III, 47) and 'the Book of God' (VIII, 67), but not even in such precise terms as Andreini's:

> The volume of the stars,
> The sovereign Author plann'd,
> Inscribing it with his eternal hand,
> And his benignant aim
> Their beams in lucid characters proclaim.
>
> (Cowper, X, 247; ll. 52–56)

And although Milton certainly means that man may admire God's handiwork in Nature, he never argues that in knowing Nature man comes to know God perfectly, as Galileo does—'God is discovered no less perfectly in the effects of Nature than in the sacred works of Scriptures.'[11] Nor could Milton allow the claims of reason to approach so near to the comprehension of faith:

> But that that same God who has endowed us with sense, with reason, and with intellect, should have wished us not to use them, giving us by some other means the knowledge that we could obtain through them, and in such a way that we should be obliged to deny the sense and reason of what natural causes or the sensations of experience or the necessities of demonstration have revealed to our eyes and mind—I do not believe it is necessary to believe this.[12]

---

[10] *Dialogue on the Great World Systems*, in the Salusbury Translation, ed. Giorgio di Santillana (Chicago, 1953), pp. 116–17.

[11] From a letter to the Grand Duchess Cristina di Lorena, in *La Prosa di Galileo*, ed. I. del Lungo and A. Favaro (Florence, 1911), p. 192.

[12] *Ibid.*, p. 192. Galileo's idea of reason goes quite beyond Milton's conception of right reason, for Galileo circumvents the notion of a hierarchy of intelligence: 'The human mind is a part of the divine mind, just as our solar system is a part of the infinite universe. The limits exist only in our understanding, which increases with every conquest of an intensive and infallible science. Consequently no mediator is needed for our cognition of the divine intelligence as soon as we possess the tools supplied by this progressive science. For Galileo metaphysics does not lie beyond physics because physics is a part of metaphysics. Thus theology and

And neither in Satan nor in Raphael, nor in his own person as the inspired poet, does Milton describe the existence of a faculty comprehending Nature and God as Galileo does with his Titanic confidence. The lack of assurance in presenting the Copernican view and the diffidence about the claims of science generally accord with the relatively modest capacities of Adam and the relatively modest claims Milton makes for reason itself. Milton does not provide the circumstances by which either Adam or Satan could perform as a protagonist in a cosmic drama in the universe Galileo was discovering.

If I may conclude, then: epic poetry always requires many actions and a variety of scenes although it may take its beginning in a single cause, Achilles' wrath or Aeneas's ambition. As incidents and characters multiply, the initial cause merges in innumerable other causes, but in the reading we discover how much all does indeed depend upon that original simplicity. In classical drama, on the other hand, it is the simplicity of the action one takes for granted and it is the complexity that grows by inference.

Milton's poem is like the classical epic in that that proclaimed initial cause, man's first disobedience, we come to see as mingling with innumerable other disobediences. And despite Milton's bent for dramatising, it does him and us a disservice to misconceive the fundamentally epic conception of *Paradise Lost*. It also leads us to overlook the power and tone of the poet who is presenting his tremendous argument as so much his own discovery. One might wish there were less of individual limitation in the doctrine, but one cannot wish for anything other than the tone of this particular poet's force and nobility, a tone that with him here was the tone of a narrator, of an epic poet.

---

natural science have, though their fields and methods are different, an identical goal'. (Leonardo Olschki, 'Galileo and the Scientific Revolution', *Philosophical Review*, 1943, No. 211, p. 363.)

Beyond Disobedience

Merritt Y. Hughes

In *Milton: The Modern Phase* Mr Patrick Murray has quoted Professor Waldock's verdict 'that, if *Paradise Lost* is really a poem about the Fall of Man with a moral of obedience, it is a failure'.[1] Discussion of that verdict is not my interest, but I am interested in the assumption about the moral itself. It seemed to Waldock to have Addison's authority behind it, for he saw a kind of official interpretation of the poem in Addison's remark in the last of his essays on it in *The Spectator* (369) that the one great moral to be drawn from *Paradise Lost* is 'the most useful that can be imagined: it is in short this, that *Obedience* to the will of God makes men happy, and that *Disobedience* makes them miserable'.

Addison thought of this as self-evident. No reader could doubt 'what was visibly the moral of the principal fable, which turns upon Adam and Eve'. He would have objected to the assumption that he intended his remark to be canonised as stating the official theme of the poem. He was careful to say that he was not hunting for any 'particular moral which is inculcated in *Paradise Lost*'. He repudiated Bossu's theory 'that an epic writer first of all pitches upon a certain moral, as the general . . . foundation of his poem, and afterwards finds out a story to it'. Addison thought that the story, the characters, and the moral or the several morals all defined themselves gradually as the poem ripened in composition.

Addison's hospitality to several morals is encouraged in our latest book on *Paradise Lost*, J. M. Steadman's *Milton and the Renaissance Hero*.[2] He sees the 'central dichotomy of obedience and disobedience in fable and episodes alike [as flanked by] other dichotomies—faith and

[1] *Milton: The Modern Phase* (London, 1967), pp. 101, 106.
[2] (Oxford, 1967), p. 198.

apostasy, righteousness and unrighteousness, truth and falsehood, peace and confusion'. Instead of disobedience and obedience he suggests impiety and piety—a suggestion which pleases me because the overtones of *disobedience* often are those of classical loyalty or love of a superior or of something like a breach of feudal fealty.

The idea of a family of morals in the poem need not clash with our new insights into its metaphorical and logical unity, but it must be acknowledged that Milton's use of the word and concept of disobedience is too vague to be very helpful to defenders of his architectonic powers and of the unity of *Paradise Lost*. Milton never defined it and he probably felt that its meaning need be no more exact than it is in the passage from *Romans*, 5 : 19, which underlies the first lines of the poem:

> For as by one man's disobedience many were made sinners, so by the righteousness of one shall many be made righteous.

In that verse *sin* and *disobedience* are interchangeable. The former is an acceptable gloss for the latter when the theme 'Of Mans First Disobedience' is announced in *Paradise Lost*. And so it is again in the overture to *Paradise Regained*:

> I who ere while the happy Garden sung,
> By one mans disobedience lost, now sing
> Recoverd Paradise to all mankind,
> By one mans firm obedience fully tri'd
> Through all temptation, . . .

To state his polar themes the poet relies on the antonyms for mutual definition and enrichment of meaning. In the account of the war in Heaven Raphael simply opposes the antonyms when he tells Adam that the 'happie state' of the loyal angels hinges on their obedience. It can last only while their obedience 'holds'. It rests upon the spontaneous love of God in which they 'stand or fall'. Raphael adds the disquieting fact that

> som are fall'n, to disobedience fall'n,
> And so from Heav'n to deepest Hell; O fall
> From what high state of bliss into what woe! (V, 537–43)

When we try to think of defining situations for *disobedience* in the poem we probably remember Professor B. Rajan's page in *Paradise Lost and the Seventeenth Century Reader* (p. 45) where he says that 'the sins of

Satan, of Adam, and of Eve . . . riot from a common stem of disobedience'. He speaks of many 'varied nuances and refinements of evil' which stem from disobedience and at the same time build up through the poem to 'a disobedience issuing in *hubris*'. But do the many varieties of evil constitute *or* derive from disobedience? Rajan was not writing as a canon lawyer nor as a criminologist. He was less interested in tying the Fall to disobedience as its cause than he was in stressing the element of arbitrary command in its context:

Obedience is claimed to an apparently arbitrary command. For Satan there is the motiveless 'begetting' of the Son, for Adam the unintelligible tabu against eating the fruit.

But what if the tabu can be thought of as less than arbitrary? The use of the term itself arouses a doubt. Anthropologists are inclined to regard many tabus as far from being the irrational restrictions of their early, narrow definition. Should the command of God respecting the interdicted tree in the Garden perhaps be viewed in the light of a test of faith like God's command to Abraham to sacrifice Isaac? Obedience to that command resulted in immediate, dramatic confirmation of Abraham's faith in a way that a lifetime of observation of the tabu in Eden could not have confirmed Adam's faith in God's goodness or wisdom. Or should the command in the Garden be compared to God's call to Abraham to leave Haran for a frontier life in a strange land? The confidence of a pioneer in his destiny does not resemble the confidence in the divine veracity a lack of which Milton thought (in *Christian Doctrine*, I, xi) contributed to Adam's fall.

The sharp difference between the commands to Abraham and Adam is of course that Adam's is for life and not for a spiritual or mundane adventure. He is potentially immortal and St Augustine repeatedly tells us—reflecting a long tradition—that his posterity also were intended to be immortal. He must consider the tabu on the tree as permanent. But can *we* accept him as having submitted to an irrational restriction of any kind as an abiding human institution? Or should he be imagined as regarding submission to God's tabu as in essence submission to the Reason which he knows is his own essence? So Tasso treated the matter in *Il Mondo creato*—making Adam's acceptance of the prohibition of the Tree of Knowledge tantamount to submission to Reason. Indications that Milton thought of it so are clear in *Paradise Lost*, but more obvious is the evidence that he thought of the tabu as an arbitrary test of the willingness of Adam's obedience. Emphatic contemporary support of that view is at hand in Mr S. E. Fish's contribution to our bumper crop of books on the poem in this jubilee year. In *Surprised by Sin*[3] he declares that:

> The freedom of the Fall (and therefore Man's responsibility for it) is a point of doctrine, and the reader must resist the temptation to submit it to the scrutiny of reason, just as Adam and Eve must maintain the irrelevancy of reason to the one easy prohibition.

I

Disobedience

Mr Fish has given a new edge to the old debate over the command which is disobeyed in *Paradise Lost* and in the account of man's Fall in *Genesis*. His defence of his view leaves little hope of compromise with those of us who would like to reconcile the ethos of the poem with that of *Areopagitica* as it is usually understood. Let us listen to the speakers in the poem who speak with most authority: We hear Adam stating it to Eve as unquestionably fair; we hear Raphael representing disobedience to it as the only danger to Adam's happiness in the Garden; we hear Adam himself accepting it from the mouth of God as the not unreasonable warrant of his citizenship in the welfare state of Eden; we hear him quoting God's words to Raphael:

> fear here no dearth:
> But of the Tree whose operation brings
> Knowledge of good and ill, which I have set
> The Pledge of thy Obedience and thy Faith,
> Amid the Garden by the Tree of Life,
> Remember what I warne thee, shun to taste,
> And shun the bitter consequence: . . .   (VIII, 322–8)

We read these key passages and others with which they resonate, and we ask ourselves how they were understood by the poet who in *Animadversions*, in his prime, condemned religious teachers who sought to 'cheat weak and superstitious fancies . . . into a blind and implicate obedience to whatsoever they shall decree'. We ask whether this is the poet who, in opening *The Reason of Church-Government*, declared:

> In the publishing of humane lawes, which for the most part aime at the good of civill society, to set them barely forth to the people without reason or Preface,

[3] (London, 1967), p. 244.

like a physicall prescript, or only with threatnings, as it were a lordly command, in the judgement of Plato, was thought to be done neither generously nor wisely.

Is this the man who in *Of Civil Power and of True Religion*, when the manuscript of *Paradise Lost* was in his desk or not long out of it, renewed his condemnation of any implicit obedience to authority? The pleasure of some leading, living Miltonists in the defence of the principle of free inquiry by the inveterate enemy of all implicit obedience in *Areopagitica*, has suffered from their sense of incongruence between his stand in that tract and his acceptance of the 'easy' but dreadfully-sanctioned prohibition of the Tree of Knowledge in *Paradise Lost*. Much discussion of the tract in college classes in America rejoices in Professor Empson's picture of Milton writing it when 'the lid was off' the explosion of revolutionary pamphlets in 1644. There is glee over Empson's echo in *Some Versions of Pastoral* (p. 186) of Dr Tillyard's bright remark that, 'If Milton had been in the Garden, he would have eaten the apple at once and written a pamphlet to prove that it was his duty'. But would the author of *Paradise Lost* have done so? Or is Professor Northrop Frye right in *Fearful Symmetry* (p. 305) when he contrasts Milton's vision of the City of God 'as a phoenix arising in the human mind from the ashes of a burned mysterious universe during the decade after the outbreak of the Civil War' with the later vision that was to make '*Paradise Lost* the song of experience following an unwritten song of triumph'?

In the poem there are two great acts of disobedience to divine commands: Satan's, and that of Eve and Adam. And there are two great acts of obedience, the Son's when he complies with the Father's expectation that he will so far empty himself of divine glory as to be able to share and cancel the penalty of death which man has incurred by disobedience, and Abdiel's when he quits the host of the rebel angels. In closing his interesting book *Milton and Christian Heroism*[4] Mr B. O. Kurth makes the point that in the cosmic setting of *Paradise Lost* its hero must be divinely obedient. To this we may add that the Son's obedience is prompted by the Father's public explanation of the reasons which might impel such an act of heroic obedience. In Abdiel's case no motives

---

[4] (Berkeley, 1959). In the coincident study of 'Heroic Virtue and the Divine Image in *Paradise Lost*', *Journal of the Warburg and Courtauld Institutes*, XXII (1959), 88–105, J. M. Steadman complemented Kurth's work with an analysis of Aristotle's relation of obedience to the supreme virtue of justice and prudence as approximating the divine.

are given for his decision to stand by his loyalty to God in the face of the disloyalty of Satan and his legions, but his reasons for it are made public later on the field between the hosts of loyal and disloyal angels. There Abdiel retorts Satan's sneer at the former's loyalty as cowardly submission to servitude:

> Unjustly thou deprav'st it with the name
> Of *Servitude* to serve whom God ordains,
> Or Nature; God and Nature bid the same,
> When he who rules is worthiest, and excells
> Them whom he governs. This is servitude,
> To serve th' unwise, or him who hath rebelld
> Against his worthier . . . (VI, 174–80)

Abdiel's retort makes Milton's own first political principle seem axiomatic. We who read are expected to share Abdiel's assumption that from the moment of the Son's presentation to the heavenly hosts Satan and his partisans should have been as sensitive to its bearing upon them as were the loyal angels. Whatever may be said in defence of their personal resentment of sudden subordination to the new head, or of their scepticism about his competence to rule, nothing can be said in defence of their indifference to the principle of obedience to virtue superior to their own. That they should understand as well as Abdiel does. With this thought in mind we may turn to the scene in Eden and to Milton's treatment of human disobedience there.

We may wonder whether Milton thought of Adam and Eve as faced by a prohibition more arbitrary than God's demand for all angels' submission to his Son—whether Milton thought of them as conceptually quite unprepared to respond to the prohibition of the Tree. Of course the situations are not strictly parallel. The first frames a demand for political obedience while the second involves more strictly legal submission. As long as Adam and Eve are alone concerned, they must submit to what the legally-minded theologians called a case of special legislation. Milton stresses the fact that the interdiction is what would in legal parlance be called a case of special legislation quite distinct from any general code of conduct. At the beginning of his chapter 'Of the Fall of our First Parents' in *The Christian Doctrine* (I, xi) he took care to make the distinction clear. First quoting the basic definition of sin in I *John* 3 : 4, 'Sin is ἀνομία, or the transgression of the law', he explained that, 'By the law is here meant, first, the rule of conscience which is innate and engraven on the mind of man; secondly, the special command which proceeded out of the mouth of God, *Genesis*, 2 : 17, "thou shalt not eat of it".' Traditional commentary had focused on the special command. A good sampling of the tradition is found in *A Treatise of Paradise*[5] by John Salkeld, a theologian of mixed Spanish-Jesuit and English-Protestant background, whom James I patronised. Most prominently among the commentaries Salkeld cited St Augustine's view of the prohibited tree as a device 'to teach us through obedience' that we need God's 'power, protection, rule and dominion over us'. And Salkeld agreed with St Gregory in his *Expositio in Job sive Moralium* liber XXXIII, x, that 'the forbidden fruit was not evill of its own nature, but was forbidden to the end, that man being created upright by nature, might increase his righteousness, by the subjection of his nature, and perfection of his obedience to the author of his nature'. No more limpid statement than this could be desired for the doctrine that to preserve his innocence man should presume not God to scan.

For an equally firm assertion much nearer home Milton needed to go no further than his own tutor at Cambridge, Joseph Mede, in the thirty-seventh of his *Discourses on Divers Texts of Scripture* (1664—p. 280). Mede was convinced that, *because* 'the Moral Law was written and engraved on the hearts of our first Parents, . . . God ordained this *Symbolical Law*, prohibiting a thing in itself neither good nor evil, neither pleasing nor displeasing unto God, but indifferent, that man's observance thereof might be a profession and testimony that he was willing to submit himself to God's pleasure, only because it was his pleasure'.

In a theoretical way both Milton and Mede regarded the Moral or Natural Law which was written in Adam's heart as distinct from the interdiction of the Tree of Knowledge. But if, though it was a positive divine law, the interdiction might also be regarded as truly symbolical, then the way opened for its involvement with the classical, Stoic doctrine of the Law of Nature inscribed by a universal mind upon the universe and the hearts of men. Such a way had actually long been recognised. It was familiar in a passage from Tertullian which Salkeld had bracketed with the two that he quoted from Saints Augustine and Gregory. Tertullian called the prohibition of the Tree 'the first principal foundation and ground from which all the [ten] Commandments be virtually included'. This meant a filiation between the peculiar, dictated law to test Adam's obedience in the Garden and the universal

[5] (London, 1617), pp. 148–52.

Stoic Law of Nature engraved on man's heart for interpretation by his Conscience. For classically trained Reformers—men like Melanchthon and Calvin—the Decalogue and the Mosaic Law generally were representative and inclusive of the Law of Nature as they had stood from the time of their first dictation to Moses. So the tabu in the Garden, if not the womb of the Law of Nature, was what Milton might have called connatural with it. Calvin put the thought boldly in his *Institute of the Christian Religion*. After declaring that the Ten Commandments were no less binding than ever on all men, he added that they were confirmed by 'that inward law which we have said to be graven and imprinted on the hearts of all men, and doth after a certain maner, enforme us of the same things that are to be learned from the two tables'. The interpreter of Natural Law was Right Reason, and its Christian counterpart was Conscience. With the least rationalisation of the myth in *Genesis* the tabu on the Tree became what Mede called a 'symbolic law'. It comprehended the prohibition of the Tree but could be hospitable to allegorisations of its breach.

An elaborate allegorisation with which Milton's thought has been compared was that in Henry More's Neoplatonic treatment of Adam as representing the human soul. In his *Philosophic Cabbala* and its *Defense* he treated Eve as 'the Feminine Faculty in the Soul of Man'. This he thought was consistent with Eve's creation out of Adam's body and with their experience in the Garden in the first three chapters of Genesis.[6] No jot or tittle of Scripture was dishonoured, but its inward meaning was modestly and tentatively revealed. More yielded to no commentator in reverence for the letter of Scripture, but he thought the Mosaic record obviously replete with allegory. Milton's respect for Scripture was no less profound, but it might be poetically elaborated and symbolically enriched with the implicit values absorbed into it during the evolution of biblical commentary and hexaemeral literary treatment. In *The Christian Doctrine*, I, x, we find him describing the forbidden Tree as a 'pledge or memorial of obedience (*pignus et monumentum obedientiae*)'. Here the Mosaic tabu is both factual and symbolic. The two conceptions are regarded as congruent. Milton implies a long-established answer to an ancient doubt. It is the reply of Adam himself when Dante questions him in the *Paradiso* (XXVI, 115–17):

---

[6] Scholium to verse 22, chapter 2. The quotation is from More's *Conjectura Cabbalistica: or, A conjectural essay of Interpreting the Mind of Moses in the first three Chapters of Genesis* (Cambridge, 1713; first published in 1653).

> Or, figliuol mio, non il gustar del legno
> fu per sé la cagion di tanto essilio,
> ma solamente il trapassar del segno.

Dante's editors have differed over these lines because he has Adam speak of the forbidden tree as a sign (*segno*) or mark which is overstepped. Rejecting the older view that to Dante the trespass meant simply a proud defiance of God, some commentators have seen it as a defiance of all law, a primal crime seminally replete with all actual crimes. Then Adam's trespass and Satan's engendering of Sin and her offspring emerge as parallel allegories in *Paradise Lost*.

So for Milton Adam's trespass was replete with more kinds of wrongdoing than are named in the Decalogue. According to *The Christian Doctrine*, I, xi, it encompassed far more offences than the ten of the Commandments. In all, eighteen are mentioned in rather haphazard order and with no thought of exhausting the world's catalogue of crimes. The list begins with parricide and includes theft, 'presumption in aspiring to divine attributes, and fraud in the means used to obtain them'. Disobedience stands inconspicuously fourth among them, following ingratitude and preceding gluttony. All alike are named as offences against the Natural Law, 'that rule of conscience which is innate, and engraven upon the mind of man'. The list seems deliberately disorderly. Its disorder reflects that of the crimes themselves. Disorder is their common link. Milton's latent image resembles the overt one in a similar list in Sylvester's translation of Du Bartas' in 'The Imposture', which calls Adam's fault

> a chain where all the greatest sins
> Were one in other linked fast, as Twinns:
> Ingratitude, pride, treason, gluttonie,
> Too-curious skill-thirst, enuie, felonie,
> Too-light, too-late belief; were the sweet baits
> That made him wander from Heav'ns holy straits.
> (*Divine Weekes* (1605), p. 262)

In *A Preface to 'Paradise Lost'* C. S. Lewis drew up a short list of the crimes which were instantly spawned in Eve's mind by the forbidden fruit. He wrote without referring to Milton's list or to disobedience as in any way related to his own. In Lewis's list pride is sire of all the other sins. Its first offspring is Eve's meditated injustice to Adam, which is to amount to tyranny over him. Then his murder becomes a possibility.

Finally, she worships the Tree of Knowledge and is visibly guilty of idolatry.

But neither in *Paradise Lost* nor in *The Christian Doctrine* was Milton interested in any domino theory of the sins comprised in the Fall. For his poetic purpose it was enough that evil was brought to the Earth by its inventors in Heaven. In the poem there are scattered suggestions that the seeds of evil had long been germinating there, but the poem is not the place to speculate about their origin. We are left to imagine it as the almost inevitable degeneration of the ties between any creature—and especially of any magnificent creature—and his creator. Such a study of the autogenesis of evil was made in Jules Douady's *Création et le fruit défendu selon Milton* in 1923. That book could hardly have been written before the development of politico-psychological fiction in the manner of Anatole France. Two years later it was overshadowed by Professor Denis Saurat's well-documented analysis of Milton's ideas about the spiritual causes of political evils on earth.

Now, in a brilliantly reasoned paper called 'Don, Amour, et Sujétion',[7] M. P. Rozenberg puts the creature's ingratitude into the key position among the evils stemming from his alienation from his Maker. As its opposite pole he can find no satisfactory attitude. He rejects obedience and submission (*soumission*) because both are too ambivalently or uncertainly linked with Milton's treatment of love.

In *Paradise Lost* God's love for man may be seriously considered as the theme, for his controlling Providence is omnipresent in the story. But man's love for God is complex. It is oftenest the love of God which is commanded first in the Decalogue, which is the delight of the first psalmist, or which is the essence of the service rendered to an overlord by a feudal vassal in a divinely ruled universe. But the love of God may also be the soul's passionate devotion to the *Summum Bonum* of a philosophical faith, immolating all lesser goods on the altar of the Highest Good and forsaking all earthly beauty to ascend the ladder of love to heavenly beauty. Or it may be the fruit of experience and thought leading to something like Spinoza's intellectual love of God, as Rozenberg believes that Milton well understood.

As a polar opposite to love no single concept or term can serve. Among the list of seventeen 'antecedents' to the Fall of man and the sins comprised in it which Arnold Williams quotes[8] from David

[7] In *Le Paradis Perdu 1667–1967*, ed. Jacques Blondel (Paris, 1967), pp. 105–40.
[8] In *The Common Expositor* (Chapel Hill, 1948), pp. 121–2.

Pareus' *Commentaries on the Genesis of Moses* there is nothing commensurate with any of the kinds of man's love for God—not even with the earthly vassal's love for his heavenly lord. Disobedience is not mentioned. Nor is pride, though the list includes 'detestable ingratitude, depravity of the will, concupiscence of the eyes, . . . idolatry', and the inevitable gluttony that was always attributed to Eve. The evidence in Pareus' *Commentaries* seems to support the conclusion of his modern countryman Max Bertschinger[9] that, 'it must be obvious for a twentieth-century reader that the word disobedience does not cover the case'. We may now wonder whether Milton himself was not of the same opinion—whether his disuse of the word after its last appearance in the prologue to Book IX may mean that he had come to understand its inadequacy.

Pareus did not compile his list of vices in the hope of finding any psychological priority among them. With no intention of that kind, he mentions 'idleness in not cultivating Paradise' as a serious 'antecedent to the sin of Eve'. This is a traditional surmise, worth a moment's digression because it cuts straight across her characterisation in *Paradise Lost*. Such idleness is the one sin impossible in her case, for it was her sincere love of her flowers that served as her plausible pretext for working alone on the day of her temptation. We remember Professor John Crowe Ransom's delightfully serious suggestion that Eve was really so dedicated to her gardening that she fell into the American infatuation with efficiency of all kinds and took the first step towards the merciless efficiency of some of our great industries.

Looking back more generally at Pareus' 'antecedent' sins, it is worth noting that their orientation is medieval and not humanistic—not like the 'Triumph of Unreason over Temperance' which Greenlaw was able in pre-Freudian times to present as the whole dark theme of *Paradise Lost*. With the advance of psycho-analysis Eve's guilt has been dissolving. Even the traditionally accepted narcissism of her first act— admiration of her reflection in a clear lake—is disputed, and so is any crucial guilt in her tasting of the forbidden fruit. Finally the guilt itself has been transformed into innocence by Bertschinger's attempt to turn her experiment with the fruit into a brave, intelligent effort to relieve what she thinks is her husband's morbid preoccupation with its tabu. Eve takes the clear short cut to a cure of Adam's psychosis by testing the fruit's alleged 'mortal taste' on her own tongue and palate. If death does not follow, she and Adam will emerge with some moral advantage

[9] In 'Man's Part in the Fall of Woman', *English Studies*, XXX (1950), 53.

over their divine threatener. If she suffers any penalty, Adam will be immune, and she will have proved herself to be a truly heroic wife. If neither is punished, they will know that they have been guilty of nothing worse than a technical breach of a park rule.

But it was not of anything like a breach of a park rule that Milton thought when in the prologue to Book IX he wrote that he must change his

> Notes to Tragic; foul distrust, and breach
> Disloyal on the part of Man, revolt,
> And disobedience.

After this point the word *disobedience* drops out of the vocabulary of the poem. The Fall is a sin against Reason and is possible only because Adam has failed to grasp Raphael's teaching that Reason is the essence of the soul's being, and that

> in the Soule
> Are many lesser Faculties that serve
> Reason as chief.   (V, 100–2)

The thought and the language itself recall classical ideals of temperance and their embodiment in images like that in the *Phaedrus*, where the soul is compared to a charioteer managing a violent horse hard to control, which is indeed a part of himself like its well-tempered teammate. The virtue symbolised is active and strenuous, but not ascetic. In the Renaissance a more disciplinary conception of it had found its favourite mythological image in Ulysses' restoration of the beasts of Circe to their lost human form. In *A Mask presented at Ludlow Castle* young Milton was severe with the beasts of Circe's son Comus, as the treatment of the Circe myth by the allegorists and the situation in the simple plot obliged him to be. His own tastes were not ascetic, nor were those of Adam and Eve and their heavenly visitor in *Paradise Lost*.

But against the background of pleasure in the world's affluent societies as they are portrayed to Adam by Michael in the eleventh book of *Paradise Lost*, temperance has to be shown as an exacting virtue. Even its ordinary dietetic standards are beyond the moral reach of too many ordinary men, as Adam finds when Michael shows him a prophetic vision of the vast hosts of humanity—more numerous than all the victims of 'violent stroke, . . . Fire, Flood, Famine'—who

> . . . shall die . . . by Intemperance . . .
> In Meats and Drinks which on the Earth shall bring
> Diseases dire.   (XI, 471–4)

If pessimism is a blight on the last two books of the poem, as it has often been said to be, it is grounded upon man's irrational disregard for the rules of temperance, first in diet and then in the pleasures which even in Michael's cinematic display of society before Noah's flood

> attachd the heart
> Of *Adam*, soon enclin'd to admit delight,
> The bent of Nature. (XI, 595–7)

Michael's rebuke of Adam is stern, but not so severe as Milton's when in the Garden—uxoriously or gregariously or devotedly, according to the school of thought about his act to which we belong—his

> Understanding rul'd not, and the Will
> Heard not her lore, both in subjection now
> To sensual Appetite, who from beneath
> Usurping over sovran Reason claimd
> Superior sway. (IX, 1127–31)

II

Beyond Disobedience

Michael's reprimand of Adam and Milton's severe judgement of him are of course for our benefit. Since Milton expected us to profit by them, he must have been to some extent what our radio announcers call 'optimistic' about their effect. Of course he despaired of the great majority of men in history, and especially of those who made history. But neglect of the rules of temperance might be mitigated by changes in men and societies. With better understanding of its principles compliance with them might make progress, and in time the Spirit of Truth might find an increasing response in men's minds. They might discover the full freedom of obedience to Reason, to the Law of Nature, and to God. Such things might still be possible, for Adam had not by any means lost all his power to conceive them. He has perhaps been helped toward imagining such things by Michael's picture of what the world might have become. Eden, he says, but for the Fall, would have been

> Perhaps thy Capital Seate, from whence had spred
> All generations, and had hither come
> From all the ends of th' Earth, to celebrate
> And reverence thee thir great Progenitor. (XI, 343–6)

Instead of having given himself time to conceive such a hope, Adam has destroyed all possibility of its realisation. And now he is to learn of the loss of all hope that men may ever visit Eden and make it the centre of a world-wide society. Michael shows him a vision of Noah's flood and of

> this Mount
> Of Paradise by might of Waves . . . moovd
> Out of his place, pushd by the horned floud,
> With all his verdure spoild, and Trees adrift
> Down the great River to the op'ning Gulf,
> And there take root an Iland salt and bare,
> The haunt of Seales and Orcs, and Sea-mews clang.
>
> (XI, 829–35)

For Adam the scene brings the full poignancy of grief over the physical effects of the Fall. But there is another side to them. If possible, it seems still more sinister, but behind it a principle is at work which is to be the means of man's recovery from the loss of Eden. The penetration of all nature by their violent effect has been shown to us when in Book X (651–4) we learn that

> The Sun
> Had first his precept so to move, so shine,
> As might affect the Earth with cold and heat
> Scarce tolerable . . .

Adam himself has seen that discord, his own discord with Eve and with himself, has spread 'through fierce antipathie' (X, 709) to the stars, the winds, and the beasts around him. He looks at the irreparable physical damage everywhere and sees that Nature's involvement in his Fall is not an imagined pathetic fallacy but actual fact. What he sees is the reverse action of the vital principle which Raphael has taught him in the Garden—the mysterious principle whereby the angel explained that his body and Eve's might

> at last turn all to Spirit,
> Improv'd by tract of time, and wingd ascend
> Ethereal, as wee, or may at choice
> Here or in Heav'nly Paradises dwell;
> If ye be found obedient, and retain
> Unalterably firm his love entire
> Whose progenie you are.
>
> (V, 497–503)

The principle in these lines has been compared with the Neoplatonic vitalism of Pico della Mirandola, the *élan vital* of Bergson, and the faith of Teilhard de Chardin in the evolution of the cosmos from biogenesis through noogenesis to Christogenesis. But its most significant kinship is with the ancient doctrine of the Great Chain of Being in which C. S. Lewis was interested less as a cosmic hypothesis placing man at the middle of creation midway between God's throne and the lowest particle of physical matter than as a setting to exhibit the absurdity of Eve's aspiration to Godhead. For most of us its most familiar application may be to Eve, who twice violates it—the second time by aspiring to superiority to her husband. But for Milton its main application in *Paradise Lost* was to Satan's revolt, and we remember that in Hell Satan himself testified that, as in Heaven,

>   Orders and Degrees
> Jarr not with liberty, but well consist.   (V, 792–3)

On Adam's level the political aspect of the Great Chain of Being is not important, though he may have meditated on Satan's failure to apply it to himself when Abdiel reminded him of it. It is the evolutionary possibility in the Chain of Being which should now vitally interest Adam. Raphael stated it to him over their meal in the Garden:

> O *Adam*, one Almightie is, from whom
> All things proceed, and up to him return,
> If not deprav'd from good, created all
> Such to perfection, one first matter all,
> Indu'd with various forms, various degrees
> Of substance, and in things that live, of life;
> But more refin'd, more spiritous, and pure,
> As neerer to him plac't or neerer tending
> Each in thir several active Sphears assign'd,
> Till body up to spirit work, in bounds
> Proportiond to each kind.   (V, 469–79)

Raphael's speech is most quoted to illustrate Milton's philosophical monism, his faith in the goodness of all matter in itself as finally divine, without reference to the possibility of a general evolution 'upwards' and sometimes downwards. Early editors compared it with one version of the Neoplatonic ladder of increasingly spiritual love of visible beauty in the universe which Spenser stated in *An Hymne of Heavenly Beautie*. Thinking of earth, sea, and air and all that the heavens encompass, he says:

> it plainly may appeare,
> That still as euery thing doth vpward tend,
> And further is from earth, so still more cleare
> And faire it growes, till to his perfect end
> Of purest beautie, it at last ascend.   (43-47)

But Spenser's cosmic spectacle is static and the degrees of heavenly beauty resemble Dante's discrete heavenly spheres more than they do Milton's, where the angels can go between Heaven and Earth on a ladder that looks like Jacob's, and where the evolution of humanity towards angelic being is possible.

There should be interest for us as well as for Adam in Raphael's doctrine of man's physical and spiritual development or evolution as an individual and as a race. In putting it into Raphael's mouth Milton must have known that he was using the Augustinian tradition which is implied in Raphael's encouragement of Adam to think that his flesh might 'at last turn all to Spirit,/Improv'd by tract of time'. In the contemporary tragedy of the Dutch poet Vondel, *Adam in Ballingschap*, a chorus of angels greets Adam and Eve with an ode inviting them as they approach their marriage altar 'in Earth's courts of love [to] Look for a fairer court in Heaven above'. They understand the implicit promise and look forward to peopling the world with immortal beings who will share their earthly novitiate on the way to the fairer court. But now Adam knows that his primal earthly immortality has been lost. He leaves the Garden to begin a life in which he knows that the outstanding event will be Cain's murder of Abel. Ineluctably he is on his way to found a race in whose history for four thousand years the most memorable event will be the Deluge, and whose climax will be the mysteriously redemptive passion of Christ. The angel's explanation of the mystery is the hardly less mysterious warning that he must not think of the promise of the bruising of the serpent's head by the seed of the woman as a prophecy of any kind of physical battle between Christ and the serpent. As a key to that final mystery he accepts the fact that destruction of its works in himself must be the means to a Paradise within him far happier than the lost Garden.

The promise of the inward Paradise is often compared with Piccarda's words to Dante in Heaven: 'In his will is our peace'. It may be better compared with the final words in *Paradise Lost*. The exiled lovers understand enough for them to become the proto-Christians; they know that their quest for the inner Paradise will not be shared by many of their descendants for a long time. They are sensitive to the Law engraved on their own hearts, but they fear that it will not be much honoured by mankind.

I am not suggesting that the last two books of *Paradise Lost* maintain a poetic level corresponding to the hope which the promised Paradise should inspire. Many strong admirers of the poem think that they do not. With Louis Martz they answer 'No' to his question in *The Paradise Within*:[10] 'Can a hundred lines of hopeful doctrine outweigh six hundred lines of visionary woe?' In reply to the rhetorical question Milton could only plead that a main strand in his story was 'tragic' in the simple, medieval sense of the word. The falls of Satan and Adam had been Chaucer's first examples of the genre. Intermixture of the theme of Redemption was not easy. An easy way out of the problem might have been through stress on the apocalyptic possibilities of a utopian eschatology—a resort to the glory of a premature hope of Christ's promised kingdom on earth. It seemed to have Scriptural encouragement, and in *Paradise Lost* there are many carefully controlled echoes of St John's Apocalypse.

Milton chose to put his stress on the very different tradition of pursuit of personal perfection—the effort to restore God's broken image in man. The two traditions could be harmoniously combined, as they were by Milton and many of his contemporaries in proportions corresponding with their variously motivated beliefs. In the impending millennium of Christ's reign on earth the world would return to its primal purity. But in ruthlessly serious entertainment of the hope there was danger. With the beginning of Christ's reign of a thousand years many of the Fifth Monarchy men expected to become powerful in the rule of his saints. Milton's famous friend, Sir Henry Vane, shared that hope and in his *Meditations* looked forward to a civil magistracy ruling with an iron sceptre if it had to be used jointly with Christ's golden one to check deviation from the approved faith and practice of the elect during his reign. Milton's sympathy with all millenarian thinking was limited by his rejection of official control of men's consciences.

We can now go back to Addison's view of *Paradise Lost* as a poem about obedience and disobedience—the obedience that is beyond disobedience. The obedience is in no danger of descending to implicit faith in any human authority or respect for any arbitrary law or tabu. So much is clear from the passage in Book XII warning against corruption of the faith into implicit acceptance of the dogmas and rules of the

[10] (New Haven, 1964), p. 163.

clerks from whose treachery to their vocation society has always suffered. George Williamson[11] looks at 'the education of Adam' as complete when Michael brings him to final understanding of the Law of God:

> Both by obedience and by love, though love
> Alone fulfil the Law.   (XII, 403-4)

Obedience yields to *love* as the right word for what is meant. And the love may be either God's providential love for man or man's devoted but not blind love for God. Or both united.

[11] In *Modern Philology*, LX (1963), p. 108.

'Within the Visible Diurnal Spheare': the Moving World of *Paradise Lost*

Philip Brockbank

Milton is an heir to the prophet Isaiah, with a comparable gift for evoking awed delight when he is performing feats of moral indictment. Therefore it is apt to begin with the prophet proclaiming the fall of the king of Babylon:

> How art thou fallen from heaven, O Lucifer, son of the morning! how art thou cut down to the ground, which didst weaken the nations!
> For thou hast said in thine heart, I will ascend into heaven, I will exalt my throne above the stars of God. (*Isaiah* 14 : 12–13)

That elementary metaphor of light falling into darkness may be counted among the sources of *Paradise Lost*; it was (and is) in touch with the natural phenomenon from which a poet's thinking about moral catastrophe may take its flight. The planet Venus can astonish us still, when it rises as Lucifer in the morning sky and sets as Hesperus in the east; the morning star fades under the stronger light of the sun, and the evening star, we may observe, in terminology ripe for allegory, declines and falls into the dark. It now needs only modest exercise of the allegorising imagination to recognise a correspondence between this cosmic movement, and our moral experience or observation in the territories of ambition, pride and emulation. The poet as prophet (as *vates*, Sidney reminds us) can refine and intensify such analogies until our moral understanding moves in harmony with our alert senses.

It is commonplace to speak of the universal scale and perspective of *Paradise Lost*, and much is known about Milton's sufficient but limited understanding of contemporary astronomical discovery.[1] I wonder,

---

[1] Readers who wish to pursue Milton's astronomy into its details should consult: Grant McColley, 'Milton's Dialogue on Astronomy: The Principal Immediate Sources', *PMLA*, LII (1937), 728–62; A. O. Lovejoy, 'Milton's Dialogue

however, if in these provinces of cosmic law and movement we are sufficiently attentive to Milton's poetic, moral and prophetic transfigurations. Milton seeks to endow the astronomical order with aesthetic and moral validity. He invites us to marvel at the comprehensive splendour and bounty of creation, at its poise, its rhythm, its justice and its miraculous solicitude for human life. I wish to move by way of a display of Milton's fascination with the diurnal rhythms of creation, towards what some may recognise as an eighteenth-century response to the poem. For the poem I am about to describe is the one that, I believe, Christopher Smart admired and imitated:

> tho' no more
> Is Paradise our home, but o'er the portal
> Hangs in terrific pomp the burning blade;
> Still with ten thousand beauties blooms the Earth,
> With pleasures populous, and with riches crown'd.
> Still is there scope for wonder and for love
> E'n to their last exertion—show'rs of blessings
> Far more than human virtue can deserve,
> Or hope expect, or gratitude return.
>
> ('On the Omniscience of the Supreme Being')

Paradise Lost is a sustained epic hymn (more sustained, that is, than any other in the language), a song of praise and adoration and gratitude. But it recognises constraints and limitations; its movement, like that of the creation it describes, is circumscribed by compasses. It declares indeed the compass of human life, and would have us free only within the boundaries of our condition. As Raphael says: 'to know That which before us lies in daily life, Is the prime Wisdom'. That seems, perhaps, too banal a truth; but Milton, I contend, made it momentous.

I begin with some stress on the sensations that Milton excites from the quotidian experience of looking at the night sky. The fall of Lucifer has a long history in moral and theological commentary, but the impulse of Milton's verse returns us to the event in space. Attendant upon the fall are multiplying possibilities of those exhilarating flights through the void, for which Milton's syntax is so fit a vehicle. Take for example

---

on Astronomy', in *Reason and the Imagination,* ed. J. A. Mazzeo (1962), pp. 129–42; Albert R. Cirillo, 'Noon-Midnight and the Temporal Structure of *Paradise Lost*', *ELH*, XXIX (1962), 372–95. I have said less than I might have done about noon in the diurnal round, as it is discussed with much refinement by Cirillo; his essay is reprinted in *Milton's Epic Poetry,* ed. C. A. Patrides (1967).

that proud sentence of Book III describing Satan's precipitant flight from 'the convex of this world's outer orb' towards Paradise:

> Round he surveys, and well might, where he stood
> So high above the circling Canopie
> Of Nights extended shade; from Eastern Point
> Of *Libra* to the fleecie Starr that bears
> *Andromeda* farr off *Atlantick* Seas
> Beyond th' Horizon; then from Pole to Pole
> He views in bredth, and without longer pause
> Down right into the Worlds first Region throws
> His flight precipitant, and windes with ease
> Through the pure marble Air his oblique way
> Amongst innumerable Starrs, that shon
> Starrs distant, but nigh hand seemd other Worlds,
> Or other Worlds they seemd, or happy Iles,
> Like those *Hesperian* Gardens fam'd of old,
> Fortunat Fields, and Groves and flourie Vales,
> Thrice happy Iles, but who dwelt happy there
> He stayd not to enquire.   (555–71)

This is occasioned, not by the fall of the evening star into darkness (that effect will be found elsewhere) but by its decline into the brightness of the western sky. The evening sky offers both the fall of Lucifer and the fable of the Hesperian Gardens—the admonition and the paradisial vision. The 'gardens fair of Hesperus' had already found a significant place in *Comus*, as the haunt of the Attendant Spirit (who delights in the 'liquid air' of the western sky), but here Milton, like Satan, stays not to enquire, and is content with a passing glance at the contiguity between biblical and pagan dream. The movement of the verse has an apt extra-terrestial felicity, letting by so many clauses towards a verb on which there is no pause but a continuing allurement, a 'winding with ease' into fresh motion. And the verbal effects collaborate; 'marble air' is not a frigid oxymoron—its Virgilian sense of 'luminous air' keeps in touch with the evening sky, and serene, smooth movement through it remains both probable and miraculous.

The exhilarations of fall and flight are not the devil's prerogative. Raphael's descent from heaven shares comparable privileges:

> Down thither prone in flight
> He speeds, and through the vast Ethereal Skie

> Sailes between worlds and worlds, with steddie wing
> Now on the polar windes, then with quick Fann
> Winnows the buxom Air. (V, 266–70)

But the sensations of space flight are only vicariously allowed to man. Eve's dreams of flight are at the devil's prompting, and are attended by the hubristic desire to escape human limitations:

> Forthwith up to the Clouds
> With him I flew, and underneath beheld
> The Earth outstretcht immense, a prospect wide
> And various: wondring at my flight and change
> To this high exaltation; suddenly
> My Guide was gon, and I, methought, sunk down,
> And fell asleep. (V, 86–92)

I shall return to Eve's unquiet night. It marks the incipient disturbance of the rhythms of Paradise. But first I wish to establish more fully what those rhythms are, and in what ways they are imaginatively and ethically satisfying.

Lucifer is sometimes called the 'day-star', but Milton's most poignant allusion to the day-star occurs in *Lycidas* where it signifies the sun:

> Weep no more, woful Shepherds weep no more,
> For *Lycidas* your sorrow is not dead,
> Sunk though he be beneath the watry floar,
> So sinks the day-star in the Ocean bed,
> And yet anon repairs his drooping head,
> And tricks his beams, and with new spangled Ore,
> Flames in the forehead of the morning sky. (ll. 165–71)

Lycidas laments the death of a poet in a world flawed by mutability, corruption and catastrophe. Milton's endeavouring art would create elsewhere in the poem a world above the sensory one and refined out of it; but here the poet's craft finds solace in expressing the diurnal movement of the sun. Again, the verse itself moves at a responsive pace—from the inauspicious stress on 'Sunk' precipitating the third line, past the subdued conjunctions opening the next three, to the triumphant verb 'Flames' which brings access of energy long with-held. The reassurance of light and life renewing themselves from darkness and death is offered again in *Paradise Lost*, but here the setting is ampler in time and space, and the related anxieties are more complicated.

The complications are familiar, but I restate them from what may be a less familiar point of view. In the span of Books IV to IX Adam and Eve are encompassed by diurnal harmonies, pervading alike the cosmos and the exquisite detail of their lives. There are, however, points of instability in the creation and the creatures that Satan locates and exploits. The myth persuades us that there is a dark nativity as well as a light, and that chaos and misery can be bred from order and felicity, as well as harmony from confusion. The fall aggravates this radical instability: the omnific word is disobeyed, the cosmic motions are dislocated, the earth tilts on its axis, and death and disease invade the world. Nevertheless, the diurnal rhythm is consolatory still; in changed form it survives the wrack, and life begins again under a new dispensation. The new life cannot be wholly satisfying in itself, but it brings prospect of satisfaction. Let me now restate these observations more amply.

In the Paradise of Book IV the sun presides over a rich and bountiful landscape populated by allegoric presences that move to the measure of Milton's verse:

> aires, vernal aires,
> Breathing the smell of field and grove, attune
> The trembling leaves, while Universal *Pan*
> Knit with the *Graces* and the *Hours* in dance
> Led on th' Eternal Spring. (264–8)

Paradise is without the seasons' change that yields so many of the poet's metaphors, and Milton must endow its 'Eternal Spring' with other modes of variety and excitement. These attend naturally and easily upon its changing times of day. After their 'sweet Gardning labour' Adam and Eve take their rest and prepare their 'Supper Fruits'; their labouring, feasting and nuptial satisfactions move to the same diurnal rhythm. They work together by day and sleep together by night. Eve's love for Adam is expressed through hyperboles that seem both to transcend and to intensify the ceremonious daily round:

> But neither breath of Morn when she ascends
> With charm of earliest Birds, nor rising Sun
> On this delightful land, nor herb, fruit, floure,
> Glistring with dew, nor fragrance after showers,
> Nor grateful Eevning milde, nor silent Night
> With this her solemn Bird, nor walk by Moon,
> Or glittering Starr-light without thee is sweet. (IV, 650–6)

Adam's love responds with a grave and marvelling account of the celestial order, and of the voices that sing to the midnight air (IV, 659-88). Milton in this passage may well be remembering Lorenzo's nocturnal courtship of Jessica in Shakespeare's Belmont; but, together with a comparable eagerness to find cosmic sanction for the tenderness of lovers, there is an austerer purpose: Milton is out to offer a humanly satisfying astronomical teleology. Eve asks disarmingly why the stars continue to shine all night when 'sleep hath shut all eyes', and Adam explains:

> Daughter of God and Man, accomplisht *Eve*,
> These have thir course to finish, round the Earth,
> By morrow Eevning, and from Land to Land
> In order, though to Nations yet unborn,
> Ministring light prepar'd, they set and rise;
> Least total darkness should by Night regaine
> Her old possession, and extinguish life
> In Nature and all things, which these soft fires
> Not onely enlight'n, but with kindly heate
> Of various influence foment and warme,
> Temper or nourish, or in part shed down
> Thir stellar vertue on all kinds that grow
> On Earth, made hereby apter to receive
> Perfection from the Suns more potent Ray.   (IV, 660-73)

The thinking is elementary, but it is not culpably naïve, and it makes an authentic claim, which Milton will struggle to vindicate, that the universe is morally coherent. As it is morally valid, so it is musically and visually satisfying, and consonant with a continuing hymn of praise. The heavenly choirs that celebrate the diurnal motion of the celestial spheres sing Eve's Hymenaean too (IV, 711), and the relationship between human love and the astronomical order is, in this movement of the poem, perfected with the prayer that preludes the 'Rites Mysterious of connubial Love':

> Thus at thir shadie Lodge arriv'd, both stood,
> Both turnd, and under op'n Skie ador'd
> The God that made both Skie, Air, Earth and Heav'n
> Which they beheld, the Moons resplendent Globe
> And starrie Pole: Thou also mad'st the Night,
> Maker Omnipotent, and thou the Day,

> Which wee in our appointed work imployd
> Have finisht happie in our mutual help
> And mutual love, the Crown of all our bliss. (IV, 720–8)

This is a more ceremonious rendering of an awareness that Lawrence in *The Rainbow* makes more actual, but in its impulse no less ideal:

> He went downstairs, and to the door, outside, lifted his face to the rain, and felt the darkness striking unseen and steadily upon him.
> The swift, unseen threshing of the night upon him silenced him and he was overcome. He turned away indoors, humbly. There was the infinite world, eternal, unchanging, as well as the world of life. (Chap. II)

Adam's solicitude and the sun's are one. Eve awakens to tell of her disquieting dream, and after some consolatory talk Adam leads her into the fields, where their Morning Hymn reaffirms the diurnal symmetries through which the goodness and bounty of God are figured forth:

> Thou Sun, of this great World both Eye and Soule,
> Acknowledge him thy Greater, sound his praise
> In thy eternal course, both when thou climb'st,
> And when high Noon hast gaind, and when thou fallst.
> (V, 171–4)

And its final prayer recovers for their thoughts 'Firm peace' and 'wonted calm':

> Hail universal Lord, be bounteous still
> To give us onely good; and if the night
> Have gatherd aught of evil or conceald,
> Disperse it, as now light dispells the dark. (V, 205–8)

In the history of astronomical lyric the hymn lies between Sir John Davies's easy familiarity with the cosmic dance (in *Orchestra*) and Addison's comfortable acclaim of 'The Spacious Firmament on high'; but it has too the psalmodic qualities of Orphic incantation (calming the troubled spirit), of 'holy rapture', looking back to Milton's own Nativity Ode and forward to the hymns and adorations of Christopher Smart. The hymn rejoices in the movements of the world because they yield its plenitude and diversity, but unlike the voice of David (in Psalm 148) the 'prompt eloquence' of Adam and Eve touches the processes by which astronomical motion cherishes life:

> Moon, that now meetst the orient Sun, now fli'st
> With the fixt Starrs, fixt in thir Orb that flies,

> And yee five other wandring Fires that move
> In mystic Dance not without Song, resound
> His praise, who out of Darkness calld up Light.
> Aire, and ye Elements the eldest birth
> Of Natures Womb, that in quaternion run
> Perpetual Circle, multiform, and mix
> And nourish all things, let your ceaseless change
> Varie to our great Maker still new praise. (V, 175–84)

But, delicately, in Paradise the cosmic rhythms remain domestic. The bounties of creation are enjoyed in response to the altitude and azimuth of the sun. When, for example, Raphael sails between world and world, passes the glittering tents of guardian angels, the 'Groves of Myrrhe' and 'Wilderness of sweets', he approaches at noon as Eve is preparing dinner. Adam sits at the door—discerning:

> *Adam* discernd, as in the dore he sat
> Of his coole Bowre, while now the mounted Sun
> Shot down direct his fervid Raies, to warme
> Earths inmost womb, more warmth then *Adam* needs;
> And *Eve* within, due at her hour prepar'd
> For dinner savourie fruits, of taste to please
> True appetite, and not disrelish thirst, (V, 299–305)

The fifty lines that follow allow Eve's hospitality all the resources of the cornucopian world—'Whatever Earth all-bearing Mother yields'; and she makes her dainty choice while the high sun continues to fertilise the ground. Adam invites Raphael to rest in a shady bower:

> and what the Garden choicest bears
> To sit and taste, till this meridian heat
> Be over, and the Sun more coole decline. (V, 368–70)

Raphael accepts with angelic propriety, and the stories of the war in heaven and of the creation discreetly become a part of the domestic day. Some two and a half books (or hours) later, the angel's tales are told; but 'Day is not yet spent' and there is time for Adam to tell his, before Raphael observes:

> the parting Sun
> Beyond the Earths green Cape and verdant Iles
> *Hesperean* sets, my Signal to depart. (VIII, 630–2)

There is much else in the clear hyaline verses of the poem to commemorate and mirror the serenities of morning, noon and night, but it is apt now to review the instabilities of creation that Satan finds and exploits. Just as Satan finds openings for malice in the created forms of toad and serpent, so he finds (like Comus) that darkness and moonlight conduce to seduction and betrayal, and that the springs of Paradise itself can be infected, through a gulf, from rising mist. But there is a more radical instability, within the rhythm of light and darkness itself, and we may locate it early in Raphael's account of the rebellion in Heaven:

> All night the dreadless Angel unpersu'd
> Through Heav'ns wide Champain held his way, till Morn,
> Wak't by the circling Hours, with rosie hand
> Unbarrd the gates of Light. There is a Cave
> Within the Mount of God, fast by his Throne,
> Where light and darkness in perpetual round
> Lodge and dislodge by turns, which makes through Heav'n
> Grateful vicissitude, like Day and Night. (VI, 1-8)

It is a central mystery of the phenomenal world and of our metaphoric thinking that light and darkness seem to be both complementary and contending essences. By one truth, reality is created out of void by the multiple unions of light and shade; by a rival truth the visible world is inescapably fashioned from invincible conflicting opposites, with shade seeking to obscure what light would reveal. We are not now concerned with the theologies that wait upon these perceptions, but with the significance and effect of the related metaphors as Milton uses them. In Raphael's presentation of the onset of the first battle, the morning is at war with the night, and diurnal harmony becomes diurnal discord almost, as the verse takes us back to the evening sky, before our eyes:

> Light issues forth, and at the other dore
> Obsequious darkness enters, till her houre
> To veile the Heav'n, though darkness there might well
> Seem twilight here; and now went forth the Morn
> Such as in highest Heav'n, arrayd in Gold
> Empyreal; from before her vanishd Night,
> Shot through with orient Beams: when all the Plain
> Coverd with thick embatteld Squadrons bright,
> Chariots and flaming Armes, and fierie Steeds
> Reflecting blaze on blaze, first met his view:
> Warr he perceav'd, warr in procinct. (VI, 9-19)

The night momentarily recovers its benign aspect when it 'over Heav'n/Inducing darkness, grateful truce impos'd,/And silence on the odious dinn of Warr' (VI 406–8); but loses it immediately when Satan 'With silent circumspection unespi'd', 'under conscious Night', prepares new instruments of destruction. The sun, that breeds life from the dark earth, and presides over the Paradisial feast of Book IV, does not bring all to light:

> This continent of spacious Heav'n, adornd
> With Plant, Fruit, Flour Ambrosial, Gemms and Gold,
> Whose Eye so superficially surveyes
> These things, as not to mind from whence they grow
> Deep under ground, materials dark and crude,
> Of spiritous and fierie spume, till toucht
> With Heavens ray, and temperd they shoot forth
> So beauteous, op'ning to the ambient light.
> These in thir dark Nativitie the Deep
> Shall yeild us, pregnant with infernal flame,
> Which into hollow Engins long and round
> Thick-rammd, at th' other bore with touch of fire [. . .]
>   (VI, 474–85)

shall 'orewhelm whatever stands Adverse'. There is, then a dark nativity as well as a bright. The earth, Satan finds by night ('conscious' when he ought to be at rest) is pregnant with gunpowder, and this assuredly is an instability in creation.

The Victor Angels rise with the matin trumpets from the dawning hills, after a restful night, but they suffer a setback from the inventions of the wakeful dark, and the battle pauses in exhausting and destructive equilibrium. God recognises the significance of the continuing conflict and resolves to end it:

> Equal in thir Creation they were formd,
> Save what sin hath impaird, which yet hath wrought
> Insensibly, for I suspend thir doom;
> When in perpetual fight they needs must last
> Endless, and no solution will be found:
> Warr wearied hath performd what Warr can do.   (VI, 690–5)

The arrival of the Messiah is like the dawn transcending twilight. The chariots of the Son of God are not the chariots of the Sun, but they are made of light and fire, and move with ease through the 'crystallin sky' to pursue 'the sons of Darkness' out of Heaven. The victory of the sons of Light would seem complete, but for our knowledge of Satan's presence as a toad in Paradise on the eve of Raphael's discourse (he fled with the shades of night), and of his imminent return on the morrow.

The sequence of night and day, then, makes its contribution to some of the more successful passages of the celestial war, and to its encompassing design; but Milton recognises that his skills are at hazard:

> Return me to my Native Element:
> Least from this flying Steed unreind, (as once
> *Bellerophon*, though from a lower Clime)
> Dismounted, on th' *Aleian* Field I fall,
> Erroneous there to wander and forlorne.   (VII, 16–20)

and he recalls his verse to a more secure and familiar movement:

> Half yet remaines unsung, but narrower bound
> Within the visible Diurnal Spheare;
> Standing on Earth, not rapt above the Pole,
> More safe I Sing with mortal voice.   (VII, 21–4)

The stress is again on the calm consolatory divine virtue displayed through the diurnal motion. The mortal voice is still attentive to Urania, Muse of the stars in their courses ('Heav'nlie born,/Before the Hills appeerd') as Milton remembers how as a poet he kept going in his years of blindness, political distress, and cultural alienation:

> In darkness, and with dangers compast round,
> And solitude; yet not alone, while thou
> Visitst my slumbers Nightly, or when Morn
> Purples the East: still govern thou my Song,
> *Urania*, and fit audience find, though few:
> But drive farr off the barbarous dissonance
> Of *Bacchus* and his Revellers, the Race
> Of that wilde Rout that tore the *Thracian* Bard
> In *Rhodope*, where Woods and Rocks had Eares
> To rapture, till the savage clamor drownd
> Both Harp and Voice.   (VII, 27–37)

That bard, of course, was Orpheus. The febrile excitements of the Restoration court would destroy the son of Calliope (Muse of epic poetry) and Milton is at bay. The allusion tunes our ears to Milton's harp and voice as he resumes his own Orphic role, but with a difference.

The difference prompts discussion of a kind of instability located, not in nature of things only, but in available accounts of that nature. It is the circumstance that requires Milton to sing of celestial motion before an audience of both Ptolemaics and Copernicans, or (to put the point more parochially) to write about astronomy for an English public whose convictions were shaped by both Alexander Ross (cosmic conservative, and sometime chaplain to Charles I) and John Wilkins of the Royal Society ('daring and sweet in thought').

Before probing the details, however, we may do well to speculate that Milton would not have been astonished or dismayed had he been exposed to the last three hundred years of astronomical theory and discovery. Destruction in Milton's space is prologue to creation, and the miracle by which a life-sustaining planet might issue from (shall we say) a galactic explosion, is no less remarkable now than was its equivalent then. The most sceptical must still find it as difficult to repudiate, as the devout to recognise, a moral dynamic at work in the inter-galactic void. Milton's space-fiction ('Measuring things in Heav'n by things on Earth') uses the immense resources of moral understanding in the traditions of Jewish, Christian and Classical thought, to contain and display the excitements of the new astronomical learning of his time. But the accomplishment requires the poet's gifts. Take Galileo's presence in *Paradise Lost*, for instance; he is held at once in awe, and in the diminishing perspective of Milton's comprehensive vision of the world:

> the broad circumference
> Hung on his shoulders like the Moon, whose Orb
> Through Optic Glass the *Tuscan* Artist views
> At Ev'ning from the top of *Fesole*,
> Or in *Valdarno*, to descry new Lands,
> Rivers or Mountains in her spotty Globe.   (I, 286–91)

And, in Book V, Raphael sees the earth from the distance that Galileo sees the moon:

> As when by night the Glass
> Of *Galileo*, less assur'd, observes
> Imagind Lands and Regions in the Moon.   (261–3)

The tensions between Ptolemaic and post-Copernican thinking are resolved with comparable art. There is tact in the assignment of rival beliefs to Adam, to Raphael, and to speculative possibility; and there is Milton's fine sense of the relationship between movement and music, playing upon the astronomical technicalities—one might call it his Pythagorean imagination. Adam's intelligence marvels that the stellar motions should be centred on the apparently negligible earth:

> this Earth a spot, a graine,
> An Atom, with the Firmament compar'd
> And all her numberd Starrs, that seem to rowle
> Spaces incomprehensible (for such
> Thir distance argues and thir swift return
> Diurnal) meerly to officiat light
> Round this opacous Earth, this punctual spot,
> One day and night. (VIII, 17–24)

Raphael's beautifully phased and phrased reply embraces a proper angelic condescension, 'To ask or search I blame thee not'; a recognition that might be found discouraging, of the necessary inadequacy of human and angelic knowledge:

> learne
> His Seasons, Hours, or Days, or Months, or Yeares:
> This to attain, whether Heav'n move or Earth,
> Imports not, if thou reck'n right. (VIII, 68–71)

and a sufficient mastery of the 'quaint Opinions' of rival astronomers, expounded under an admonitory ethical precept:

> consider first, that Great
> Or Bright inferrs not Excellence: the Earth
> Though, in comparison of Heav'n, so small,
> Nor glistering, may of solid good containe
> More plenty then the Sun that barren shines,
> Whose vertue on it self works no effect,
> But in the fruitful Earth. (VIII, 90–6)

The possibility that life flourished elsewhere fascinated the more 'roaving' thinkers of the seventeenth century, but I take it that Raphael's questioning, warning voice can still be heard:

> What if the Sun
> Be Center to the World, and other Starrs
> By his attractive vertue and thir own
> Incited, dance about him various rounds? (VIII, 122–5)

> what if sev'nth to these
> The Planet Earth, so stedfast though she seem,
> Insensibly three different Motions move?
> Which else to several Sphears thou must ascribe,
> Mov'd contrarie with thwart obliquities,
> Or save the Sun his labour, and that swift
> Nocturnal and Diurnal rhomb suppos'd,
> Invisible else above all Starrs, the Wheele
> Of Day and Night. (128–36)
>
> What if that light
> Sent from her through the side transpicuous aire,
> To the terrestrial Moon be as a Starr
> Enlightning her by Day, as shee by Night
> This Earth? reciprocal, if Land be there,
> Feilds and Inhabitants. (140–5)

Whatever the possibilities, we are returned to a human centre on this diurnal planet, to its tender, poised, solicitude of movement:

> Whether the Sun predominant in Heav'n
> Rise on the Earth, or Earth rise on the Sun,
> Hee from the East his flaming rode begin,
> Or Shee from West her silent course advance
> With inoffensive pace that spinning sleeps
> On her soft Axle, while she paces Eev'n,
> And bears thee soft with the smooth Air along,
> Sollicit not thy thought with matters hid. (VIII, 160–7)

Once again we sense the continuities between the rhythms of the stars and the rhythms of human affection:

> Of other Creatures, as him pleases best,
> Wherever plac't, let him dispose: joy thou
> In what he gives to thee, this Paradise
> And thy faire *Eve*. (VIII, 169–72)

Creation, however, is not as poised and secure as these passages alone would suggest; the world of Raphael's 'friend with friend' discourse with Adam is still unfallen. What sustains it, we may ask again, and what threatens it? To the answers already entertained, we may now add another of perhaps greater conceptual complexity. It is an axiom of

Old Testament thought that wisdom was, and is, antecedent to creation. The passage of *Proverbs*[2] in which Wisdom itself makes this claim, is the source of Milton's great compass symbol in Book VII:

> When he prepared the heavens, I was there:
>   when he set a compass upon the face of the depth:
> When he established the clouds above:
>   when he strengthened the fountains of the deep.
>
> (*Proverbs* 8: 27–8)

It therefore happens that the *constraint* of chaos, the act of setting bounds upon it, becomes in *Paradise Lost* a condition of life. *Proverbs*, more explicitly than Milton, makes a first principle of the elements' obedience to the ordinance of God:

> When he gave to the sea his decree,
> That the waters should not pass his commandment:
>   when he appointed the foundations of the earth.
>
> (*Proverbs* 8: 29)

If we reflect upon the metaphors of *Proverbs* and of Milton, relating them to what we know of obedience to law in the physical and human world, we may catch a glimpse of the analogue between modes of obedience on which the allegory of *Paradise Lost* largely rests. The omnific word that decrees the laws of motion determines at the same instant the nature of the moral order. It may be said in passing that among Milton's contemporaries, Thomas Hobbes attempted to ground a moral system in a principle of obedience to the laws of motion, but he lacked an astronomical imagination, and his account of motion seems to me to subserve his ethical and political purposes.

In *Paradise Lost* moral offences are attended by mutations in creation; disobedience first in heaven and then on earth, changes the physical nature of the cosmos and its moral teleology. Morally speaking, the first change (the fall of Lucifer and his starry hosts) is towards a more prolific cosmos, creating 'out of one man a Race/Of men innumerable' (VII, 155) who will ultimately inherit 'joy without end'. The second change, following the fall of Adam and Eve, is towards a more tragic but richer fulfilment of the possibilities of human freedom. The corresponding changes in the physical nature of the cosmos are teleological because they are designed to fulfil the precedent moral ends.

---

[2] I quote the Authorised King James version; the gloss against 'a compass' reads, 'Or, a circle'.

It is a defect of the myth that light and darkness are quintessences of Heaven (and mountains and fields among its properties) before the sequence of the narrative allows 'Light Ethereal, first of things' to be created, but it is not a damaging one. Language itself must embody an element of translation of the invisible into the visible, and Milton is at ease with the phenomenon. Book VII deals pre-eminently with the creation of the solar and stellar systems out of chaos—it is God's response to the population loss in Heaven. The effect is to multiply the possibilities of both good and evil—night and day find fresh dominions, and new substances are discriminated in the cosmos. The process is initiated with the inscription of that circle on the deep, but Milton enriches it by ranging from the mechanical bounding of energy (the compasses) to images of incubation—at once formidable and tender:

> Thou from the first
> Wast present, and with mighty wings outspred
> Dove-like satst brooding on the vast Abyss
> And mad'st it pregnant. (I, 18–22)

The incubation is more technically described in Book VII, and it is there that we can recognise a substantial counterpart to the darkness that in the earlier books contends with light:

> but on the watrie calme
> His brooding wings the Spirit of God outspred,
> And vital vertue infus'd, and vital warmth
> Throughout the fluid Mass, but downward purg'd
> The black tartareous cold infernal dregs
> Adverse to life: then founded, then conglob'd
> Like things to like, the rest to several place
> Disparted, and between spun out the Air,
> And Earth self-ballanc't on her Center hung. (VII, 234–42)

The purging of 'black tartareous cold infernal dregs' reminds us of the potential of the universe for 'dark nativity' and is analogous to the principles by which the hell of 'burning marl' in the vast abyss was conceived in Book I. The substantial counterpart of light is 'liquid, pure, Transparent, Elemental Air'. The visible world is therefore attended with new antitypes, new sources of conflict.

The second change in the physical order of the cosmos is described with eloquent precision in Book X. The knowledge of good and evil that contaminates with evasion, shame and guilt, the innocent naked intimacies of Adam and Eve, reacts upon the total system of the world. Why should this be so? Milton has the tact (some of the time) to let the fable carry its own significance, but from its ethical and imaginative sequences we may abstract a variety of answers. We may say that consciousness of good and evil embarrasses, complicates and often destroys human intimacy, as curiosity about the cosmos discovers its disturbing complexities and apparent disorders—and how can we be sure that what consciousness discovers it has not helped to create? Or we may say that since the boundaries of human and cosmic possibility were circumscribed by the same act, human transgression of those boundaries must have cosmic consequences. The great topic or *topos* of which we are now speaking, however, might lead us to recall from Book VIII (150) that 'Male and Femal Light' (Sun and Moon) are the 'two great Sexes' that 'animate the World', and to recognise a richer correspondence between the fall of man and the emergence of the new cosmos—the rhythmic relationships between man and woman grow more complex under the new treaty between diurnal and nocturnal light.

The new cosmos calls for a technical explanation too (Milton delighted in physics) and again the pre-Copernican and post-Copernican possibilities are left side by side, both to be wondered at. The Copernican account finds that the earth moves about the sun at an obliquity to the axis of the ecliptic of 23°27'; while the more antique account takes the apparent movement of the sun across the equinoctial to be real and epicyclical:

>   Som say the Sun
> Was bid turn Reines from th' Equinoctial Rode
> Like distant bredth to *Taurus* with the Seav'n
> *Atlantick* Sisters, and the *Spartan* Twins
> Up to the *Tropic* Crab; thence down amaine
> By *Leo* and the *Virgin* and the *Scales*,
> As deep as *Capricorne*, to bring in change
> Of Seasons to each Clime; else had the Spring
> Perpetual smil'd on Earth with vernant Flours,
> Equal in Days and Nights. (X, 671–80)

The earth, alas, is invaded by weather. 'Thus began Outrage from liveless things', and it is co-incident with other forms of moral catastrophe —the insinuation of fear, terror, suffering, sin and death, variously among animals and men, the creatures as the creation.

The dislocation of the cosmic diurnal movement is attended by dislocations of the human one. The passage in Book IV that dwells on the mysterious satisfactions of evening light may be called to witness, with its grave postscript where Adam tells Eve that they must sleep. With that caressing gravity, so fitting in a world where man and angel talk together, and which is the source of so much of the poem's indulgent good humour, Adam makes the delight of sleep almost a cosmic obligation:

>   Fair Consort, th' hour
> Of night, and all things now retir'd to rest
> Mind us of like repose, since God hath set
> Labour and rest, as day and night to men
> Successive, and the timely dew of sleep
> Now falling with soft slumbrous weight inclines
> Our eye-lids.   (IV, 610–16)

The night of Book X is, in contrast, a physical and moral ordeal; Adam's stricken psyche finds torment in the dark:

> Thus *Adam* to himself lamented loud
> Through the still Night, not now, as ere Man fell,
> Wholsom and cool, and mild, but with black Air
> Accompanied, with damps and dreadful gloom,
> Which to his evil Conscience represented
> All things with double terror: On the ground
> Outstretcht he lay, on the cold ground, and oft
> Curs'd his Creation.   (X, 845–52)

The 'cold infernal dregs' are again a presence in the creation from which they were cast down, and they contaminate and afflict the human consciousness.

When Michael makes his prophetic survey of the human state after the fall, he tells of many that shall suffer extremities of deprivation and pain; but even those more fortunate, he warns Adam, must undergo the distresses of age:

> So maist thou live, till like ripe Fruit thou drop
> Into thy Mothers lap, or be with ease
> Gatherd, not harshly pluckt, for death mature:
> This is old age; but then thou must outlive
> Thy youth, thy strength, thy beauty, which will change
> To witherd weak and gray.   (XI, 535–40)

'A melancholy damp of cold and dry' waits to weigh our spirits down, and 'last consume/The Balme of Life'. It is not difficult to recognise here the specific exacerbations of Milton's old age, together with its heroic sense of life-transcending purpose; like Adam, Milton can patiently attend his dissolution. But the bleakness and nihilism that will loom in *Paradise Regained* and in *Samson Agonistes* is kept at its proper distance in *Paradise Lost*, in part by Michael's injunction:

> Nor love thy Life, nor hate; but what thou livst
> Live well, how long or short permit to Heav'n: (XI, 553–4)

and in part by the conviction that eternal life will prevail over pain and confusion. The conviction springs less fully than it might from Milton's understanding of the Divine and human sacrifice, enacted and symbolised by the death and resurrection of Christ.

I hope no astringent and watchful theologian will call me to account for this, I hope, traditional and acceptable way of putting it; for I speak of the effects of the poem rather than of its doctrines, and in particular of the effects owed to its handling of diurnal rhythms. The divinely human love of Jesus is, from this point of view, less present in our experience of the poem than it might have been. Milton relies on metaphors of creation and re-creation, and on the renewal of human affection (momentarily shattered), to convey the divinely heroic ends of life.

Book X ends with the renewal of life and hope for Adam and Eve out of their imminent despair. 'Childless thou art', cries Eve with nihilistic resolution:

> Childless remaine: So death
> Shall be deceav'd his glut, and with us two
> Be forc't to satisfie his Rav'nous Maw. (989–91)

But Adam sees that this is not an authentic self-effacing disdain of life:

> But self-destruction therefore sought, refutes
> That excellence thought in thee, and implies,
> Not thy contempt, but anguish and regret
> For loss of life and pleasure overlov'd. (X, 1016–19)

He goes on to see new possibilities and opportunities in the asymmetries of the post-lapsarian world: Eve's pain in childbirth will be compensated by its joy; Adam's labour will be hard but sustaining; the new ordeals of the weather, and of the extremities of night and day, will occasion new discoveries of the potentials of creation. Adam, our primordial technologist, retaining his prelapsarian wonder and *gravitas*, but now more bent on practical needs, plans to light a fire before it gets dark:

> ere this diurnal Starr
> Leave cold the Night, how we his gatherd beams
> Reflected, may with matter sere foment,
> Or by collision of two bodies grinde
> The Air attrite to Fire. (X, 1069–73)

The next dawn over the fallen world is consolatory still, and brings promise of continuing contentment:

> for see the Morn,
> All unconcerned with our unrest, begins
> Her rosie progress smiling; let us forth,
> I never from thy side henceforth to stray,
> Wherere our days work lies. (XI, 173–7)

But the illusion cannot last, and its end is prefigured by the coming of Michael in a movement of light contrary to diurnal expectation:

> Who knows, or more then this, that we are dust,
> And thither must return and be no more.
> Why else this double object in our sight
> Of flight persu'd in th' Air and ore the ground
> One way the self-same hour? why in the East
> Darkness ere Dayes mid-course, and Morning light
> More orient in yon Western Cloud that draws
> Ore the blew Firmament a radiant white,
> And slow descends, with somthing heav'nly fraught.
> (XI, 199–207)

The banishment from Paradise is decreed; the idyllic scene that was once actual becomes a dream, plangently and nostalgically remembered:

> Must I thus leave thee Paradise? thus leave
> Thee Native Soile, these happie Walks and Shades,
> Fit haunt of Gods? where I had hope to spend,
> Quiet though sad, the respit of that day
> That must be mortal to us both. O flours,
> That never will in other Climat grow,
> My early visitation, and my last

> At Eev'n, which I bred up with tender hand
> From the first op'ning bud, and gave ye Names,
> Who now shall reare ye to the Sun, or ranke
> Your Tribes, and water from th' ambrosial Fount?
>
> (XI, 269–79)

Michael counsels patience, detecting in Eve's voice a strain of self-regard:

> Lament not *Eve*, but patiently resigne
> What justly thou hast lost; nor set thy heart,
> Thus over-fond, on that which is not thine;
> Thy going is not lonely. (XI, 287–90)

And for this span of the poem (that is, from Michael's appearance to the end of his Old Testament narrative) the dominant idea of virtue is classical (often Stoic) calling for the exercise of fortitude, patience, moderation, temperance and self-control. The voices of praise are muted or subdued. The diurnal rhythm, however, keeps its sway: the evening star, 'Love's Harbinger', rises over the revellers in the tents of wickedness (XI, 588); the sun dries up the deluge, and the rainbow promises that:

> Day and Night,
> Seed time and Harvest, Heat and hoary Frost
> Shall hold thir course, till fire purge all things new,
> Both Heav'n and Earth, wherein the just shall dwell.
>
> (XI, 898–901)

    Book XII opens with a pause in Michael's discourse (added in the second edition), 'As one who in his journey bates at Noone'; a pause 'Betwixt the World destroyd and World restor'd'—a line that offers another description of the poem's movement. The world restored by Noah's surviving kin is ravaged by Nimrod, whose arrogation of 'Dominion undeserv'd' is in the high and mighty line from Lucifer to Charles I; but it is reclaimed to the rule of law by Moses and the Israelites in the wilderness.

    None of these lesser recessions and renewals of divine life in man, however, is graced with metaphors of returning light, which are reserved (perhaps deliberately withheld) until Christ rises again on the third day:

> so he dies,
> But soon revives, Death over him no power

> Shall long usurp; ere the third dawning light
> Return, the Starres of Morn shall see him rise
> Out of his grave, fresh as the dawning light. (XII, 419–23)

If it is a less climatic passage than it might have been, it is because the dawn is not unique enough (in the poem) adequately to mark what Michael's next pause recognises as 'the Worlds great period'. But Adam can fittingly acclaim the event as:

> more wonderful
> Then that which by creation first brought forth
> Light out of darkness! (XII, 471–3)

Thus it comes about that Adam, from Michael's sombre but—let us reclaim the bruised word—*uplifting* vision, Adam can depart 'Greatly instructed . . . in peace of thought'. Eve has been similarly composed by sleep. They are ready, hand in hand, to take their solitary way. But it is for us to notice that the descending Cherubim signal their departure by way of a diurnal metaphor:

> on the ground
> Gliding meteorous, as Ev'ning Mist
> Ris'n from a River ore the marish glides,
> And gathers ground fast at the Labourers heel
> Homeward returning. (XII, 628–32)

But the western sky bears now the 'brandisht Sword of God'; for Adam and Eve there is no 'homeward returning'; the freedom of the world is open to them, but as darkness comes on they must still choose their place of rest.

I have tried to let the poem make its own presence felt by disengaging one of its topics, but I have exhausted neither the topic nor the poem.[3]

---

[3] Literary treatments of the diurnal topic are inexhaustible, but a larger essay about them would include much from Virgil (e.g. *Aeneid,* IV, 522 ff.), from Dante (e.g. *Inferno,* II, i ff.), and from Shakespeare (e.g. *3 Henry VI,* II, v, 1–40). For some lyric treatments see Donne's 'Good Friday, 1613. Riding Westward', Vaughan's 'The Night', Blake's 'Night' (*Songs of Innocence*), and Wordsworth's 'A slumber did my spirits seal'. Donne's poem is discussed by A. B. Chambers, *ELH,* XXVIII (1961), 45–46. For a rival treatment of the Paradisial world and its fall, including a highly imaginative and resourceful account of the physical and moral history of both the fall and the deluge, see Thomas Burnet, *The Sacred Theory of the Earth* (1681–9).

I would wish to be among those who, three hundred years later, find *Paradise Lost* still alive in their consciousness of the astronomical and moral coherence of things. In spite of its lapses, its occasional weariness, its confession of certain human inadequacies, the poem (if we reflect upon it) makes a continuing contribution to the sum of tenderness, fealty and intellectual adventure in the world.

SPECIAL CONTRIBUTION

The Iconography of the Fall of Man

J. B. Trapp

> . . . What *Adam* dreamt of when his Bride
> Came from her Closet in his side:
> Whether the Devil tempted her
> By a *High Dutch* Interpreter:
> If either of them had a navel;
> Who first made Musick malleable:
> Whether the Serpent at the Fall
> Had cloven feet, or none at all . . .   Samuel Butler, *Hudibras*

At intervals along the path up the Sacro Monte at Varallo Sesia are forty-three chapels, constructed and embellished at various times from the sixteenth to the nineteenth century. They tell, by means of life-size wood and plaster figures standing on their floors and frescoes painted on their walls, the story of the life and death of Christ, beginning with the Annunciation and culminating in the Last Judgement in the cupola of the basilica at the summit. The first of the chapels, however, does not belong to the New Testament at all: it portrays the Fall of Man, so that the story of Redemption opens with the event that made the Sacrifice necessary: 'as in Adam all die, even so in Christ shall all be made alive'.[1]

Grateful acknowledgement is made to the following for permission to reproduce objects in their ownership or charge: the Earl of Crawford and Balcarres; the Trustees of the British Museum; the Bodleian Library; Stichting Johan Maurits van Nassau, The Hague; Bibliothèque nationale, Paris; Bayerische Staatsbibliothek, Munich; Kupferstichkabinett der Landesgalerie, Stuttgart; the Courtauld Institute, London.

[1] There is no satisfactory account of the iconography of the Fall, any more than any comprehensive history of Old Testament illustration (cf. n. 3 below).

At Varallo, Adam and Eve stand on either side of an apple tree, round which is twined the Serpent. Eve hands the forbidden fruit to Adam across the tree. Animals cluster about the pair, while on the wall behind are also frescoed God forbidding them to taste of the tree and Adam and Eve hiding themselves in the Garden.[2]

I use this somewhat provincial and late, but engaging, example both because it makes use of the most common visual formula for picturing the Fall itself—borrowed, as we shall see, from pre-Christian antiquity —i.e. that which shows our first parents one on either side of a serpent-entwined tree; and because it serves to press home the point that, in any work of art made by or for a Christian which portrays the Fall, there must always be a more or less explicit proleptic reference to Redemption and/or Judgement.

In art-historical terms this means that it almost invariably forms part of a cycle, full and sequential or condensed and episodic, which may

---

This essay is no more than a sketch and summary, much indebted to the help of L. D. Ettlinger, Otto Kurz and C. A. Patrides. Useful collections of material are: T. Ehrenstein, *Das Alte Testament im Bild* (Vienna, 1923), pp. 37 ff. (out-of-date, with indifferent reproductions); *The Old Testament in Art*, ed. M. Brion with notes on the plates by H. Heimann (London, 1956), pls. 1 ff. Both these aim to cover the field from early Christian times to the present. The entries *Adam und Eva, Baum*, and others, in the *Reallexikon zur deutschen Kunstgeschichte* (Stuttgart-Munich, 1938 ff.—which has reached only the letter F—are, though not even in quality, always informative and often extend beyond the art of Germany itself. L. Réau, *Iconographie de l'art chrétien*, vol. ii, part 1 (Paris, 1956), pp. 77 ff., is the fullest of the manuals, and the most recent H. Aurenhammer, *Lexicon der christlichen Ikonographie* (Vienna, 1959 ff.—in progress), *s.v. Adam und Eva* etc.; but still indispensable are K. Künstle, *Ikonographie der christlichen Kunst*, vol. i (Freiburg i. B., 1928), pp. 259 ff.; and W. Molsdorf, *Christliche Symbolik der mittelalterlichen Kunst* (Leipzig, 1926). The best recent surveys are Sigrid Esche, *Adam und Eva. Sündenfall und Erlösung* (Düsseldorf, 1957), and E. M. Vetter, 'Necessarium Adae peccatum', in Ruperto-Carola, xxxix (1966), 144–81, superseding e.g. L. A. Breymann, *Adam und Eva in der Kunst des christlichen Altertums* (Wolfenbüttel, 1895), and J. Kirchner, *Die Darstellung des ersten Menschenpaares in der bildenden Kunst* (Stuttgart, 1903). J. Flemming, *Die Ikonographie vom Adam und Eva in der Kunst von 3. bis zum 13. Jh.*, Diss., Jena, 1953, unpublished, was not available to me.

[2] The chapel of the Fall was constructed in 1567. It contains statues by Tabacchetti and Michele Prestinari, both of the seventeenth century; and its frescoes are by Domenico Alfano (sec. xvi) and Francesco Burlazzi (sec. xix). See P. Angelo Trovati, *Il Sacro Monte di Varallo, Guida illustrativa* (Varallo, 1963), and Marziano Bernardi, *Il Sacro Monte . . . Varallo* (Turin, 1960). The account by Samuel Butler, *Ex Voto* (London, 1888), is agreeable reading.

take in all or part of the Old Testament narrative before passing to the antitypes of the New, or may content itself with this single scene by way of preamble to the story of Salvation, with the events of *Genesis* 3 : 1–24, or even of *Genesis* 1 : 1 to 3 : 24, often condensed into one picture. Such cycles more frequently represent the story in the order of the Biblical narrative, or of the liturgy, or of the devotional practices of the Church in outline rather than convey much in the way of doctrinal subtlety. Sometimes, then, Creation and Fall, with succeeding events, are given full and detailed expression as equal components in a series ending in Crucifixion, Resurrection or Last Judgement. Sometimes the whole drama of Salvation is condensed into a single picture: Salvation, or its means, writ large, but its antecedent crime merely stated, as it were, in the margin. This, and the multiplicity of monuments on which the Fall is shown, are what makes it difficult to compress the essential iconography of the Fall of Man into a small space and to write its history without at the same time writing a history of Old Testament illustration, or even the history of Christian art itself. I shall have to select most rigorously, but I hope that what follows, being intended for literary rather than art historians, will have some use as an indication of the works of art that are most important and typical in the tradition of Old Testament illustration in particular.[3]

For each example, I have tried to give in the footnotes a reference to the most recent and comprehensive book or article. I go no further in time than the seventeenth century for two reasons. First, there is little or nothing in the way of innovation or of iconographic interest in representations after this; and second, since this account forms part of a volume on Milton, there seems little point in carrying it beyond him. The illustrators of *Paradise Lost* I likewise leave on one side.[4]

---

[3] There is no satisfactory general account of Old Testament illustration and its history. M. R. James, *The Illustration of the Old Testament*, in introduction to S. C. Cockerell, *A Book of Old Testament Illustrations of the thirteenth Century* (Roxburghe Club, 1927), though now a little outdated, is still useful.

[4] They have been catalogued by C. H. Collins Baker, in *The Library*, 5th ser., III (1948), 1–21, 101–19. On the first and undistinguished illustrator, J. B. Medina, see Helen Gardner, in *Essays and Studies*, IX (1956), 27–38 (reprinted in her *A Reading of 'Paradise Lost'* [Oxford, 1965], pp. 121 ff.). On John Martin, see Kester Svendsen in *Studies in English Literature*, I, i (1961), 63–74; and on Fuseli and Martin Ruthven Todd, *Tracks in the Snow: Studies in English Science and Art* (London, 1946). On the Expulsion see Merritt Y. Hughes in *Journal of English and Germanic Philology*, LX (1961), 670–79.

I

Reference to the Redemption in picturings of the Fall, then, may be taken to be always present. Thus on the Ghent altar-piece by van Eyck, for instance, the upper right and left of the extended wings show the single figures of Adam and Eve, with the figure of God the Father in the centre above and the Mystic Lamb below.[5] So too the Malvagna triptych by Mabuse[6] shows our first parents in the Garden entwined with each other and reaching up into the tree for the fruit, with the Expulsion in the background—all this on its outside: within is the Madonna enthroned with the Child, and saints in Paradise. The door closed by Adam and Eve is opened by Christ and the Virgin. Likewise on the podium of Mantegna's Madonna della Vittoria, in the Louvre (Pl. 1), is pictured the Fall, quite small and in grisaille, the antecedent of the triumphant pair above.[7]

Even the very earliest surviving illustrations of the Fall reflect the prolepsis. The wall-paintings in the catacombs of Rome[8] and in the Christian baptistery at Dura Europos[9] in the Syrian desert, half-way between Aleppo and Baghdad on the bank of the Euphrates, which date from the beginning of the third century onwards and are the representatives of the Western and the Eastern traditions—together with the

[5] Ghent, S. Bavon; reprod. L. Baldass, *Jan van Eyck* (London, 1952), Cat. no. 1, pls. 14 ff.

[6] Palermo, Galleria Nazionale della Sicilia, Inv. no. 75; R. Delogu, *La Galleria nazionale della Sicilia* (*Itinerari dei Musei, Gallerie e Monumenti d'Italia*), 1962, pls. 71–72 (open); *Jan Gossaert genaamd Mabuse*, Catalogue of the Exhibition at Rotterdam and Bruges (1965), plates 1a–c.

[7] Painted in 1495 for Gian Francesco Gonzaga. E. Tietze-Conrat, *Mantegna* (London, 1954), pp. 194–5, plates 126–8.

[8] P. Testini, *Le Catacombe e gli antichi cimiteri cristiani in Roma* (Bologna, 1966), the most recent handbook, has excellent bibliographies for each catacomb and a handy list of publications on the iconography of the various subjects represented in the wall-paintings, not including the Fall. It does not replace the older standard works, such as J. Wilpert, *Die Malereien in den Katakomben Roms* (Freiburg i. B. 1903; also published in Italian at Rome in the same year), and P. Styger, *Die römischen Katakomben. Archäologische Forschungen über den Ursprung und die Bedeutung der altchristlichen Grabstätten* (Berlin, 1933), but it allows the student to bring these works up to date where necessary.

[9] See now Carl H. Kraeling, *The Christian Building* (*The Excavations at Dura-Europos, Final Report*, viii, 2; ed. C. B. Welles), New Haven 1967, pp. 55–57; 200–2; 214–15; 231–2; pls. xvii–xlv.

early Christian sarcophagi, which are a mixture of both—are already evidence of this. Opinion varies on which is the first in point of time. It may be the painting in the *cubicolo superiore* of the Ipogeo degli Aureli in Via Luzzatti at Rome, of between A.D. 161 and 235, and perhaps Gnostic.[10] Here Adam and Eve stand together to the left of the tree, Eve closer to it. They are turned, even seem to step, towards it, as if eager to taste, and a small Serpent rises at Eve's feet, its mouth open, to allow its forked tongue to be seen. (This detail, according to Wilpert, was an indication of the Gnostic character of the paintings in the Ipogeo: it indicated that the Serpent was speaking to Eve and imparting to her the true *gnosis*. But cf. p. 228 below.) Such an asymmetrical arrangement of our first parents and the tree, though less common than the symmetrical—with the pair placed one on either side of the tree— is nevertheless not infrequent, especially in the earliest period of Christian art. The scene in the Ipogeo degli Aureli is important both because of its early date and because it exemplifies the tendency, in picturing the the Fall, to contract or telescope the episodes of the Temptation of Eve, the Temptation of Adam, the Fall itself, and the Hiding of Nakedness, into one or at most two scenes. Especially noticeable in early Christian art, the tendency never really loses its strength. A similar scene to that in the Ipogeo degli Aureli is found in one of the niches in Gallery K of the catacomb of Sta Priscilla in Via Salaria at Rome, dating from the end of the third or beginning of the fourth century, which is so badly damaged that all that can be made out is the figure of Eve, full-face to the spectator, hiding her nakedness with a leaf or leaves.[11] To the right is the Serpent, as if raised on its tail—whether merely to give it prominence or to suggest that it has not yet suffered the effect of God's curse. To the right of the Serpent is the tree and to the right of the tree Jonah, the prophet of Christ, reclines under his gourd. Similarly, in the catacomb of SS Marcellino e Pietro in Rome,[12] the fourth-century painting shows the pair, clutching their aprons to them and turned towards one another, on either side of the tree, round which the Serpent

[10] Near Via Manzoni. Testini, *Le Catacombe* . . ., p. 157; J. Wilpert, 'Le Pitture dell'Ipogeo degli Aureli presso il Viale Manzoni in Roma', in *Atti della Pont. Accademia Romana di Archeologia*, ser. iii, Memorie, vol. i, part ii (Rome 1924), pp. 1 ff., 10; fig. 4, pl. 1; C. Cecchelli, *Monumenti cristiani-eretici di Roma* (Rome, 1944), pp. 82 ff., pl. iii.

[11] Testini, pp. 166–7 and the literature cited there; Wilpert, *Malereien*, pl. lxx, 2.

[12] Testini, pp. 157–9; C. Cecchelli and E. Persico, *SS. Marcellino e Pietro. La Chiesa e la Catacomba* [*Le Chiese di Roma illustrate*, xxxvi] (Rome, 1938), p. 83, fig. 14; Esche, *Adam und Eva*, pl. 5.

is twined, his head half-way down it close to the right hand of Eve, which seems to be brazenly indicating it to Adam, whose eyes are modestly downcast.

Earlier than any of the catacomb paintings may be those in the barrel vault of the aedicula, on the west wall, of the Christian baptistery at Dura Europos,[13] showing the Fall of Man below (Pl. 2) and the Good Shepherd above, which date from the very early years of the third century. (The Fall pictured in the catacomb of S. Gennaro in Naples,[14] which belongs to the same iconographic type as that of Dura Europos, may also antedate the representation in the Ipogeo degli Aureli. No serpent is visible. It may also perhaps be worth noting here that the catacomb paintings, and indeed all the earliest Christian wall-paintings of the Fall, do not show the Serpent as proffering the fruit to Eve in its mouth. This detail, as far as I can discover, occurs only on the sarcophagi among the earliest monuments of Christian art). What may be called, then, the Dura Europos type is next to invariable in Western art for well over a thousand years—at least as regards the placing of Adam and Eve. Its treatment of the Serpent rapidly and almost invariably gives way to that which shows the creature twined about the Tree and offering the forbidden fruit to Eve, by way of its mouth in the early representations, and often, after the twelfth century, by way of the hand which it has acquired along with its human head or torso (see below, p. 262). The Dura painting, it is now argued, was an addition to the original decorative scheme of the baptistery, introducing an element which makes that scheme conform more closely to the theology current in the churches of the contemporary Mediterranean world. The pair are shown in a garden, flanking a central tree on which grow two dark red fruit, and themselves flanked at the edges of the scene by the trunks of trees which were formerly taken for the walls of the terrestrial Paradise. They stand, full-face, Eve, slightly the smaller, to the left. Leaves cover their genitals and each raises the arm nearer the Tree to reach into its branches. A long Serpent slithers away on the left—a specifically Eastern feature. The space to the right of this scene is empty and may have been intended for an Expulsion.

Variations on this basic formula are many, even in early Christian art. The scene in the S. Gennaro catacomb, for example, omits the serpent, and Adam and Eve are not reaching into the branches; and

[13] Kraeling, *Christian Building*, pl. xxxii, 1 and 3. I summarise Kraeling's account of the content and meaning of the Fall painting, below, pp. 231.

[14] H. Achelis, *Die Katakomben von Neapel* (Leipzig, 1936), p. 44, pl. 8.

1 Mantegna, *Madonna della Vittoria*. Paris, Louvre.

2 *Fall of Man*. Dura Europos, Christian Chapel, wall-painting.

3 *'Adam and Eve'*. (*below left*) Cameo. Paris, Bibliothèque Nationale, Cabinet des médailles.

4 *Fall of Man*. Detail from the sarcophagus of Junius Bassus. Vatican, Grotte Vaticane.

5 *Temptation of Eve, Fall of Man, Rebuke, Expulsion and Toil of Adam and Eve,* from the Grandval Bible. London, British Museum, MS. Add. 10546, fol. 5v.

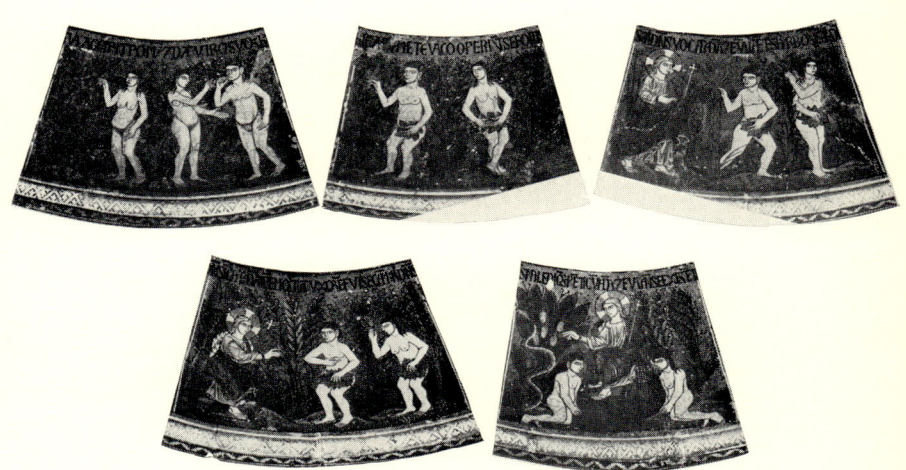

6 *Temptation* and *Fall of Man.* Detail from the mosaics of the narthex, Venice, S. Marco.

7 *Temptation* and *Fall of Man.* Octateuch. Istanbul, Seraglio Library, cod. viii, fol. 43v.

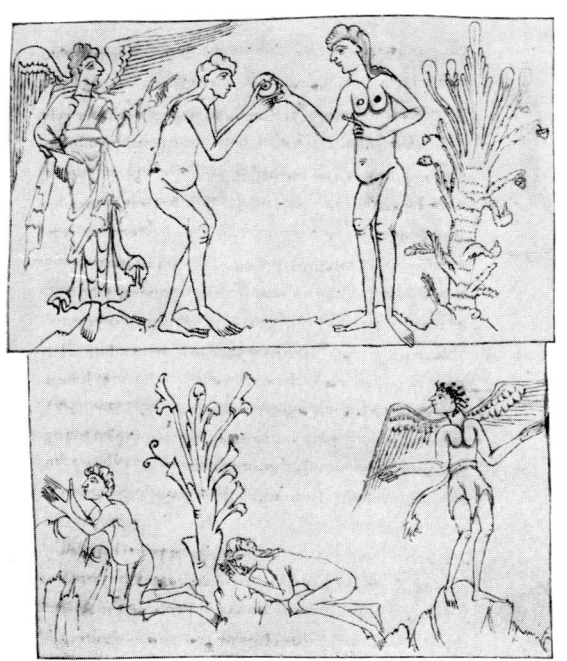

8 *Temptation* and *Fall of Man* from the 'Caedmon' MS. Oxford, Bodleian Library, MS. Junius xi, p. 31.

9 *Fall of Man* from the St Albans Psalter, Hildesheim, St Godehard, p. 17.

10 *Temptation of Eve, Fall of Man, Rebuke* and *Expulsion*, from the *Très riches heures du duc de Berry*. Chantilly, Musée Condé, MS. 1284 [65], fol. 25v.

11 Fall of Man and moralizations, from the *Bible moralisée (Gen.* 3). Oxford, Bodleian Library, MS. Bodl. 270b, fol. 7v.

12 Temptation of Eve, from *Speculum humanae salvationis.* Paris, Bibliothèque Nationale, MS. lat. 9584.

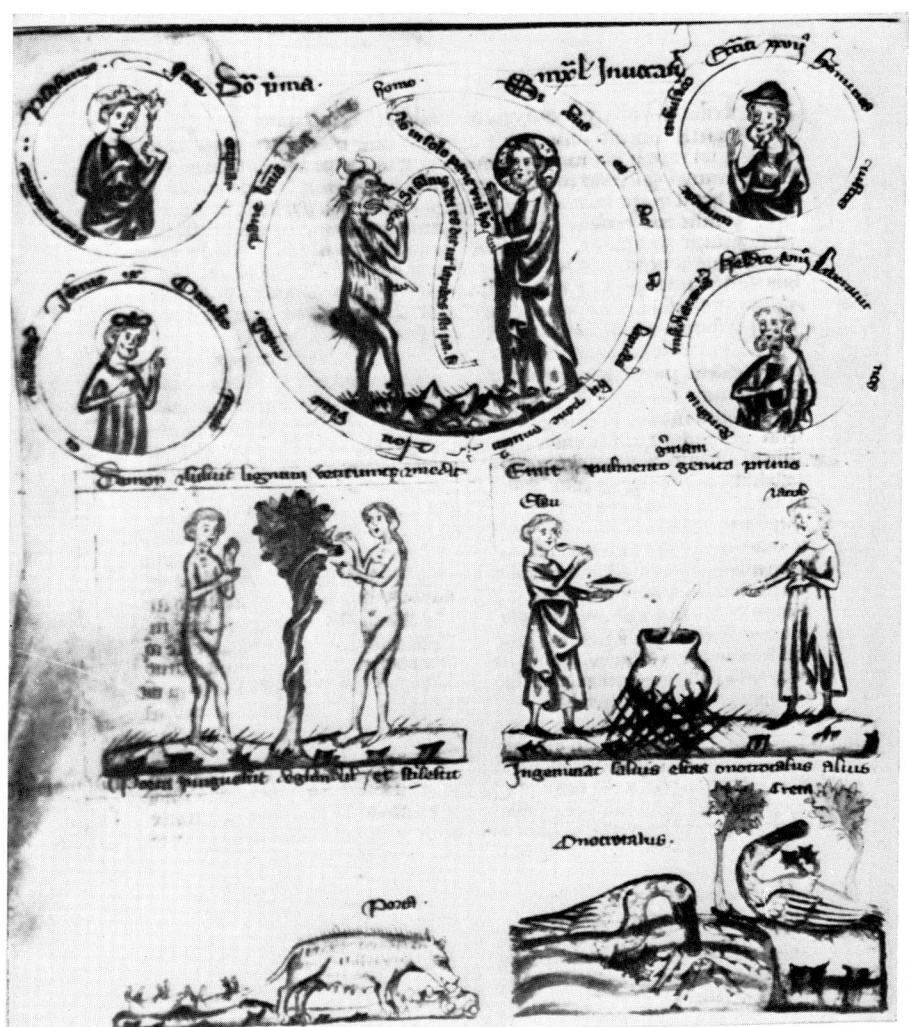

13 The First Temptation of Christ and its types, from the *Concordantia caritatis*. Lilienfeld, Stiftsbibliothek, MS. 151, fol. 33.

14 *Fall of Man* and *God's Rebuke of Adam and Eve*. Hildesheim Cathedral, bronze door, detail.

15 Ghiberti, *Creation of Adam and Eve, Fall* and *Expulsion*. Panel from the 'Porta del Paradiso' of the Baptistery, Florence.

 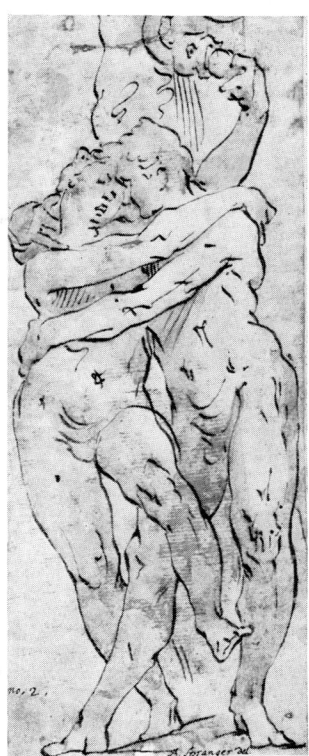

16 Dürer, *Fall of Man*. (*above left*) Woodcut from the *Small Passion*.

17 Bartholomaeus Spranger, *Adam and Eve*. (*above right*) Drawing. Stuttgart, Kupferstichkabinett.

18 Michelangelo, *Fall and Expulsion*. (*below*) Vatican, Sistine Chapel, Ceiling fresco.

19 Raphael, *Fall of Man*. Vatican, Stanza della Segnatura, Ceiling.

20 Titian, *Fall of Man*. Madrid, Prado Museum.

21 Rubens (with Jan Breughel), *Paradise*. The Hague, Mauritshuis.

22 Tintoretto, *Fall of Man, with Expulsion*. Venice, Accademia.

23 Hans Holbein the Younger, *Fall of Man* and *Toil of Adam and Eve*. Woodcuts from the Dance of Death—Old Testament suite.

24 Rembrandt, *Fall of Man*. Etching.

25 Berthold Furtmeyer, *Tree of Life and Death*. Munich, Staatsbibliothek, clm 15710, fol. 60v.

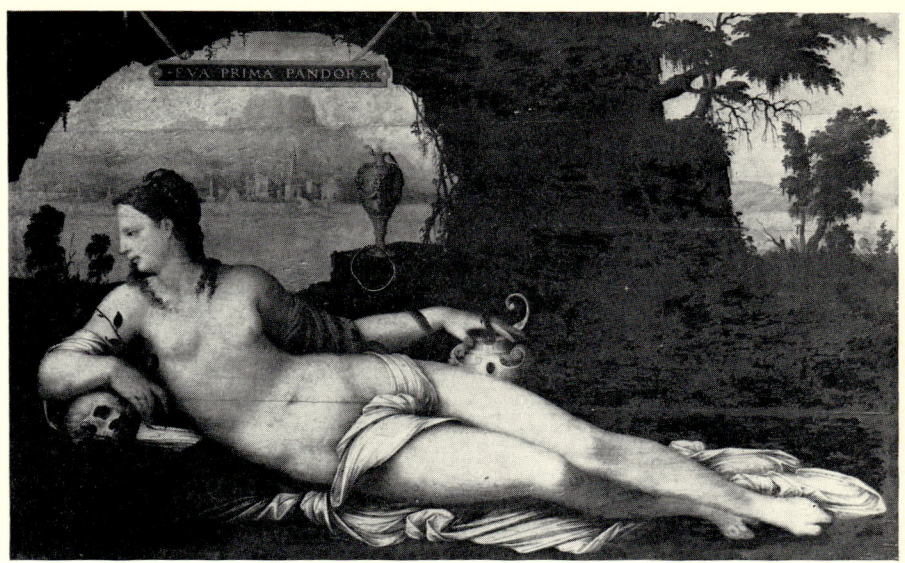

26 Jean Cousin, *Eva prima Pandora*. Paris, Louvre.

27 *Adam and Eve,* attributed to Bronzino. Balcarres.
Collection of the Earl of Crawford and Balcarres.

28 Lucas Cranach the Elder, *Fall of Man*. University of London, Courtauld Institute Galleries, Lee Collection.

most of the later catacomb paintings show the two in profile or at least less frontally—but the symmetrical grouping remains the same. As a visual formula it is of great antiquity: it goes back to the art of Assyria and Babylonia where it is found on cylinder seals, for example. The intermediaries by which it was adopted into early Christian art were, however, the more usual ones, the descendants of the motif in late Graeco-Roman art—just as the Good Shepherd was, in the most common manifestation, adapted from the Graeco-Roman *criophoros*, or the Creation of Man on the Prometheus sarcophagi of late Antiquity served as a model for artists who had to depict the Christian version of the legend. Some Athenian coins of Imperial times[15] show Poseidon and Athena, contenders for the office of patron of the city, each clasping the outstretched hand of the other across the upright trunk of an olive tree, round which is twined a serpent. One antique representation of this scene was indeed later taken to be a Fall of Man. It is a cameo,[16] an oval sardonyx, and is now in the Bibliothèque nationale at Paris, having been, with an interruption, in the French royal collections since 1379. At some time during the fifteenth or sixteenth century it was altered to conform with its supposed content (Pl. 3). The trident which Poseidon once held in his upraised right hand and the prow of the ship on which his left foot was placed, as well as the lance of Athena, were all erased. Athena's helmet was rather inexpertly transformed into a flowing head of hair, her owl, perched in the tree, was replaced by other birds and a vine, and various animals were added in the exergue. Round the edge of the cameo have been inscribed, in Hebrew characters, the first words of *Genesis* 3 : 6, 'And when the woman saw that the tree was good for food, and that it was pleasant to the eyes . . .'

Similarly *à propos* are the reliefs on sarcophagi depicting the Labours of Hercules which show the hero obtaining the golden apples of the Hesperides.[17] The coincidences in subject matter—the dragon,

---

[15] e.g. the Antonine coin in B. V. Head, *Catalogue of Greek Coins in the British Museum*, vol. x, *Attica, Megaris, Aegina*, ed. R. S. Poole (1888), p. 98, no. 707, pl. xvii, 4.

[16] E. Babelon, *Catalogue des Camées antiques et modernes de la Bibliothèque nationale* (Paris, 1897), pp. 18–21; pl. v, fig. 27; *Bibliothèque nationale, Paris. Cabinet des médailles et des antiques. Les pierres gravées. Guide du visiteur* (Paris 1930), no. 27, pp. 84–87.

[17] Carl Robert, *Die Antiken Sarkophag-Reliefs*, Vol. iii, part 1 (Berlin, 1897), pp. 114 ff., Abb. 106a, 113c, 120, and perhaps 137; cf. Esche, *Adam und Eva*, pl. 4: her illustration (Robert, Abb. 113c) is taken from a seventeenth-century drawing of a sarcophagus relief, for which see now Cornelius C. Vermeule, III, 'The Dal

the tree round which he twines to guard the golden apples, the forbidden fruit itself, growing in a paradisial garden—may well have aided the adaptation of the scene to a Christian context. It is, in fact, also depicted, along with other exploits of Hercules, other pagan subjects, two representations of the Fall and many Christian scenes, in the catacomb of Via Latina.[18] In composition, it is an almost exact counterpart of the symmetrically arranged Adam and Eve: some versions even showed the almost naked Hesperid to the left, her left arm raised towards the central tree, her right arranged in the classic *pudicitia* gesture, the tree with its fruit and the serpent twined down it and the naked Hercules on the right, his left arm raised towards the tree to defend himself against the serpent.

The central tree type is frequent on Christian sarcophagi of the fourth and fifth centuries. For example, the sarcophagus of Junius Bassus,[19] who died Prefect of the City in 359, shows Adam to the left and Eve to the right of a fig-tree, fruitless, clasping their aprons to them (Pl. 4). Only the mid-part of the serpent's body, twined round the tree-trunk, is preserved. Beside Adam is a sheaf of corn and beside Eve a lamb, in allusion both to the labour with which they are to be afflicted, and to the sacrifice of Cain and Abel. Here the scene, telescoped and proleptic as it so often is in early Christian art, is nevertheless, in one sense, complete in itself, just as in the paintings at Dura and in the Roman catacombs. All of these represent, in one scene, all or many of the separate episodes of the Biblical narrative of the Fall—the Temptation of Eve, the Temptation of Adam, the taking of the Fruit, shame at nakedness—explicitly or by allusion or implication—God's curse on the Serpent and the Toil of Adam and Eve. None show scenes anterior to the Temptation of Eve, though some have separate scenes of the Expulsion or of Adam and Eve disconsolate. In other words, the Fall itself is thrown into the highest relief: 'For by one man's disobedience many were made sinners, so by the obedience of one shall many be

---

Pozzo-Albani Drawings of classical Antiquities in the Royal Library at Windsor Castle', in *Transactions of the American Philosophical Society*, N.S., LXVI: 2(1966), p. 18, no. 8300.

[18] A. Ferrua, S.J., *Le Pitture della nuova Catacomba di via Latina* (Città del Vaticano, 1960), esp. pp. 78–79; pls. lxxvi, lxxix–lxxxi, cxiii; pp. 43, 51, 56, 74, pls. v, xxix, xxxix, lxviii, xcv; Testini, *Le Catacombe* . . . p. 156.

[19] Esche, pl. 1; F. Gerke, *Der Sarkophag des Iunius Bassus* (Berlin, 1936); C. R. Morey, *Early Christian Art* (Princeton, 1942), p. 271, fig. 141, and on the sarcophagi in general, pp. 103 ff.

made righteous'. It is as if nothing is to be interposed between our sin in the sin of our first parents and our redemption.

This is so only in a limited sense, for there are both exceptions which survive and exceptions whose early existence may be conjectured from other works of art, both manuscripts and monuments. Moreover, these contracted representations are only less proleptic in character for stating less explicitly than a full cycle that the Fall is the essential, even the happy, preliminary to salvation and eternal bliss. Rather than illustrations of the Old Testament they are witnesses—catechetical, dogmatic, almost liturgical in content—of eschatalogical expectations, which are emphasised by the juxtaposition, both in the catacomb paintings and on the sarcophagi, of the Fall with other scenes. It should be noted that the context both of these reliefs and paintings is a funerary one. The other scenes are sometimes pagan and syncretist in character, but are chiefly prophetic, 'typical', Old Testament episodes and—more frequently—New Testament or Christological illustrations. At Dura, the Good Shepherd (*John* 10 : 11–15) is shown immediately above the Fall, while the surviving decoration of the chapel has, besides David and Goliath, the Healing of the Paralytic, Christ walking on the water, the Women at the Sepulchre and the Woman of Samaria. The catacomb of Via Latina has episodes from the stories of Noah, Abraham, Lot, Isaac, Jacob, Moses, Balaam, Samson, Daniel, Susanna and others, the Adoration of the Magi, the Woman of Samaria, the Sermon on the Mount, the Miracle of the loaves and fishes, the Raising of Lazarus, the Good Shepherd, Jesus teaching, Jesus and the disciples, and other scenes —besides many other mythological subjects, pictures of animals, plants, human figures and the like. True, the catacomb subjects are not usually many: those just given, with the addition of the Baptism of Christ, the prophecy of the Denial of Peter, the three Hebrews in the fiery furnace, the Woman with the issue of blood, and some scenes from the apocryphal Acts of Peter, effectively exhaust the repertoire, including the less popular ones. Much ingenuity is often required to arrange them in more or less symmetrical patterns according either to the narrative of the Bible or to the requirements of anything like a strict 'typological' scheme, or to bring the representations into line with doctrinal differences or subtleties.

The sarcophagi too insist more upon the broad theme of deliverance, echoing the catacomb paintings in their choice and arrangement of subject and in their emphasis on the Fall as the preliminary to Redemption rather than to Judgement. They may perhaps assert the Christian themes in a slightly more overt way, being mainly intended for the use of the wealthier Christians and in cemeteries above ground[20]—a sign that the edicts of tolerance under Constantine and the imperial conversion have freed the faith from the more or less furtive practice underground of its early years, under the threat of persecution. The surviving sarcophagi are, generally speaking, of two types. The first is the adaptation of the older Roman frieze type in which six to nine of the popular subjects are arranged, sometimes in two registers, across the front of the sarcophagus without division of any kind in a continuous band. Sometimes a single popular subject, such as Jonah, occupies the whole band. The other type is the Roman adaptation of the Asiatic columnar sarcophagus, with scenes arranged, generally in two registers, one above the other, each within an architectural framework. In this type, scenes from both the native Roman iconography and the Asiatic were often mixed together—as on the sarcophagus of Junius Bassus, which has the Sacrifice of Abraham, Christ enthroned, Adam and Eve, and Daniel, along with the Arrest of Peter, Christ before Pilate, Job, the Entry into Jerusalem, and Paul led to execution. The columnar sarcophagi use the formula for the Fall with the central, serpent-entwined tree exclusively and show no other scenes involving our first parents. The frieze sarcophagi, on the other hand, having a continuous narrative to work with, are freer: they both depict additional episodes from the story of Adam and Eve and vary the formula of the central tree. On a fourth-century sarcophagus in the Lateran Museum,[21] for example, the story begins with the Lord laying his hand upon Adam's shoulder—perhaps an allusion to the Creation or the Expulsion—and continues with the familiar central-tree Fall, with Eve on the other side. Another,[22] also fourth century, begins with the Creation of Adam and Eve, followed by the bestowal of the fruits and beasts of the earth upon a naked Adam and Eve standing on either side of an angel. On Eve's left is the tree, entwined by the Serpent with a fruit in its mouth. This part of the story is ended at this point by the medallion with portraits of the dead. Below are the Adoration of the Magi and other New Testament scenes.

[20] Morey, p. 67.
[21] Morey, p. 257, pl. 57.
[22] Esche, pl. 2; J. Wilpert, *I Sarcofagi cristiani antichi* (Rome, 1926–36), pl. 96.

II

These more or less monumental treatments are the major evidence that we possess for the representation of the Fall in the earliest Christian art. I have dwelt on them at some length because of their importance in the establishment of forms of expression and modes of thought about the Fall and its consequences. Others exist, such as the agreeable example of the symmetrical, central tree type, in Roman gilt glass[23] of the fourth century showing, as invariably in early Christian art, an ideally handsome pair, Adam stalwart and beardless (there are some exceptions to this, which may represent the Eastern tradition), and Eve beautiful and long-haired. The distinctive feature of this representation is that Eve is dressed as a bride, wearing necklace and nuptial crown and veil, which may indicate knowledge of the Jewish tradition based on *Ezekiel* 18: 13 according to which Eve was conducted to Adam by God as his bride.[24] It remains an isolated and uninfluential instance. Equally interesting and more indicative of an artistic tradition is the scene in the cupola of a funerary chapel at El Bagawat in Libya,[25] dating from the fourth or fifth century. It forms part of a larger programme of decoration, consisting of episodes from *Exodus*, the story of Jonah, Jeremiah, Susanna, Rebecca sought in marriage, Noah and others. The Adam and Eve episode seems to depend on a Judaeo-Christian biography of Adam and—as far as can be judged from its fragmentary condition—shows the estate of man before the Serpent entered Paradise. Below the Heavenly Jerusalem, beside which stands a clothed figure with a rod, are, from left to right: the Serpent (?) upright and (?) hanging from the wall of Paradise; a figure labelled Adam, and another labelled ZΩH (i.e. Life=Eve),[26] both wearing long tunics; and two small bushes alternating singly with two larger trees, one of them perhaps a

---

[23] Esche, p. 19.

[24] L. Ginzberg, *The Legends of the Jews* (Philadelphia, 1947), I, 68; V, 90.

[25] The dome of the Chapel of Peace has a simple central serpent-tree, with Adam and Eve on either side of it. See Ahmed Fakhry, *The Necropolis of El-Bagawat in Kharga Oasis* (Cairo, 1951), frontispiece and p. 71. The Chapel of Exodus has the scene described above; see Fakhry, p. 57, fig. 40, pl. xviii.

[26] L. Troje, *Adam und Zoe: Eine Szene der altchristlichen Kunst in ihrem religionsgeschichtlichen Zusammenhang*, in *Sitzungsberichte der Heidelberger Akademie der Wissenschaften*, Phil.-hist. Kl., Jg. 1916, 17. Abh.

fig and the other perhaps a vine. It is at least possible that we have here the first attempt—not frequently followed, even much later—to differentiate between the Trees of Life and Knowledge.

The pictures of the Fall in surviving early Christian manuscripts, which are the witnesses of a tradition which goes back in time much beyond them, are somewhat different in character. For one thing they form part of substantial cycles of Old Testament illustration and follow the order of the Scriptural narrative, so that their soteriological reference is not so immediately apparent. It is now generally agreed that three traditions of Old Testament illustration can be documented for the early Christian period,[27] though only two of them are represented by manuscripts or fragments of manuscripts made within centuries of their origin. The first is Syrian, perhaps Antiochene, and its representative is the elaborate *codex purpureus* known as the Vienna *Genesis*, the earliest surviving illustrated Bible manuscript, perhaps of the fifth century.[28] The second is attested by the fragments known as the Cotton *Genesis*,[29] is Alexandrian in origin and probably contained some three hundred and thirty scenes. The fragments themselves belong to the fifth or sixth century and it has long been recognised that many if not all of the scenes which originally composed its cycle of illustrations could be reconstructed from later cycles dependent on it. These are all Western: the mosaics in the narthex dome of S. Marco in Venice, dating from before 1220;[30] the frescoes in S. Paolo fuori le Mura at Rome, of the fifth century;[31] the ninth-century Turonian Bibles—

[27] The best account of these is Kurt Weitzmann, 'Observations on the Cotton Genesis Fragments', in *Late classical and mediaeval Studies in honor of A. M. Friend Jr.*, ed. K. Weitzmann (Princeton, 1955), pp. 112–31. E. B. Garrison, 'Note on the iconography of the Creation and of the Fall of Man in eleventh and twelfth-century Rome', in his *Studies in the History of mediaeval Italian Painting*, iv (Florence, 1961), pp. 207 ff., argues for the early existence of an Italian modification so strong as to amount to a recension.

[28] H. Gerstinger, *Die Wiener Genesis. Farbenlichtdruckfaksimile der griechischen Bilderbibel aus dem 6. Jhdt. n. Chr., cod. vindob. theol. graec. 31* [Nationalbibliothek, Vienna] (Vienna, 1931).

[29] British Museum, MS. Cotton Otho B. vi.

[30] Otto Demus, *Die Mosaiken von San Marco in Venedig, 1100–1200* (Baden bei Wien, 1935), and, for illustration, Sergio Bettini, *Mosaici antichi di S. Marco in Venezia* (Bergamo, 1944); W. Weidlé, *Les Mosaïques vénitiennes* (Milan, 1956).

[31] Destroyed. See J. Garber, *Wirkungen der frühchristlichen Gemäldezyklen der alten Peters- und Pauls Basiliken in Rom* (1918), pp. 7 ff.; S. Waetzoldt, *Die Kopien des 17. Jhdts. nach Mosaiken und Wandmalereien in Rom* (Vienna-Munich, 1964), pp. 55 ff., Abb. 329 ff.

THE ICONOGRAPHY OF THE FALL OF MAN 235

Grandval (Alcuin);[32] Vivian;[33] Bamberg;[34] S. Paolo fuori le Mura;[35] the Caedmon MS, of about 1025;[36] the ivory *paliotto* at Salerno, of the eleventh century;[37] the St Albans Psalter of before 1123;[38] the twelfth-century mosaics at Palermo[39] and Monreale;[40] and the twelfth-century illustrations of the Millstatt *Genesis*[41] and the *Hortus Deliciarum* of Herrad of Landsberg[42]—manuscripts and monuments, in other words, from both north and south of the Alps. Some of them are more explicitly soteriological in orientation than others and there are certain differences in the formulae used to picture the Fall—a number of these, perhaps, arising from the attempt to show the Temptation rather than the Fall itself, or the Fall without the Temptation, as in the Millstatt *Genesis*—but this does not affect the integrity of the tradition. The third great family of Old Testament illustrations is Constantinopolitan in origin and ancient, but its earliest surviving witnesses are the Byzantine

[32] British Museum, MS. Add. 10546, fol. 5v. For the Carolingian Bibles, see W. Köhler, *Die Karolingischen Miniaturen*, I: *Die Schule von Tours* (Berlin, 1930–3); Text, part ii, pp. 118 ff.; and for a recent summary, A. Grabar and C. Nordenfalk, *Early Mediaeval painting, from the fourth to the eleventh century* (Geneva, 1959), pp. 136 ff.

[33] Bibliothèque nationale, Paris, MS. lat. 1 (Bible of Charles the Bald), fol. 10v.

[34] Bamberg, Staatl. Bibliothek, MS. bibl. 1, fol. 7v.

[35] Rome, S. Paolo fuori le Mura, fol. 7v.

[36] Oxford, Bodleian Library, MS. Junius XI, pp. 3, 13, 16, 17, 20, 24, 28, 31, 34, 36, 39. Executed about 1025.

[37] Salerno, Cathedral, antependium. Eleventh century. See A. Goldschmidt, *Die Elfenbeinskulpturen der romanischen Zeit, xi–xiii Jh.*, iv (Berlin, 1926), no. 126, 7; and cf. now Herbert L. Kessler, 'An eleventh Century Plaque from Southern Italy and the Cassinese Revival', in *Jahrbuch der Berliner Museen*, viii (1966), pp. 67–95.

[38] Executed before 1123. Hildesheim, St Godehard, p. 17.

[39] Palermo, Cathedral, Cappella Palatina. O. Demus, *The Mosaics of Norman Siciliy* (London, 1950), p. 44, pl. 28b.

[40] Monreale, Cathedral, Navata maggiore. Demus, p. 122, pl. 97a; E. Kitzinger, *The Mosaics of Monreale* (Palermo, 1960), pp. 51 ff., pl. 13. Adam is bearded.

[41] Klagenfurt, Kärntner Landesarchiv, cod. VI.19, fol.11. See H. Voss, *Studien zur illustrierten Millstätter Genesis*, [*Münchener Texte und Untersuchungen zur deutschen Literatur des Mittelalters*], (Munich, 1962), esp. fig. 21; and, now, the facsimile of the MS., *Millstätter Genesis und Physiologus-Handschrift*, [*Codices selecti*, x] (Graz, 1967). The trees are differentiated and there is no Serpent.

[42] Formerly Strasbourg, Bibl. de la Ville. Destroyed. See A. Straub and G. Keller, *Herrade de Landsberg, Hortus Deliciarum* (Strasbourg, 1899), p. 7, pl. 8; and Rosalie B. Green, 'The Adam and Eve Cycle in the *Hortus Deliciarum*', in *Late classical and mediaeval Studies in honor of A. M. Friend Jr.* . . . (1955), pp. 340–7.

Octateuchs of the eleventh to thirteenth centuries.[43] Let us look at the three traditions one by one.[44]

On the first surviving pages of the Vienna *Genesis* are depicted the Fall and Expulsion, within half-page miniatures placed below the text. There are four episodes, over which presides the Hand of God. In the first, Adam and Eve stand on either side of the tree. Adam has just accepted the fruit—perhaps a pomegranate. There is no sign of the Serpent, despite the text written above. Leaves conveniently stretch out from adjacent branches to hide the pudenda of Adam and Eve. In the next episode they cover their nakedness with leaves taken from another tree, perhaps a fig, which may indicate an attempt to show correctly the tree from which the aprons were plucked; and in the third scene, they flee to hide themselves in the Garden. The fourth scene, on the second page, shows first a fruit-bearing tree with a Serpent twined about it, and then Adam and Eve going towards the gate of Paradise, with a flaming wheel—standing for the sword that turned every way—outside it and the angel before the door. At the far right the pair, dressed in skins, are led away.

What may be called the Cotton *Genesis* tradition of Old Testament illustration is best studied in the monument from which the full cycle was first reconstructed[45]—the San Marco mosaics—and in the Carolingian Bible manuscripts already mentioned. True, the two differ in the mode in which they present the story; the Bible manuscripts are, as it were, much straighter tellings of the story of Genesis, less concerned to show the Fall, for example, exactly in its place in the scheme of Redemption. The Bibles, to take the earlier and less comprehensive first, show the Creation and the Fall as a frontispiece to the *Book of Genesis*, is a continuous series of scenes, arranged in three or four registers on each page, opening with the Creation of Adam and passing through the Expulsion to the Toil. The Grandval Bible, of about

---

[43] e.g. Istanbul, Seraglio, cod. VIII, fol. 43v; T. Ouspensky, *L'Octateuque du Sérail à Constantinople* (Sofia, 1907), and K. Weitzmann, in *Münchner Jahrbuch der bildenden Kunst*, 3. Folge, iii–iv (1952–3), fig. 26; and Smyrna, Evangelical School, fol. 13r; reprod. D. C. Hesseling, *Miniatures de l'Octateuque grec de Smyrne* (Leiden, 1909).

[44] In addition to the literature cited in n. 27 above, see G. Henderson, 'Late-antique Influences in some English mediaeval illustrations of Genesis', in *Journal of the Warburg and Courtauld Institutes*, XXV (1962), 172–98.

[45] J. J. Tikkanen, *Die Genesismosaiken von S. Marco in Venedig*, Acta Societatis Scientiarum Fennicae, xvii (1889), pp. 10 and *passim*.

840,[46] in the register showing the Fall itself (Pl. 5) uses the asymmetrical arrangement—the less usual—beginning with the tree with the Serpent twined about it, and Eve, naked and unashamed, taking the fruit from its mouth. The next scene shows Eve and Adam together, Adam eating the fruit. Then comes a tree, then God rebuking the pair, now wearing their large leaves, with the Serpent, standing on its tail, at Eve's left hand. The Bamberg Bible,[47] of about the same date, has a similar version, but the scene of the Temptation and Fall is telescoped, so that Eve takes the fruit from the Serpent in the tree with her right hand and passes it direct to Adam with her left. Then the two are shown hiding their nakedness, rebuked and expelled. The Vivian Bible,[48] of about 846, seems to use a kind of conflation of the symmetrical and asymmetrical arrangement: the Fall is represented, as in the Grandval Bible, with the addition of a tree between Adam and Eve, as Eve takes the fruit from the Serpent at left and hands it to Adam at right; and the Temptation of Adam and of Eve is represented, as in the Bamberg Bible, with two instead of three figures. On the other hand, the Bible of S. Paolo fuori le Mura,[49] of about 870, uses the 'condensed' iconography, with the central tree which we have already encountered at Dura, in the catacombs and on the sarcophagi—Adam and Eve eat the fruit, cover themselves, and are rebuked, in the same scene. In the previous scene, where God is forbidding them to taste of the tree, the arrangement is the same: they are placed on either side of it, whereas in the Vivian, Grandval and Bamberg Bibles they are placed together at one side. These variations are reflected in the other monuments of the Cotton *Genesis* group already mentioned, and in the present state of our knowledge there is little point in particularising further. The major representative of this Alexandrian tradition must nevertheless be described, for its historical importance. This is the mosaic cycle in the dome of the narthex of the atrium at S. Marco in Venice (Pl. 6), where a vast and detailed composition begins with the Creation of Light and ends with the Toil.[50] In turn, it forms only part of a much vaster complex of Old- and New-Testament scenes, with Saints, embracing the

---

[46] See W. Köhler, *Die Karolingischen Miniaturen*, Text, i, 1, pp. 194–209; i, 2, pp. 20–22, pl. 50.

[47] Köhler, Text, i, 1, pp. 209–34; i, 2, pp. 102 ff.; pl. 56a.

[48] Köhler, Text, i, 1, pp. 250–5; i, 2, pp. 32–36; pl. 70. Bibliothèque nationale, *Les MSS à peintures en France du viie au xiie siècle*, Exhibition (Paris, 1954), no. 32.

[49] Grabar and Nordenfalk, *Early medieval Painting* (1959), p. 151.

[50] Demus, *Mosaiken von San Marco*, pp. 53 ff., 98 f., pl. 27; Bettini, pl. 1, liii ff.; Weidlé, pl. 110 ff. See n. 30.

whole process of Redemption. Here the Fall is shown more fully, with the Temptation of Eve (Adam beside her), the plucking of the fruit, the Temptation and Fall of Adam, the hiding of nakedness, the Inquisition and Rebuke of the Lord, the prayer for forgiveness, the cursing of the Serpent, the Clothing and Expulsion, and the Toil. The story takes its place here much more explicitly as the depiction of the steps by which that innocence was lost which the Sacrifice of Christ is to restore.

Of the third tradition of *Genesis* illustration—the Constantinopolitan—the only memorials left are the miniatures in the Octateuchs, richly but less comprehensively illustrated, produced at Constantinople from the eleventh to the thirteenth centuries.[51] As far as the Fall is concerned, their iconography varies little, though some cycles of illustrations are fuller than others. They begin with the first day of Creation, and the miniature showing the Fall, which follows that of Adam naming the animals, has Eve standing beside a tree, with the Tempter at her other side in the form of an animal with a camel's body and a neck and head formed of a serpent (Pl. 7; see below, p. 261). Then come Adam and Eve on either side of a small bush; then a scene showing Eve reaching up into the branches of a tree and Adam either eating or merely standing in horror at the other side of the tree. The pair are naked.

III

In these Bible manuscripts we are dealing with the illustration of the Old Testament: so far at least no explicit connexion with the New Testament is made and certainly no specific system of types and antitypes has yet appeared. The case is rather different with the mosaic cycles such as those at Palermo, Monreale, S. Marco or the Baptistery in Florence,[52] as it is with the medieval bronze doors, to be mentioned later, at Monreale, Hildesheim and S. Zeno in Verona. In these the whole nature of the cycle, and the fact that it is not represented on the successive pages of a book, involves a stronger and more obvious accent on the soteriological implications of the Fall. Nevertheless, there are early medieval manuscript representatives of the Cotton *Genesis* recension in which we obtain the first known pictures of the Fall which specifically illustrate the theme of *Felix culpa*. These are the six of the

[51] Ouspensky, p. 115, pl. 25; Hesseling, fig. 19.
[52] A. de Witt, *I Mosaici del Battistero di Firenze* (1954-9), vol. iv, pl. iv.

Exultet rolls,[53] which were executed in Southern Italy at various dates from the eleventh to the thirteenth centuries, where the Temptation and Fall are shown, in one or two episodes, at 'O certe necessarium Adae peccatum, quod Christi morte deletums et! O felix culpa . . .' of the Paschal Proclamation on Holy Saturday. Two of these six pictures—the earliest, of the eleventh century from Montecassino[54] (now British Museum Add. MS. 30337 and Vatican Library, Barb. lat. 592)—are much more strongly Constantinopolitan in character than the others, except that the Serpent is a true snake, its tail entwined round Eve's ankles. The other four, at least so far as the Fall is concerned,[55] are more strongly reminiscent of the Italian modification of the tradition, especially as it is represented in the Carolingian Bibles. One of the rolls now in Pisa[56]—also of the eleventh century—has an interesting variant: the Serpent seems to be standing on its tail to the left of the tree, to either side of which stand Adam and Eve, wearing a sort of bathing trunks.

It is true that other, more oblique, allusions to the repair of the Fall in the Crucifixion had begun to appear. There is something of the kind on one of the Monza ampullae[57] of the seventh century, and a more explicit example in the Fulda sacramentary[58] of about 975, in which Adam and Eve emerge from their tombs below the Cross on Golgotha and a serpent twines round the upright of the Cross; or the Evangelary of the tenth century in Kassel,[59] where Mother Earth lifts Adam up towards the crucified Christ, with a serpent at the base of the Cross;

---

[53] The fundamental work on the Exultets is still E. Bertaux, *L'Art dans l'Italie méridionale*, i (1904), pp. 216–40, in default of the promised text volume to Myrtilla Avery's corpus of their illustrations, *The Exultet Rolls of Southern Italy*, ii (Princeton, 1936). The Fall is shown only in rolls belonging to the Vulgate recension, not the Vetus Itala group.

[54] Avery, pls. xlix, cl. On these two manuscripts see P. Baldass, in *Scriptorium*, viii (1954), pp. 75–88, 205–19.

[55] They fall into two groups. The Pisa pair shows Eve handing the fruit to Adam, while the pair from Fondi and Lucca has them both reaching for the fruit: Avery, pls. lxxvi, clxxix; xcii, ci. Adam and Eve, fig-leaved and rebuked, appear at *Adae debitum* in the Troia roll, Avery, pl. clxxvii.

[56] Avery, pl. xcii.

[57] A Grabar, *Les Ampoules de Terre-Sainte* (Paris, 1958), p. 56.

[58] Göttingen, Universitätsbibliothek, cod. theol. 231, fol. 60; A. Goldschmidt, *Die deutsche Buchmalerei* (1928), vol. ii, pl. 106.

[59] Kassel, Landesbibliothek, cod. theol. 2°, 60, fol. 1; A. Goldschmidt, *Die deutsche Buchmalerei* (1928) vol. i, pl. 82; *Kunst und Kultur im Weserraum, 800–1600*, Exhibition, Corvey, 1966; Catalogue, Münster/Westf., 1966 (ii), no. 173.

or the crucifix of Adalbero,[60] on which are shown Adam and Eve, sorrowful, seated on either side of the tree beneath the Cross. The Munich manuscript of the *Laudes sanctae Crucis* has a miniature showing the fallen and aproned Adam indicating a leafy Cross, behind which stands Ecclesia.[61] Other scenes from Adam's life are shown above and below.

The most remarkable treatment of the Fall in the manuscript illustration of the early Middle Ages is one that makes no explicit reference to Redemption or to Judgement. It is the extensive series of drawings in the 'Caedmon' MS.—MS. Junius XI in the Bodleian Library, dating from the second quarter of the eleventh century but perhaps copied from a manuscript of up to a century earlier[62] (Pl. 8). The drawings illustrate the Anglo-Saxon paraphrase, *Genesis B*, not the Biblical text, but they do not do so without some variation. The text of *Genesis B*, for example, makes Adam the subject of the Tempter's first essay, which is resisted. The drawings, no doubt because of the strength of the tradition of illustrating the Bible itself, show Eve tempted first. The series is also noteworthy as the first example where the story begins with the Revolt of the Angels—an opening which, as we shall see, was popular in later psalters and typological compilations—and one of the very few which distinguish Tempter and Serpent. Almost everywhere else, even in very full cycles, Satan and Serpent are the same from the beginning. The very first drawing of the 'Caedmon' series is of the Deity enthroned above Chaos. This is followed by the Revolt of the Angels, the Creation, and other scenes; then Adam and Eve in the Garden, each pointing to a tree at either side of the picture (the Trees of Life and Death according to the poem—v, 460 ff.); then Satan's emissary escaping from his bonds and tempting Eve in the shape of a serpent; next Adam and Eve together, pointing to a tree, Eve taking the fruit from the emissary of Satan who is now disguised as an angel; then Adam withstanding temptation, Adam succumbing, the remorse of Adam and Eve, and the triumph of the evil angel now shown in his

[60] About 1000. Metz, Bibliothèque de la Ville. See A. Goldschmidt, *Die Elfenbeinskulpturen der karolingischen und sächsischen Kaiser, viii–xi Jhdt*, i (Berlin, 1914), no. 78.

[61] *Reallexikon zur deutschen Kunstgeschichte*, i (1938), s.v. Adam, Abb. 19; Munich, Bayer. Staatsbibliothek, clm 14159; A. Boeckler, *Die Regensburger-Prüfeninger Buchmalerei des xii. and xiii. Jahrhunderts* (Munich, 1924), pp. 34 f., 96 f., pl. 30; late twelfth century.

[62] I. Gollancz, *The Caedmon MS. of Anglo-Saxon Biblical Poetry* . . . (Oxford, 1927), pp. xli–xliii.

THE ICONOGRAPHY OF THE FALL OF MAN 241

true guise; Adam and Eve conscious of their nakedness and clothing themselves in leaves; Satan's messenger reporting his success; Adam (now bearded) and Eve contrite, and hiding themselves; judgement passed on the pair and on the serpent; the Toil; and the Expulsion. Some connexion with early Christian MS. tradition here seems certain, even though the artist was illustrating a paraphrase rather than a text of the Bible.

A clearer relationship with Late Antique tradition is apparent when we come to consider one of the other great monuments of English early medieval art, the St Albans Psalter.[63] All the evidence points to the conclusion that the Cotton *Genesis* recension was known in England by the end of the first quarter of the twelfth century, when the manuscript was made. Of Old Testament subjects, this Psalter illustrates only the Fall and the Expulsion in the first two of the full-page miniatures by the Alexis Master.[64] The Fall miniature (Pl. 9) shows Adam and Eve naked and seated, each on a hillock, on either side of a central tree, from the branches of which a winged devil hangs by his feet, a serpent protruding from his mouth—a kind of hybrid of the figures in the Caedmon manuscript and the much more usual single Serpent. From the mouth of this serpent Eve takes a fruit, which she hands on to Adam, who eats—a feature typical of the Cotton *Genesis* recension, which tends to place this kind of explicit stress on the sequence of the transmission of evil.[65] The Expulsion miniature is a conflation of the Guarding of the Gate and the Expulsion (in reverse order, as at S. Marco), with the Expulsion being performed, as usual in the Cotton recension, by God and not by his Archangel.[66] Other more or less contemporary renderings of the Expulsion, such as those in the Millstatt *Genesis* and the *Hortus Deliciarum*, belonging to this recension, show the correct sequence of events.[67]

To return to the miniature of the Fall, it can be said that it represents a rare example—unique in its specific combination of creatures and method of distinction—of differentiation between Tempter and Serpent.[68] Almost all such examples of differentiation are English. A

---

[63] O. Pächt, C. R. Dodwell and F. Wormald, *The St Albans Psalter*, [*Studies of the Warburg Institute*, xxv], (London, 1960).
[64] Pächt, *et al.*, pls. 14, 15a; pp. 56–57, 80–81.
[65] Pächt, p. 57.
[66] Pächt, p. 81.
[67] Pächt, *ibid*.
[68] Pächt, p. 57.

mid-eleventh-century Spanish ivory in Leningrad[69] may be an exception to this rule, but otherwise there survive only the 'Caedmon' illustrations—the most elaborate set of changes—and the miniatures in Queen Mary's Psalter as well as the opening miniatures of the manuscripts of the *Speculum Humanae Salvationis* (see below, p. 245). These *Speculum* miniatures are clearly influenced by the tradition of Psalter illustration which begins in Late Antique times and has affinities with the Cotton *Genesis*, as represented by the St Albans Psalter (in a truncated form) and by Queen Mary's Psalter (in a more extended form). This method does not, like the Utrecht Psalter for instance, illustrate the Psalms themselves. The tradition involves, in a series of miniatures which precede the text but follow the calendar, incidents from the Old Testament and thereafter scenes from the life of Christ and the Last Judgement. In other words, it reflects the use of the Psalter as a book of devotion, and survives into late medieval Books of Hours, such as, for example, the late Franco-Flemish *Très riches heures* of the Duc de Berry (see below, p. 243). The impulse to differentiate between Tempter and Serpent at the particular time that the St Albans Psalter was made may also be reflected, as Pächt[70] has pointed out, in the fact that in the mid-twelfth-century *Jeu d'Adam* the character Diabolus acts out the Temptation, while the Serpent silently passes the apple to Eve only after Diabolus has finished speaking.

Queen Mary's Psalter[71] is a richly illustrated product of a scriptorium in East Anglia at the beginning of the fourteenth century. Its illustration opens, like that of the Caedmon MS., with the Fall of the Angels and proceeds in the Old Testament as far as the Death of Solomon, a favourite stopping point for such series.[72] It too shows devils as the tempters of Adam and of Eve, who stand on either side of a central tree. The pair are naked. Adam is eating a fruit which has been given into his right hand by Eve. The Serpent, twined round the tree, has the face of a woman (see below, p. 262). In the next miniature the Serpent,

---

[69] A. Goldschmidt, *Die Elfenbeinskulpturen aus der romanischer Zeit,* iv (Berlin, 1926), no. 92.

[70] Pächt, p. 57, n. 3.

[71] British Museum, MS. Royal 2 B. VII, fols. 1v, 2, 2v, 3, 3v, 4. See G. F. Warner, *Queen Mary's Psalter. Miniatures and Drawings by an English Artist of the fourteenth century* (London, 1912), pp. 55–56; M. Rickert, *Painting in England: the Middle Ages* (*The Pelican History of Art,* Z5), 2nd ed. (Harmondsworth, 1965), pp. 127–8. For the 'Old Testament' system of psalter-illustration, see M. R. James, *The Illustration of the Old Testament* . . . (n. 3 above), pp. 26 ff.

[72] James, *Illustration of the O.T.*, p. 15.

its work done, is slithering from the tree to live out its curse, while Adam and Eve, clutching their fig leaves, are expelled by the Archangel.

This type of Psalter illustration survives longest in France, and is still active in the books of devotion that begin to be produced in larger numbers, especially with the invention of printing, in the fifteenth century. A well-known and luxurious example is the *Très riches heures*[73] just mentioned, of the first quarter of the fifteenth century, where the elaborate calendar illustrations are followed by the famous circular miniature of the Fall, its composition less comprehensive than Ghiberti's was to be on the Porta del Paradiso, but more faithful to the Biblical narrative (Pl. 10). Like Ghiberti's, the story moves down and round, towards the Expulsion by the fiery angel on the right. At the upper left is Eve alone, taking the fruit from the Serpent, who has a woman's head and torso; below, she tempts Adam by coming to him unawares from behind as he kneels. At the upper right the pair are rebuked and cover their genitals with their hands. Expelled, they clutch their fig leaves to them. This miniature is in turn followed, at intervals, by the Fall of the Rebel Angels, by Purgatory and by Hell—each on single full pages—a much more condensed and minatory cycle than we find, for example, in the earlier English psalters, but none the less having affinities with them.

The pattern insists on the scheme of Salvation—or damnation—but far less explicitly than the systems of interpretative or typological decoration of Bible manuscripts which were developed, first in France with great beauty and elaboration of sentiment and artistic execution, and later in Germany with rather less of either, from the thirteenth century onwards, to illustrate such works as the *Bible moralisée* and the *Biblia pauperum, Speculum humanae salvationis* and *Concordantia caritatis*. Of these the earliest are the huge early thirteenth-century

---

[73] By the Brothers Limbourg, all dead, the book unfinished, by 1416. It is now Chantilly, Musée Condé, MS. 1284, and the Paradise miniature is on fol. 25r. For recent literature on Jean and his patronage of the arts, see J. Porcher, *French Miniatures from illuminated MSS.* (London, 1960), pp. 65 ff.; and his catalogue *Les Manuscrits à peintures en France du xiiie au xvie siècle* (Paris, 1955), nos. 182 ff., and now, for the earlier period, Millard Meiss, *French Painting in the time of Jean de Berry: the late fourteenth Century and the Patronage of the Duke* (London, 1967); but the fundamental work and reproduction remains P. Durrieu, *Les Très Riches Heures du Duc de Berry* (Paris, 1904): for the Paradise miniature see pp. 55, 167–8, and pl. xviii. For Adam's attitude, see O. Brendel, *Studies in the History of Art presented to R. Wittkower* (London, 1967), pp. 63–4.

Bibles moralisées,[74] luxury manuscripts *par excellence*, of which probably only a very few copies were made. These are richly and comprehensively illustrated with medallions, arranged in pairs, with a text setting forth both incident and spiritual meaning, each of which has a medallion to itself (Pl. 11). The Fall serves both for signifier and signified—what were to be called type and antitype. Thus the three medallions illustrating *Genesis* 3 are paired with three others; the Fall signifies all those who for secular concupiscence transgress the commandment of the Lord and obey the will of the Devil. The Devil rewards them by binding them mouth, neck, reins, legs and feet and casting them into infernal darkness (as shown). Adam, who on being 'rebuked by the Lord, excuses himself by blaming the woman', is the aggregate of those sinners who, 'menaced by the Lord, say that, because they were born at such and such an hour, they must necessarily be grasping, thieves, lustful, murderers . . .', and the Expulsion signifies 'Christ driving sin out of the Kingdom of the church into eternal Hell'. Clearly, the Fall is losing the intrinsic prominence it once had, in Old-Testament illustration for example, at the expense of a stress on the Redemption by Christ. Moreover, the Fall, with its episodes condensed, recurs several times in unexpected contexts in the *Bible moralisée*. Combined in the same medallion with the Expulsion it occurs at *Deuteronomy* 22:13 ff., 'If a man take a wife and find her not a maid . . .'—an incident moralised as referring to Adam, who sinned against God, and Eve, who first seduced man and thus offended God by disobedience. It recurs at 2 *Samuel* 4: 5–8, where the captains kill Ish-bosheth and thus signify the Devil who slew man with an apple. There is also an explicit allusion, merging the Fall and the Redemption, at 2 *Samuel* 24: 16: the anger of God kindled against Jerusalem signifies the anger of Christ against the people for Adam's sin; while David's acknowledgement of his sins and prayer for the people signify Christ's intercession for mankind. The 'application' medallion shows God above the angel putting Adam back from the Cross and Christ kneeling to intercede. Illustrations to *Job* use the image of the Fall and of Adam covering his nakedness. The most easily intelligible of these uses occurs as signifier at *Job* 14: 1 ('Man that is born of woman . . .'): the moralisation speaks of progression in putrescence, of the tree hewn down and of Christ's sacrifice on the Cross. These instances by no means exhaust the occasions when the *Bible moralisée*

---

[74] A. de Laborde, *Étude sur la Bible moralisée* (Paris, 1911–27), pls. 7, 89, 149, 160, 215, 226, 242, 358, 429, 500.

THE ICONOGRAPHY OF THE FALL OF MAN   245

shows or moralises the Fall, illustrating it each time (cf. below, p. 259).

The *Bible moralisée* is, as M. R. James remarks, rather interpretative than typological in character.[75] The great typological systems of illustration—less rigid than received scholarly opinion is apt to suppose—develop a little later in time, probably in Germany. The oldest is the *Biblia pauperum*,[76] which first appears in Germany about 1300. It uses Scriptural subjects only and is arranged in forty sets of three—two types to one antitype, each with a short text consisting of four prophetic quotations and some rhyming explanations in Latin. The next in point of time is the *Speculum humanae salvationis*,[77] a rhyming Latin poem of nearly five thousand lines, composed about 1324 possibly by Ludolf of Saxony, with three types for every antitype, the types being drawn from Scripture, legend and secular history. As the Prologue affirms, the Holy Scripture is like soft wax which will take any seal impressed upon it, so that any occurrence can prefigure any other. Accordingly, after the Proem, the illustration begins with eight miniatures for the Prologue, and both Proem and miniatures 'introduce the scheme of Redemption by explaining the need for it'[78]—much the system of that type of Psalter illustration we have been dealing with (Pl. 12). The Old-Testament cycle in the *Speculum* is indeed almost identical with that in Psalters contemporary with its composition, e.g. Queen Mary's Psalter, the East Anglian work mentioned earlier, which also has explanatory texts to its Old-Testament miniatures, in that it opens with the Fall of the Angels and progresses to the Creation of Eve, the presentation of Eve to Adam, the Temptation of Eve by an upright and often beautiful woman-headed dragon ('Quoddam ergo genus serpentis sibi diabolus eligebat, Qui tunc erectus gradiebatur et caput virgineum habebat'[79]), the Fall itself, the Expulsion, the Toil, and so on as far as Rebecca giving drink to Eliezer. (No other miniature showing the Fall

---

[75] M. R. James, *Illustration of the Old Testament*, p. 51.

[76] Gerhard Schmidt, *Die Armenbibeln des xiv. Jhdts.* (Graz-Cologne, 1959); F. Unterkircher and G. Schmidt, *Die Wiener Biblia pauperum, cod. vind. 1198* (1962).

[77] J. Lutz and P. Perdrizet, *Speculum humanae salvationis. Kritische Ausgabe. Übersetzung von Jean Mielot (1448). Die Quellen des* Speculum *und seine Bedeutung in der Ikonographie* (Leipzig, 1907–9); and M. R. James and B. Berenson, *Speculum humanae salvationis, being a reproduction of an Italian MS of the fourteenth century* (Oxford, 1926).

[78] M. R. James, Introduction to *Speculum* (n. 77), p. 8.

[79] Lutz-Perdrizet, I, pp. 4 ff., 122 ff.; cap. i–ii, pp. 181 ff., pls. 1–4 etc. James-Berenson, *Speculum*, pp. 13 ff., figs. 1 ff. On the use of the *Speculum* in the Alsace glass of the fourteenth century see Lutz-Perdrizet, i, p. 28.

occurs in the *Speculum*: the types of the Temptation are Daniel destroying Bel and the Dragon, David slaying Goliath and David killing the lion and the bear—all in allusion to Christ's slaying the Devil by resisting temptation.) The *Speculum* then leads us to the New-Testament story, which is arranged in the order of the Gospel narrative, by way of the Conception and Birth of the Virgin. The narrative of the Life of Christ treats the Infancy and Passion very fully but virtually omits the Ministry. It takes the story as far as the Ascension, which is followed by Pentecost, the life and death of the Virgin, her intercession for mankind, Christ's mediation with the Father, the Last Judgement, Hell and Heaven. There follow the Hours of the Passion and the Joys and Sorrows of Mary. The *Speculum* is a Dominican compilation—written by a religious, for religious, says Perdrizet—and manuscripts of it range in artistic quality from the dismal early German example (Munich, Staatsbibliothek clm 146) to the very beautiful and elaborate fifteenth-century French translation (Paris, Bibliothèque Nationale, fr. 6275)—both reproduced by Lutz and Perdrizet—and the fine Italian fourteenth-century codex edited by James and Berenson.

The *Biblia pauperum*, compiled a little earlier, on the other hand, does not lay such prominent stress on the Fall. Here Adam and Eve—standing naked on one side of the central tree round which is twined the Serpent with a woman's face—are, together with Esau tempted by Jacob to sell his birthright, the types of the Temptation of Christ,[80] which is shown in its correct position well along in the Bible narrative. The Fall does not occupy the prominent initial position that it does in the *Speculum*. The *Biblia pauperum* usually opens with the Annunciation, one of the types of which is the Lord in or beside the tree cursing the serpent on the ground beside it or wound round it.[81]

The third of these typological compilations comes out of Austria in the fourteenth century—the *Concordantia caritatis*,[82] put together between 1351 and 1358 by Ulrich, Abbot of Lilienfeld. The *Concordantia* is for the greater part dependent on the earlier *Concordantiae veteris et novi Testamenti*, which is in turn the descendant of the twelfth-century English text *Pictor in carmine*,[83] an unillustrated set of

---

[80] Schmidt, *Armenbibeln*, pl. 11a.

[81] Schmidt, pl. 8a.

[82] The best account of the *Concordantia(e) caritatis* is by A. A. Schmid in *Reallexikon zur deutschen Kunstgeschichte*, vol. iii (Stuttgart, 1954), cols. 833–54, which has a good conspectus of the literature.

[83] M. R. James, 'Pictor in Carmine', in *Archaeologia*, XCIV (1951), 141–66.

instructions for depicting five hundred and eight types of one hundred and thirty-eight New Testament subjects, all Scriptural or believed to be so. James noted the similarity of many types to those in the twelfth-century stained glass at Canterbury.[84] In the *Pictor*, the first temptation of Christ *de gula* is likened to, among others, the Temptation of Eve by 'diabolo de gula per serpentem dicenti: In quacumque die comederitis'; the temptation *de vana gloria* is again the Temptation of Eve, by which she is told 'Eritis sicut dii'; and the third temptation *de avaritia* is the Temptation of Eve by the devil in serpent form saying: 'Scientes bonum et malum'.[85]

The *Concordantia* (Pl. 13) was intended as a preachers' manual for the lower clergy and differs from the other typological compilations in that it is arranged in the sequence of the Missal and Breviary. Instead of following the order of the Scriptural narrative of the Life of Christ, the New Testament scenes are arranged according to the church year. Four types are given for each antitype: two from the Scriptures and two from natural history—the latter the enlargement of the tradition of the *Physiologus*. Here, once more, the Fall does not occupy the prominent position it does in the *Speculum*. It, and Esau selling his birthright are the Old-Testament types of the first Temptation of Christ—as in *Pictor*—the natural history types being the pregnant sow which miscarries through eating too many acorns and the spoon-billed bird which lives by fishing in the water but expires when it greedily seeks more food on dry land.[86] The other two temptations in the *Concordantia* are not associated with the Fall, but with other Old-Testament types mentioned by *Pictor*—the implication being, at least for the *Concordantia*, that gluttony was indeed the first sin.

IV

These typological manuals are, it should be emphasised, on the one hand *sui generis* and, on the other, systematisations of earlier cycles, less detailed but equally comprehensive of the whole pattern of Salvation. Their character and influence are perhaps in the direction of solidification and reinforcement rather than of innovation. They treat every event of the story of Christ, where larger, more monumental, cycles

---

[84] James, *ibid.*, pp. 154–5.
[85] *ibid.*, pp. 148 ff.
[86] *loc. cit.*, cols. 839–40, nos. 533–5.

are forced to select. So the sculptures of the north portals at Autun[87] and Chartres,[88] for example, are intended to lead us, by way of Old-Testament stories and types, to the Christ in majesty of the West front. So too the great bronze doors of the Cathedral at Hildesheim,[89] of S. Zeno at Verona,[90] of the Cathedral of Monreale,[91] and of the Baptistery at Florence[92]—covering a span in time of over four hundred years, from the early eleventh to the mid-fifteenth century—represent the scheme of Salvation even as they reinforce, augment and repeat its details as expressed in the sculpture, mosaic or wall-painting within or without the building itself. The door at Hildesheim (Pl. 14), echoing the Late Antique manuscript tradition already noted, terminates its series at 'Noli me tangere'. It has the Creation of Adam, the Temptation of Eve, the Fall, Rebuke and Expulsion—Temptation and Fall in a continuum as it were—with Eve tempted by the Serpent in the tree at right, handing the fruit across a second tree to Adam at left. At Verona, the Fall is again shown below the Creation of Eve, but on one panel and more simply: two figures, both female in appearance, on either side of the tree, from which the serpent reaches out with the fruit in its mouth. The Rebuke has a panel to itself, with Eve and a now bearded Adam holding leaves to themselves; and the Expulsion, again on a separate panel, shows the pair, clothed, and dismissed by the angel. This Old-Testament cycle on the left leaf of the doors is paralleled on the right leaf by a series of New-Testament scenes in which the Annun-

[87] D. Grivot and G. Zarnecki, *Gislebertus, Sculptor of Autun* (London, 1960), pp. 151 ff.

[88] A. Katzenellenbogen, *The Sculptural Programs of Chartres Cathedral* (Baltimore, 1959), in general; but for the Creation and Fall in the North Portal, of the thirteenth century, E. Houvet, *Cathédrale de Chartres; Portail Nord* (Chartres, n.d.), p. 2, pl. 34.

[89] One of the rare examples of an Old Testament cycle in Ottonian art. See A. Goldschmidt, *Die deutschen Bronzetüren des frühen Mittelalters* [*Die frühmittelalterlichen Bronzetüren*, i] (Marburg, 1926), pp. 14–25, pls. xii ff.; F. J. Tschan, *St Bernward of Hildesheim* (Notre Dame, 1942–52), ii, pp. 141 ff., esp. 181 ff.; iii, pls. 115 ff. Tschan ingeniously sees an ageing—to represent the debilitating effects of sin—of the pair in the panels succeeding the Fall.

[90] A. Boeckler, *Die Bronzetüren von Verona* (Marburg, 1931), p. 17, pls. 1–3, 40–42; p. 41, pls. 52–53. The Fall is also shown in the sculpture in relief on the west front adjoining the doors.

[91] Porta principale, 1186, probably by Bonanus of Pisa. See A. Boeckler, *Die Bronzetüren des Bonanus von Pisa und des Barisanus von Trani* (Berlin, 1953), pp. 18 ff., pls. 36, 38, 49–50; R. Salvini, *Il Chiostro di Monreale e la scultura romanica in Sicilia* (Palermo, 1962), pp. 231 ff., pl. xlix.

[92] R. Krautheimer, *Lorenzo Ghiberti* (Princeton, 1956), pp. 159 ff., pls. 81 ff.

ciation is placed opposite the Creation of Adam, the Nativity against the bringing of Eve to Adam, the Crucifixion opposite the Fall, the Adoration of the Magi against the Rebuke (cf. the Porta di S. Ranieri of the Cathedral at Pisa, made c. 1180 by Bonanus of that city,[93] where the Magi are shown riding over the cavern where Adam and Eve were buried: the Temptation, Fall and Expulsion are counterpointed with the Journey of the Magi), and the Presentation in the Temple opposite the Expulsion.

The selection of scenes is much more eclectic at S. Zeno, where episodes from the lives of the saints and little 'genre' scenes are incorporated in addition to those from the Old and New Testaments.

In Florence, four hundred years later, on the other hand, when in the 1420s Ghiberti[94] came to begin work on the Old-Testament east door—the Porta del Paradiso—not only had he an internal mosaic cycle already *in situ*, including a bare and schematic Fall in an Old-Testament series which included a life of Joseph as well as a life of John the Baptist and of Christ and a Last Judgement,[95] but he could also build, so to speak, on to two other doors.[96] One was his own north door, put in place and consecrated in 1424 (the contract is dated 1403), the other the door of Andrea Pisano of 1329-38. Andrea's door shows, in seven registers of four scenes each, virtues and the life of John the Baptist. Ghiberti's north door shows the life of Christ in five rows of four episodes each, reading across and upwards and culminating in the Pentecost. Below, as a sort of base, are two further registers, one with the Evangelists and the other with the Doctors of the Church—an arrangement also found in the late Gothic stained-glass cycles of Northern France. The programme devised in 1424 by Leonardo Bruni for the Porta del Paradiso, we remember, was again of this conventional type: two registers of prophets, followed by five registers, also of four plaques of single scenes each, telling the Old-Testament story, beginning with the Creation of the Heavens, Adam and Eve, the Fall, and the Expulsion, and ending with the story of Solomon. But the door as it was made is a revolutionary composition in a series of ten panels, reading across from the top, beginning with the Creation and ending with Solomon and Sheba. Ghiberti was justly proud of his

[93] A. Boeckler, *op. cit.* n. 91, pp. 9 ff., pls. 1, 9. This door is almost entirely New Testament in its choice of subjects represented.
[94] Krautheimer, *loc. cit.*
[95] A. de Witt, *I Mosaici del Battistero di Firenze* (Florence, 1954-9).
[96] Krautheimer, *op. cit.*, pp. 101 ff.

first panel, which 'shows the creation of Man and Woman and how they disobey the creator of all things; in the same scene you see them driven out of Paradise on account of the sin they committed; thus in one and the same panel no less than four acts are portrayed.'[97] The Fall itself is shown in the middle left-hand area of the panel: Eve hands the fruit across a serpent-entwined tree to Adam with her right hand, while reaching for more with her left (Pl. 15).

The figures of Adam and Eve in the depictions of the Fall have always, as we have seen, been shown naked. One reinforcing reason for its so frequent representation in art may, indeed, have been the opportunity it offered for an unrebuked display of skill in depicting the nude. However, it is next to impossible to conclude anything on the score of whether these figures are an exact reflection of current ideals of beauty or to draw conclusions from any real or suspected expressions of face, pose or gesture. With the fifteenth century and the sixteenth, we seem perhaps to be on firmer ground—the figures in the *Très riches heures* and in Ghiberti's panel seem to be reasonably specific statements in themselves.

By the beginning of the sixteenth century we have figures of Adam and Eve which are explicitly intended as expressions of an ideal beauty and proportion—at least of body. Among them are the most celebrated northern representations, namely Albrecht Dürer's. The most famous of these is the single engraving of 1504[98] in which the careful balance of the composition is enriched, in Panofsky's view,[99] by a whole set of iconological contrasts. Thus the serpent from which Eve takes the fruit with her right hand, while concealing and being concealed by another fruit and branch on her left, seems to be curled round a fig-tree. On the other side of this tree, Adam holds the branch of a rowan, which grows beside him. The whole represents mankind still uncorrupted: the humours, sources of the sins, are exactly balanced. In the pair of paintings made in 1507 and now at the Prado,[100] Adam and Eve are likewise constructed as perfectly proportioned human beings, though slenderer, more softly modelled and 'proto-mannerist' in representation and pose. The 'yearning sigh'[101] of Adam is perhaps borrowed from the Adam by Rizzo on the Doges' Palace at Venice. A sixteenth-

---

[97] *Commentario* ii, fol. 12r.; ed. J. von Schlosser, *L. Ghibertis Denkwürdigkeiten* [*I Commentarii*] . . . (Berlin, 1912), vol. i, p. 49; Krautheimer, pl. 82.

[98] E. Panofsky, *Albrecht Dürer* (Princeton and London, 1948), ii, Cat. no. 108; figs. 117, 132.

[99] Panofsky, vol. i, pp. 84–87.

[100] Panofsky, vol. ii, Cat. no. 1; figs. 164–5; i, pp. 119–21.

[101] Panofsky, i, p. 120.

century description of an Adam and Eve by Dürer insists on a quality of lifelikeness and 'inbred beauty', the ruddy, sanguine complexion of the figures and their expression 'wonderingly looking at the Tree placed in the centre, gaping ever so slightly as if attracted to the Tree all the time.'[102] But as no tree is visible in the present state of the Prado pair of pictures, the reference may well be to a different version. The copy now in the Pitti Gallery in Florence has parrots, a lion and partridges added to the Eve, and a stag and a pheasant to the Adam, to indicate, according to Panofsky, choler and blood[103]—sensuality in the one, and melancholy and phlegm in the other. Later, in the drawing of 1510,[104] now in the Albertina, Dürer introduces a new variant on the old asymmetrical formula for posing the pair—a variant which he uses again with minor modifications, in the second woodcut of the Small Passion of 1509–11.[105] In the 1510 drawing the pair are seen from behind, Eve's arm round Adam's neck, his round her waist, their free hands holding the same one large fruit before them; while the female-headed Serpent is twined round the tree above, and an elk and a lion are in the background. But the woodcut (Pl. 16) shows the pair from the front. Adam, bearded, has the same pose, but now Eve alone is taking the fruit from the mouth of a Serpent (which is no longer woman-headed), while a badger, a bison and a lion peer out from the forest. Like the Large Passion of about 1511, the Small Passion opens with the Man of Sorrows; but where the Large Passion goes directly on to the Last Supper and the events following from it, ending with the Resurrection, the Small Passion follows the Man of Sorrows with the Fall and the Expulsion before proceeding to the much longer series which opens with the Annunciation and terminates with the Last Judgement. Dürer in his woodcuts of the Fall may be hinting at the belief in the predominance of sexuality in the compendium of sins which make up the first sin.[106] Certainly as the sixteenth century pro-

[102] This occurs in the commentary of Johannes Dubravius to his edition of Martianus Capella, *De nuptiis Mercurii et Philologiae* (Vienna, 1516), sig. G4.

[103] Panofsky, ii, p. 3. On the significance of apes and monkeys in representations of the Fall see H. W. Janson, *Apes and Ape-Lore in the Middle Ages and Renaissance* [*Studies of the Warburg Institute*, xx], (London, 1952), pp. 91 ff., 107–44.

[104] Panofsky, ii, Cat. no. 459—cf. no. 457 and fig. 96—and i, p. 144.

[105] Panofsky, ii, Cat. no. 236, fig. 194; i, pp. 139–45, 157.

[106] Milton, *De doctrina christiana*, in *Works*, XV, 181–83. See, for the doctrine, Julius Gross, *Geschichte des Erbsündendogmas. Ein Beitrag zur Geschichte des Problems vom Ursprung des Übels* (Munich-Basel, 1960 ff.); and the literature cited in C. A. Patrides, *Milton and Christian Doctrine* (Oxford, 1966), p. 98, n. 1.

gresses there is what looks like strong emphasis on sexuality, especially in the work of northern artists, for example, among those clearly influenced by Dürer's woodcut, such as the Antwerp painter Bartholomaeus Spranger (Pl. 17). [107]

There are, however, two much larger and more comprehensive cycles than Dürer's, perhaps even more influential and certainly the best known of all: that by Michelangelo in the Sistine Chapel, executed between about 1508 and about 1512;[108] and that by Raphael in the ceiling of the Stanza della Segnatura of the Vatican Palace (1509–11)[109] —as well as the suite designed by Raphael but completed by his pupils in the Logge (1519).[110] These form the logical conclusion to the great cyclical portrayals of the Middle Ages. In Michelangelo's ceiling the whole culminates in the thunderclap of the Last Judgement on the altar wall, which is what the visitor instinctively and by training turns to on entering the chapel. On the ceiling itself, reading West from the Last Judgement, are the great images of the Division of Light from Darkness, the Creation of Sun and Moon, the Division of the Waters and the Earth, the Creation of Adam, the Creation of Eve, the Fall and the Expulsion (Pl. 18)—in one compartment—the Offering of Noah, the Flood and the Drunkenness of Noah, with the *ignudi*, the ancestors and prophets of Christ, the sibyls in spandrels and lunettes, the Jonah and the Zachariah, and the miraculous deliverances of Israel. Michelangelo's Serpent is more woman than her predecessors: she has arms and reaches down the fruit to Eve, who takes it from a recumbent contrapposto pose, stretching up her hand for the fruit which Adam, standing over her, greedily reaches into the tree to pluck.[111] To the

[107] Stuttgart, Kupferstichkabinett, Inv. 1729. A. Niederstein, 'Das graphische Werk des Bartholomäus Spranger', in *Repertorium für Kunstwissenschaft*, lii (1931), fig. 11, p. 27, no. 23. The pose is, in fact, taken from the group of Cupid and Psyche in the Capitoline Museum in Rome, Gabinetto della Venere, 3 (H. S. Jones, *Catalogue of the ancient Sculptures preserved in the municipal collections of Rome: The Sculptures of the Museo Capitolino*, [Oxford, 1912], pp. 185–6, pl. 45). Cf. also the drawing, popular and copied in its own day by the Austrian Daniel Fröschl (1572–1613), whose copy is now in the Albertina, Vienna (*Beschreibender Katalog der Handzeichnungen in der Albertina: Die Deutschen Schulen* [1933], no. 457), formerly in the collection of Sir Robert Mond.

[108] C. de Tolnay, *Michelangelo*, vol. ii, *The Sistine Ceiling* (Princeton, 1945), General view (folding plate) and pls. 1 ff.; L. Goldscheider, *Michelangelo* (London, 1954), pls. 38, 44.

[109] A. Rosenberg, *Raphael* [*Klassiker der Kunst*] (Stuttgart and Berlin, 1922), pl. 58.

[110] Rosenberg, *Raphael*, pl. 177.

[111] Tolnay, pp. 31 ff., 134 ff., pl. 40; Goldscheider, pl. 178.

right is the Expulsion: the angel drives out the pair, naked still and despairing, into an unseen and terrible world—as in Masaccio's Expulsion in the Brancacci Chapel of the Chiesa del Carmine in Florence, of about 1425, which is the ancestor of Michelangelo's design.[112] It is the Judgement—as in the Psalters—rather than the hope of Christ which informs the whole: Adam appears again on the altar wall, as he has done in earlier Last Judgements or Harrowings of Hell, with his coat of skins.[113]

The Stanza della Segnatura also represents the Renaissance summing-up of a long tradition: its decoration is one of the last of those great encyclopaedic cycles in which the arts and sciences, handmaids to theology, were blended, crossed with and set over against the events of the Old and New Testament in a vast and coherent complex. On the walls the Disputa del Sacramento, the School of Athens, the Parnassus, and the Virtues and Laws, are the exemplars of theology, philosophy, poetry and justice respectively—a lesson repeated in the circular medallions of the ceiling, which depict the allegorical figures of those disciplines. In the mosaic panels of the ceiling, placed between the medallions in the corners and, as it were, connecting them, are the Judgement of Solomon, the Fall, the story of Marsyas and the figure of astronomy, exempla of justice, theology, poetry and philosophy respectively. Raphael's Fall (Pl. 19) is a less original composition than Michelangelo's but equally influential. It reverts, for one thing, to the central tree formula, with the Serpent very definitely a woman in head and torso. Eve, standing, hands the fruit to Adam, who is sitting on a grassy bank, raising his face and hand towards Eve.

The Logge cycle, on the other hand, though in details it owes much to Michelangelo, is a much less unified and compelling whole than either the Sistine Ceiling or the Stanza della Segnatura decorations. It is a series of Old- and New-Testament scenes in separate compartments, beginning with the Division of Light from Darkness and ending with the Last Supper. Little more need be said about the Fall here than that it has marked similarities with the fresco in the Stanza, just as the Expulsion has affinities with Michelangelo and so with Masaccio.

From the sixteenth century on, little that is new and significant is added to the Fall in any medium, including book-illustrations. Single pictures incorporating the whole or part of the story of the Creation,

---

[112] U. Procacci, *All the Paintings of Masaccio* (London, 1962), pl. 51.
[113] S. Esche, *Adam und Eva*, pl. 45; cf. p. 257 below.

Fall and Expulsion—even statues of Adam and Eve, or smaller representations incorporated in background, border decoration, architectural motif, back or podium of throne or the like of paintings of the Virgin and Child—all these abound. For example, there is the splendid Cranach[114] of 1532, in the Kunsthistorisches Museum in Vienna, where the whole story, from the Creation of Adam to the Expulsion, is told in a single picture, its central foreground point showing God joining Adam and Eve. There is the Titian of about 1570,[115] now in the Prado (Pl. 20)—where Rubens's copy of it also hangs[116]—showing the Fall only, the Tempter being a horned putto- or faun-serpent who is handing the fruit down out of the tree to Eve, who reaches up for it from a standing position, while Adam, seated, puts out a hand apprehensively as if to restrain her. Rubens's own splendid Paradise (Pl. 21) of about 1620[117] shows the Fall at its left foreground, the rest of the picture being occupied with garden, animals and birds. The pair are long-haired, blond and beautiful, still in their state of innocence, figures in a paradisial landscape. So they had been, seventy years earlier, for Tintoretto[118] (Pl. 22), though the Venetian achieves his effect from another atmosphere altogether, moister and richer, and from a moment in the action which is later than Rubens's. The picture is the epitome of Venetian mid-century figures-in-a-landscape painting, the bright hard body, seen from behind, of Adam standing out, like the rounded softness of Eve, by contrast with the darker woods of the Garden behind them, where the fiery Expulsion is writ small.

V

If we now turn again briefly to the illustration of the Old Testament after the invention of printing, we find a tradition that begins, for the printed book at least, with the Cologne Bible of 1480 and is preserved in the edition of Niccolò Malermi's Italian translation printed at

[114] M. J. Friedländer and J. Rosenberg, *Die Gemälde von Lukas Cranach d. Ä.* (Berlin, 1932), no. 167.
[115] H. Tietze, *Titian* (London, 1950), pl. 270.
[116] No. 1692. See F. J. Sánchez Cantón, *Museo del Prado. Catalogo de los Cuadros* (Madrid, 1952).
[117] The Hague, Mauritshuis. Rosenberg, *Rubens* (1905), pl. 220; Oldenbourg, *Rubens* (1921), pl. 219.
[118] Venice, Accademia. H. Tietze, *Tintoretto* (London, 1948), pl. 30.

Venice in 1490 and in the Lübeck Bible of 1494.[119] The early emphasis is thrown on to two scenes, which also appear at the beginning of the incunable World Chronicles and occasionally elsewhere. The first is a circular medallion, generally incorporating in its frame scenes of the first days of Creation, but still insisting on the responsibility of Eve by having as its centrepiece her emergence from Adam's side. The second is a Fall and Expulsion, the conventional condensed version of the Fall with central Tree and female-headed Serpent, and our first parents driven out of an enclosed Paradise. The Malermi Bible has a frontispiece divided into six compartments, one for each day of Creation, the last devoted to the Creation of Eve. This is followed, with only an initial N (showing God the Father, with angels) intervening, by the head-piece to Chapter III—a small oblong cut showing the Fall in an enclosed Paradise and the Expulsion thence. The pair are naked in the Fall section of the cut, and fig-leaved in the Expulsion.[120] Thus the emphasis is still strongly on the Creation of Eve as the preliminary to the Fall, whereas later illustration, as for instance Bernard Salomon's in France in the 1550s,[121] tends to lessen the stress on and prominence of Eve. Salomon's series opens with a rectangular cut of the Creation of Adam, followed by another of Adam vivified, the Creation of Eve, the Fall—which owes more in its composition to Raphael than to Holbein— and the Death of Abel. Later still Theodore de Bry,[122] following Salomon with variations, opens with a synoptic Creation cut (light and darkness, waters and firmament, sun and moon, land, plants, animals), followed by single copper-plates of the Creation of Adam and Eve, and the Fall. De Bry's Fall also owes something to Raphael's rendering

[119] There is not a very satisfactory summary treatment in James Strachan, *Early Bible Illustrations. A Short Study based on some Fifteenth and early Sixteenth Century printed Texts* (Cambridge, 1957), see esp. pp. 11 ff., 25 ff., 36 ff.

[120] Venice, 1490, fols. a8v, b1, b1v. See M. Sander, *Le Livre à figures italien, depuis 1467 jusqu'à 1530: Essai de sa bibliographie et de son histoire* (Milan, 1942), i, no. 989.

[121] *Biblia Sacra* (Lyons, 1554 etc.). A fuller series of nearly two hundred scenes is used in C. Paradin, *Quadrins historiques de la Bible* (Lyons, 1553 etc.). The first four cuts are the same as in the Bible, but they are followed by five others before the Death of Abel cut, viz. the Donning of the Aprons, the Rebuke, with the Serpent, no longer woman-headed, elegantly gliding away, the Expulsion (by the Archangel, with Death gambolling between the pair, as in the Holbein), the Toil, and the Sacrifice of Cain and Abel. Cf. Ruth Mortimer, *Harvard College Library, Department of Printing and Graphic Arts. Catalogue of Books and Manuscripts. I. French sixteenth-century Books* (Cambridge, Mass., 1964), nos. 80 ff.

[122] *Biblia Sacra vulgatae editionis . . . cxxxx figuris illustrata* (Mainz, 1609), p. 3.

and is mentioned here because it was widely diffused and frequently imitated by painters and miniaturists. It found its way as far as Armenia and was copied in seventeenth-century Bible manuscripts from that area.[123]

Perhaps the most famous Bible illustrations of all, however, are those of Hans Holbein,[124] which depend in part on the tradition established by the Cologne and Malermi Bibles, but transform it, and are hugely influential. Some editions of the Old Testament, such as those published at Lyons by Trechsel in 1538 and by Frellon in 1551, use as frontispiece to *Genesis* a rather stiff cut, showing Adam fig-leafed, Eve reaching into an apple tree between the two of them and a large worm-like Serpent, crowned and woman-faced and wearing a severe expression, standing on its tail between Eve and the tree and leadenly contemplating the scene. But the woodcuts which usually open the series, first published thus in 1538—ninety-eight in all, including the purely decorative blocks—are the four grim and powerful but eminently tragic and human images which also open the Dance of Death suite, first published in the same year. The first is the Creation, with the Creation of Eve placed centrally. The second is the Fall, with a half-lying Eve surrounded by animals and passing an apple up to Adam who is reaching into the tree himself, while the Serpent, its woman's mouth open as if to cry out in triumph, coils down the tree towards Eve (Pl. 23). In the Expulsion miniature Death has been brought into the world: he dances mockingly ahead, while the terrified Adam and Eve flee after him from the sword of the angel above. In the picture of the Toil, finally, Eve is suckling a child, her spindle beside her, while Death helps Adam, in his dress of skins, to delve and overturn a tree.

---

[123] Sirarpie Der Nersessian, *Armenian Manuscripts in the Freer Gallery of Art*, [Smithsonian Institution, Freer Gallery of Art, Oriental Series, vi] (Washington, D.C., 1963), pp. 84–85, fig. 287. De Bry's Bible seems also to have been known at Constantinople in the early seventeenth century, as well as to the painters of New Julfa, perhaps through the intermediary of the Armenians of Poland—see S. Der Nersessian, *A Catalogue of Armenian MSS. in the Library of A. Chester Beatty* . . . (Dublin, 1958), vol. i, pp. xlii, 5.

[124] Conveniently published in A. M. Hind, *Hans Holbein the Younger: his Old Testament Illustrations. Dance of Death and other Woodcuts*, [*Great Engravers*] (London, 1912); A. Woltmann, *Holbein und seine Zeit*, 2nd ed. (Leipzig, 1874–6), Katalog 92–149; the *Dance of Death* Fall in J. M. Clark, *The Dance of Death by Hans Holbein* (London, 1947), p. 40. For other examples of the introduction of Death (and Time)—some earlier than Holbein—see S. C. Chew, *The Pilgrimage of Life* (1962), pp. 6 ff., figs. 9, 11–12, 15.

The tradition of representation with which we have been dealing leaves us unprepared for the extraordinary etching by Rembrandt (Pl. 24), signed and dated 1638.[125] Its execution dates from the earlier years of the most mature period of the etchings, when worldly success had begun to desert the artist. It seems not to be related in any way to any cycle but to stand on its own as the most sinister and powerful single vision of the Fall that has ever been produced. This is hardly because of the huge and menacing dragon, so different from the beautiful creature either of earlier art or of Milton (it is borrowed from the Christ in Limbo of Dürer's Small Passion, as the figure of Eve is perhaps taken from Altdorfer's Fall and Redemption series). Nor is it the ruggedness of the Paradise behind the figures which is so disturbing. It is the protagonists themselves: their appearance, gesture, and pose, the choice of the exact moment as Adam's left hand is about to close on the apple while his right seems to express the hesitation and fear that he is bound by the prohibition of God to feel. This is the true tragedy for all mankind.

VI

Certain aspects of the story of Adam and Eve—or rather of the Fall and Restoration—can be mentioned here only briefly. A little has been said already about the iconography of Adam-Christ,[126] the *Vetus* and the *Novus Adam* for example. There are, in addition, such themes as the sanctity of Adam and Eve—*felix culpa* wrought to its highest pitch— which is an Eastern tradition found at El Bawit[127] in the fifth or sixth century, and perhaps in Tintoretto[128] in the sixteenth; or the salvation of the two at the Last Judgement, which seems not to be current in western art before the twelfth century, when it is represented in manuscripts and mosaics, but occurs as late as Michelangelo[129] and

---

[125] L. Münz, *A critical Catalogue of Rembrandt's Etchings and the Etchings of his School* . . . (London, 1952), Cat. no. 177, pl. 197.

[126] A useful starting-point is the article *Adam-Christus* in the *Reallexikon zur Deutschen Kunstgeschichte*, i (1938), col. 157 ff.

[127] A. Grabar, *Martyrium* . . . (Paris, 1946), ii, pp. 297, 300; Esche, *Adam und Eva*, p. 34.

[128] In a Coronation of the Virgin in the Louvre; H. Tietze, *Tintoretto* (1948), pls. 242, 244.

[129] Esche, *Adam und Eva*, pl. 45.

Rubens.[130] But two other topics must be touched on. Both are expressly mentioned by Milton. One, noteworthy for the frequency of its occurrence, is the equation Eve-Mary[131]—the reverse of the antifeminist trend—which has its greatest flowering in the later Middle Ages and Renaissance. The other, equally noteworthy because it is only once represented in art, is the equation Eve-Pandora.[132].

Milton refers several times to the notion of Mary as the second Eve:

> So spake this Oracle, then verifi'd
> When *Jesus* son of *Mary* second *Eve*,
> Saw Satan fall like Lightning down from Heav'n . . .[133]

It is present early in the Fathers—for example Justin Martyr, Tertullian and Irenaeus[134]—and is a constant tradition, reinforced by such statements as contained in the ninth-century hymn 'Ave, maris stella':

> . . . Sumens illud Ave
> Gabrielis ore,
> funda nos in pace,
> mutans nomen Evae . . .[135]

i.e. by reversing *Eva* into the *Ave* of the angelic salutation. Its earliest occurrence in art, however, seems to be in the double-page dedication miniature of the so-called *Kostbares Evangeliar* of St Bernward of Hildesheim (c. 1015) which shows Bernward presenting his book to the Virgin and Child enthroned.[136] Mary and Eve appear in medallions on either side of the framing arch, with the purport made quite plain by the inscription on the *porta clausa* (*Ezekiel* 44: 1–3—a symbol of virginity):

PORTA PARADISI PRIMAEVAM CLAUSA PER AEVAM:
NUNC EST PER SANCTAM CUNCTIS PATEFACTA MARIAM.

---

[130] The 'Great Last Judgement', 1615–16, Munich, Alte Pinakothek; see A. Rosenberg, *Rubens* (1905), pl. 107; R. Oldenbourg, *Rubens* (1921), pl. 118.

[131] A full study of the iconography of this is E. Guldan, *Eva und Maria: eine Antithese als Bildmotiv* (Graz-Cologne, 1966); and for the literary background in the Fathers, L. Cignelli, *Maria nuova Eva nella Patristica greca* (Assisi, 1966).

[132] E. and D. Panofsky, *Pandora's Box: the changing Aspects of a mythical Symbol* (New York and London, 1956), pp. 62 ff., 71.

[133] *Paradise Lost*, X, 182–4; cf. V, 387; XII, 327.

[134] Cignelli, *op. cit.*

[135] F. J. E. Raby ed., *The Oxford Book of medieval Latin Verse* (Oxford 1959), p. 410.

[136] Hildesheim, Domschatz, cod. 18, fols. 16v–17; see F. J. Tschan, *St Bernward of Hildesheim* (Notre Dame, 1942–52), vol. ii, pp. 36–37, 46–47; iii, pl. 57–58.

On Bernward's bronze door, too, roughly contemporary, we have Eve nursing her children set over against the Virgin and Child. The typological compilations already referred to, especially the *Bible moralisée*, continue the tradition. In one of the *Bible moralisée* medallions,[137] Eve is shown with the Serpent in the tree, taking the fruit, while the angel of the Annunciation stands to the right of the tree and at the far right Mary receives the naked Christ-child, holding a wafer (?), from Heaven. One further example must suffice: the very elaborate and beautiful miniature in the five-volume Missal made before 1481 by Berthold Furtmeyer of Regensburg for Bernhard von Rohr, Archbishop of Salzburg, and his successor Johann Peckenschlager (Pl. 25). It shows the Tree of Life and Death, with a crucifix in one half of its foliage, from which Mary hands down the food of life to kneeling suppliants, an angel behind them. On the other side of the tree, the foliage of which supports a skull, is Eve, naked, taking from the mouth of the Serpent the fruit of death and damnation, while Death stands over those who receive it. The moral is hammered home with mottoes and further scenes.[138] Similarly, the woodcut executed by Hans Schäufelein in 1516 shows a composite Tree[139]—olive-tree to the left, with an angel in its branches and Mary with churchmen below; apple tree to the right, some of its fruit bearing a death's head, with Adam and Eve at its foot, Adam handing the fruit to a crowned figure. These German trees are elaborations of the Trees of Life, always bearing the crucified Saviour, which appear in the fourteenth century in Italy and elsewhere. Pacino di Bonaguida[140] provides one example, based on the *Lignum vitae* of St Bonaventure, where the tree is said to have twelve branches (the number of the Apostles, months, tribes of Israel, and so on). On the branches hang round medallions showing scenes from the life of Christ. But the German trees also have affinities with the Trees of Vices and Virtues and others illustrating such didactic texts as the *Speculum virginum*[141] or the ps.-Hugo of St Victor's *De*

[137] Oxford, Bodleian Library, MS. Bodley 270b, fol. 208r, *c.* 1240; Laborde, *Bible moralisée*, pl. 208; Guldan, *Eva und Maria*, no. 30.
[138] Munich, Staatsbibliothek, clm 15710, fol. 60v; *Bayerns Kirche im Mittelalter: Handschriften und Urkunden*, Exhibition (Munich, 1960), no. 268, pl. 60; Guldan, frontispiece, pp. 142, 161.
[139] M. Geisberg, *Der Deutsche Einblattholzschnitt in der ersten Hälfte des 16. Jhdts.*, no. 1049.
[140] F. Hartt, '*Lignum vitae in medio Paradisi*: The Stanza d'Eliodoro and the Sistine Ceiling' in *Art Bulletin*, XXXII (1950), 140.
[141] Eleanor Simmons Greenhill, *Die geistigen Voraussetzungen der Bilderreihe des*

fructibus carnis et spiritus,[142] which often show Adam and/or Eve at the foot of the evil tree and Christ at the root of the good tree. In the same context may perhaps be mentioned the Trees of Life and Knowledge in Guillaume de Déguileville's *Pèlerinage de la vie humaine*: in their post-lapsarian state the one is still green and fruitful, the other withered.[143] There are also Trees of Death, among the most startling those of Hans Sebald (1543), and [144] Bartel Beham, the latter a copy after the former.[145] The trunk of the Tree is a human skeleton, growing out of a clump of grass, a Serpent entwined in the bones with its head emerging at the neck of the skeleton to offer the apple to Eve, who is standing to one side, with Adam to the other. A variant by Hans Sebald Beham shows the deadly tree as an ordinary apple, crowned with a death's head.[146]

The equation of Eve and Pandora, not infrequent in literature, is rare in art. Milton has two references to it, one of them in *Paradise Lost*:

> . . . Here in close recess
> With Flowers, Garlands, and sweet-smelling Herbs
> Espoused *Eve* first deckd her Nuptial Bed,
> And heav'nly Quires the Hymenaean sung,
> What day the genial Angel to our Sire
> Brought her in naked beauty more adornd,
> More lovely than *Pandora*, whom the Gods
> Endowd with all their gifts, and O too like

Speculum Virginum [*Beiträge zur Geschichte der Philosophie und Theologie des Mittelalters* xxxix, 3] (Münster/Westf., 1962), pls. 3–4.

[142] A. Katzenellenbogen, *Allegories of the Virtues and Vices in medieval Art* [*Studies of the Warburg Institute*. x] (London, 1939), figs. 66–67; and, for a twelfth-century example, Leipzig, Universitätsbibliothek, cod. mscr. 305, illustrated in *Reallexikon zur deutschen Kunstgeschichte*, i, cols. 163–4.

[143] On Guillaume and his illustration see, in general, *Guillaume de Déguilleville, Le Pèlerinage de la Vie humaine*, ed. J. J. Stürzinger (Roxburghe Club, 1897); and now Rosemond Tuve, *Allegorical Imagery: Some Medieval Books and their Posterity* (Princeton, 1966), pp. 145 ff. For the episode in question, e.g. MS. British Museum, Add. 38120, fol. 155; MS. Bodleian Library, Oxford, Douce 305, fol. 51v; and ed. Paris, 1511, fol. xlviii.

[144] G. Pauli, *Hans Sebald Beham: Ein kritisches Verzeichniss seiner Kupferstiche . . .* [*Studien zur deutschen Kunstgeschichte*, xxxiii] (Strassburg, 1901), no. 7. On the Tree of Death, see S. C. Chew, *The Pilgrimage of Life* (1962), pp. 6 ff., figs. 1–7.

[145] G. Pauli, *Barthel Beham, Ein kritisches Verzeichnis seiner Kupferstiche* [*Studien zur deutschen Kunstgeschichte*, cxxv] (Strassburg, 1911), Cat. no. 1.

[146] Pauli, *Hans Sebald Beham*, no. 687; Geisberg, *Einblattholzschnitt*, no. 163.

In sad event, when to th' unwiser Son
Of *Japhet* brought by *Hermes*, she ensnar'd
Mankind with her faire looks, to be aveng'd
On him who had stole *Joves* authentic fire.[147]

The equation goes back to Tertullian, Gregory Nazianzenus and Origen,[148] among others, but there is, as far as I know, only one visual statement of it. This is the panel by Jean Cousin (Pl. 26), of about 1548, now in the Louvre, which is modelled on Cellini's Nymph of Fontainebleau and is a kind of *memento mori* picture.[149]

The Serpent and its transformations make another interesting subject for investigation. The early Christian monuments—wall-paintings, sarcophagi, and manuscripts of the Cotton and Vienna *Genesis* recensions and their dependents—all have a Serpent, generally large and usually twisted round the Tree, and proffering the fruit in its mouth to Eve. At Dura the Serpent, already cursed, is slithering away on its belly: at El Bagawat (the Exodus Chapel), it may be trying to enter or to leave Paradise. There is no sign of any attempt to show Satan and Serpent as different beings, which indeed is not warranted by the text of the Bible. In the Byzantine Octateuchs, and in them only, the Tempter is a composite, long-necked quadruped, with a camel's body and the head of a snake, the body of the snake forming the neck of the camel (Pl. 7). This is Jewish in origin: it goes back to apocryphal biographies of Adam and the Haggadic literature.[150] There is no sign of any such creature in Eastern or Western monuments of any other sort: at Aght'amar, for example, the creature to whom Eve is kneeling[151] seems to be the usual Serpent. All early examples of differentiation between Devil and Serpent are English and range from the early eleventh to the fourteenth century. The earliest and most elaborate is the series in the 'Caedmon' MS., the initial pages of which also have close affinities with the 'Old-Testament' tradition of Psalter illustration (see above, p. 242). The tradition may be English in origin: at all events it reappears in Queen Mary's Psalter in the fourteenth century and is taken over into the illustration of the *Speculum humanae salva-*

---

[147] *Paradise Lost*, IV, 708–19. Cf. *The Doctrine and Discipline of Divorce*, ii, 3.
[148] Panofsky, *Pandora's Box*, p. 64.
[149] *ibid*.
[150] K. Weitzmann, most recently in his 'Die Illustration der Septuaginta', in *Münchner Jahrbuch der bildenden Kunst*, 3. Folge, iii–iv (1952–3), p. 119, fig. 26.
[151] Sirarpie Der Nersessian, *Aght'Amar, Church of the Holy Cross* (Cambridge, Mass., 1965), p. 19, pl. 46–48—executed about 920.

tionis. Between the 'Caedmon' MS. and Queen Mary's Psalter lies, chronologically, the only other instance of differentiation: the St Albans Psalter, with its Serpent being spewed out of the Devil's mouth. The *Speculum* illustrations indeed differentiate, but not between devilish-human Satan and Serpent: they have rather a female-headed glittering dragon in the Temptation scene and either an ordinary or a female-headed Serpent in the Fall itself. Indeed, from the late twelfth century on, the most frequent mode of representing the Serpent is with a woman's head or torso and with the body of serpent, dragon or even salamander, sometimes crowned. This used to be thought of as the result of performances of mystery plays (cf. above, p. 242), since Tempter or Serpent was a speaking part.[152] It first comes to literary prominence in the West in the commentary on *Genesis* by Petrus Comestor (ob. 1179) who makes Bede the authority for the serpent's 'virgineum vultum' . . . 'quia similia similibus applaudunt'—a tradition which in the East goes back to the apocryphal legends of Adam.[153] Its first appearance in art is on the altar by Nicolas of Verdun, at Klosterneuburg, another detailed analysis of the Old Testament in terms of Redemption, which is dated 1181.[154] This is the form which is extremely popular throughout the Middle Ages and Renaissance, though not invariable, as a glance at the illustrations to this article will show. The *Très riches heures,* Michelangelo and Raphael, for example, have a whole female torso, something like a mermaid, though terminating in serpent coils instead of the tail of a fish. Hugo van der Goes has an upright, giant salamander with a woman's face,[155] supporting itself against the tree. The Grimani Breviary[156] has an upright, long-tailed figure, based on Hugo's, which seems to be a boy from the waist up

[152] John Bonnell, 'The Serpent with a human Head in Art and Mystery Plays', *American Journal of Archaeology,* XXI (1917), 255 ff.

[153] *Historia Scholastica, Liber Genesis,* in Migne, *Patrologia latina* (ed. 1855), vol. cxcviii, col. 1072. Cf. *The Book of the Cave of Treasures: a History of the Patriarchs and the Kings their Successors from the Creation to the Crucifixion of Christ* [perhaps sixth century], trans. by E. A. Wallis Budge (London, 1927), p. 64: 'And when she turned round towards him she saw her own form reflected in him and she talked to him'.

[154] F. Röhrig, *Der Verduner Altar, Stift Klosterneuburg* (1955), p. 74, pl. 29; C. Drexler and T. Strommer, *Der Verduner Altar* (Vienna, 1903), pl. 28.

[155] Robert A. Koch, 'The Salamander in van der Goes' *Garden of Eden*', *Journal of the Warburg and Courtauld Institutes,* XXVIII (1965), 322 ff.

[156] Venice, Biblioteca Marciana, fol. 286v; Koch, pl. 48c. For bibliography see *Mostra storica della miniatura italiana, Rome, Palazzo Venezia, 1953, Catalogo* (Florence, 1953), no. 735.

and a salamander in its lower part. Lucas van Leyden[157] uses a bloated, obscene, hairless, large-eared, tailed creature, part animal, part reptile, part human, clinging to the Tree. Sometimes, as in the panel attributed to Michael Coxie now in the Wallraf-Richartz-Museum in Cologne,[158] the Serpent has a plumed, beaked head—half-way between a peacock's and a vulture's—perhaps to indicate that the Fall was the result of pride and its sequel debased appetite. Titian's horned putto-devil is, as far as I know, unique, though in the painting by Hendrik Goltzius[159] the Serpent has the torso of a hornless putto. A fully-grown serpent-devil sometimes also appears, as in the panel attributed to Jan Cornelisz Vermeyen[160] at Innsbruck. Sometimes the Serpent has a worm-like body and the face of a man rather than of a woman—as perhaps in the drawing after Rembrandt, attributed to Philip Koninck, at Melbourne Hall.[161] The use of a man's face for the Serpent is infrequent, and I know of no certain instance before the Renaissance; for the Middle Ages usually seized this opportunity for yet another denunciation of woman as the source of Evil. It is possible that a masculine sex for the Serpent is intended in some medieval representations, but there is no way of being sure, just as in the grisaille on the podium of the throne in Mantegna's Madonna della Vittoria of 1495,[162] one cannot be certain that the face is male. But in the sixteenth century there are undoubted instances. In a picture of the mid-century sometimes attributed to Bronzino,[163] for example, the Serpent has the face of one of the painter's handsome young men (Pl. 27); and in a slightly earlier one, of the School of Fontainebleau, he cranes his more mature head just into the picture.[164] But in the late sixteenth century the artists return, on the whole, to the Serpent as serpent, and this is the tradition which persists through the seventeenth century and beyond. Exceptions, such as Rembrandt's ugly, threatening, swinish dragon crouching in the tree, become rarer.

All these visual representations of the Fall give few particular

[157] About 1508. M. J. Friedländer, *Lucas van Leyden* (1963), pp. 12 ff., fig. 2.
[158] Netherlandish (Malines), 1499–1592.
[159] Leningrad, Hermitage, dated 1608. O. Hirschmann, *Hendrik Goltzius als Maler, 1600–1617* (The Hague, 1916), no. 11, pl. 2.
[160] Tiroler Landesmuseum Ferdinandeum, Inv. 105; M. J. Friedländer, *Die altniederlandische Malerei*, vol. xii (Leiden, 1935), p. 200, no. 305, as by Jan van Scorel.
[161] Collection of the Marquess of Lothian, Melbourne Hall.
[162] E. Tietze-Conrat, *Mantegna* (1955), pl. 128.
[163] Collection of the Earl of Crawford and Balcarres.
[164] Paris, Art Market, 1965.

indications of dogma, especially with regard to the nature of man's first disobedience. As so often, the artists meet the subtleties of theological speculation on this point by blandly ignoring them. True, there seems in the late fifteenth and early sixteenth centuries to be an increasing tendency to emphasise the sexual element.[165] Dürer's embracing pair are enormously influential, and the immediate intentions of the couple in the drawing by Spranger and the paintings of the Fontainebleau School, of 'Bronzino' and of Tintoretto are transparently obvious. The difference is in the atmosphere: quick and nervous in the Fontainebleau painting, languorous in the Bronzino, calm and voluptuous in the Tintoretto. It is also at this time perhaps that frequent use is made of the single picture showing our first parents and the Fall, with a consequent de-emphasis of the Redemption or Judgement. However, the stress on Judgement remains always strong. Something of the conviction that evil was transmitted from Eve to Adam may be seen ever since the earliest monuments, in that it is Eve who is shown plucking the fruit or receiving it from the Serpent and handing it to Adam. On the other hand, this attitude is balanced by the number of times Adam and Eve are shown jointly reaching into the tree after the fruit or grasping it with one hand from either side. In the broadest terms, too, it may be said that the respective roles of Adam and Eve pass from something approaching equality (in the earliest monuments), through Eve's primacy, back to something like equality (e.g. in the Rembrandt etching). While in the earliest representations Adam expresses little if any doubt or dismay at the prospect offered him, in later renderings, especially those of the sixteenth century, he runs the gamut from doubt and hesitation (Pl. 28) to fear and recoil.

One painting of the effects of the Fall may here be mentioned, the triptych by Albrecht Altdorfer. Its centrepiece is the Fall, showing Adam indicating the Serpent and the apple; its two wings are the resultant evils: drunkenness, represented by a plump Bacchus and a drunken rout; and war and strife, represented by Mars and a warring crowd. Nothing is known of the context in which it was produced, but it has been dated between 1526 and 1528.[166]

---

[165] But note the emphasis on the 'compendium' of sins in the Fall, shown in the illustrations mentioned by S. C. Chew, *The Pilgrimage of Life* (1962), p. 2, fig. 8.

[166] L. von Baldass, *Albrecht Altdorfer* (Zürich, 1941), pp. 17 ff., pls. 306–8, dates the picture, now in the Kress Collection at the National Gallery of Art, Washington, D.C., about 1526–8. E. Rühmer, *A.A.* (Munich, 1965), cat. no. 12, is unenlightening.

The legend of the Fall and its illustration is too vast a subject for the compression attempted here. Anyone who ventures even such a summary and imperfect account as the present one may well feel that the Zoroastrian Satan, Ahriman, would have been a keener and subtler tempter than the Christian Devil. This insidious creature assumed the guise of an old man and seduced the first man and woman, Mesha and Meshyana, who had already lived fifty years without the need of food and drink and free of pain and sorrow. He demonstrated how the eating of a pomegranate changed him once more into a young and handsome man.[167]

[167] Sir T. W. Arnold, *The Old and New Testaments in Muslim Religious Art* (London, 1932), pp. 21 f., pl. 5. This is an illustration of al-Biruni on the chronology of the world in a manuscript of 1307. For other examples of the primal pair in Muslim art, see *ibid.*, pp. 22 f.; and *id.*, *Painting in Islam* (Oxford, 1928), p. 51 (a false identification); pp. 100, 103.

DATE DUE

MAY 24 '73			
GAYLORD			PRINTED IN U.S.A.